Economic History of Early India

Economic History of Early India

R.S. SHARMA

Viva Books

New Delhi | Mumbai | Chennai | Kolkata | Bengaluru | Hyderabad | Kochi | Guwahati

Publisher's note

First Published 2011
Reprinted 2015, 2017, 2018, 2024, 2026

Viva Books Private Limited

- 4737/23, Ansari Road, Daryaganj, New Delhi 110 002
  Tel. 42242200, 23258325, 23283121, Email: vivadelhivivagroupindia.net
- 76, Service Industries, Shirvane, Sector 1, Nerul, Navi Mumbai 400 706
  Tel. 27721273, 27721274, Email: vivamumbaivivagroupindia.net
- Jamals Fazal Chambers, 26 Greams Road, Chennai 600 006
  Tel. 28294241, 28290304, Email: vivachennaivivagroupindia.net
- B-103, Jindal Towers, 21/1A/3 Darga Road, Kolkata 700 017
  Tel. 22816713, Email: vivakolkatavivagroupindia.net
- 7, GF, Sovereign Park Aptts., 56-58, K. R. Road, Basavanagudi, Bengaluru 560 004
  Tel. 26607409, Email: vivabangalorevivagroupindia.net
- 101-102, Moghal Marc Apartments, 3-4-637 to 641, Narayanguda, Hyderabad 500 029
  Tel. 27564481, Email: vivahyderabadvivagroupindia.net
- First Floor, Beevi Towers, SRM Road, Kaloor, Kochi 682 018
  Tel. 0484-2403055, 2403056, Email: vivakochivivagroupindia.net
- 232, GNB Road, Beside UCO Bank, Silpukhuri, Guwahati 781 003
  Tel. 0361-2666386, Email: vivaguwahativivagroupindia.net

www.vivagroupindia.com

ISBN: 978-81-309-1012-3

Published by Vinod Vasishtha for Viva Books Private Limited
4737/23 Ansari Road, Daryaganj, New Delhi 110 002

Printed and bound in India by Replika Press Pvt. Ltd.

S0000/S0300/S0600

Contents

Transliteration of the Devanagari Alphabet into Roman Characters

अ-a,
आ-a,
इ-i,
ई-i,
उ-u,
ऊ-u,
ऋ-ri,
ए-e,
ऐ-ai,
ओ-o,
औ-au,
अं-am,
अः-ah,
क-ka,
ख-kha,
ग-ga,
घ-gha,
ङ-na,
च-ca,
छ-cha,
ज-ja,
झ-Jha,
ञ-n,
ट-T,
ठ-tha,
ड-da,
ढ-dha,
ण-na,
त-ta,
थ-tha,
द-da,
ध-dha,
न-na,
प-pa,
फ-pha,
ब-ba,
भ-bha,
म-ma,
य-ya,
र-ra,
ल-la,
व-va,
श-sa,
ष-sa,
स-sa,
ह-ha,
ड-r

Preface

I am glad to present my work before those interested in early Indian economy. The book contains eleven chapters written for different occasions. In Chapter One the material background of the vedic warfare has been presented on the basis of literary references and hitherto discovered archaeological finds. Chapter Two deals with as many as seven stages of ancient Indian economy viz., (i) Harappan (ii) Ṛgvedic, (iii) later Vedic, (iv) the period of *c*.500–322 BC, (v) Mauryan, (vi) post-Mauryan (200 BC–AD 200) and (vii) Gupta. The various modes of production are discussed in Chapter Three, while the fourth chapter draws the north Indian economic life during the Gupta period.

In the fifth chapter eight economic aspects of the caste system have been pointed out, while the sixth chapter presents the early medieval land grants with Rāṣṭrakūṭa examples. In the seventh chapter problems regarding the peasant protest in early medieval India have been brought to light. Chapter Eight deals with usury in early medieval times. In Chapter Nine different aspects of urbanism in early historic India are discussed, while the urban growth and decline have been explained in Chapter Ten. The economic trends and prospects in India upto AD 1200 have been stressed in Chapter Eleven with the cooperation of Professor D.N. Jha and bibliographical assistance of Dr B.K. Pandeya.

CHAPTER 1

Material Background of Vedic Warfare

Beginning with Oppert in 1880, several monographs have been written on war in ancient India, which also finds mention in books on polity and interstate relations in ancient India. Most books are concerned with proving that early Indian rules of war were as good as modern ones, perhaps far more civilized, and some of them try to demonstrate that ancient Indian weapons were perhaps as effective as modern ones. None of them examine ancient weapons or allied antiquities discovered from different parts of the country and preserved in the museums. Yet, since warfare is an inseparable part of material culture, a study of the literary and linguistic evidence in relation to archaeological evidence is essential. Apparently, because of the preoccupation of the scholars with the Aryans, Wheeler warns against such an attempt, but even without introducing the Aryans into the picture one could think of possible connections between the tools and weapons mentioned in the Vedic texts and those uncovered as a result of excavations. This is precisely what Dr Singh sets out to do in his book.[1] He reinforces his arguments by drawing upon military developments among the pre-Aryans and

[1] Sarva Daman Singh, *Ancient Indian Warfare: With Special Reference to the Vedic Period*, E.J. Brill, Leiden, 1965, pp. xiv; 203.

Aryans in western Asia. The picture that emerges may be partly provisional on account of many uncertainties, both linguistic and archaeological, but his technique is commendable and needs to be followed.

Initially, the study of the period 1500–1600 BC was the monopoly of the philologists; archaeologists appeared on the scene rather late. But if these two streams of knowledge have to be utilized for reconstructing a total, meaningful picture, trained historians will have to chanalize them into the mainstream of history. We cannot afford to be carried away by the enthusiasm of archaeologists who postulate as many as half a dozen theories in pursuit of the Aryans in India, nor by the uncritical linguists who ignore the relatives chronology of the various strata of the *Ṛgveda* and other texts, and play too much on the meaning of words. It will be interesting to investigate the motives and objectives which inspired and informed the progress of Indian archaeology in the last 20 years, and to see how they influenced the interpretation of excavation results. Some archaeologists seem to be too much obsessed with the idea of the Aryans. Perhaps a more fruitful pastime will be to look for the archaeological counterpart of the later Vedic culture, which may be seen as a synthesis of Aryan and non-Aryan elements. However, since the Vedic texts range over nearly 1,000 years, and since the same text reveals several stages in linguistic and literary development and in the extension of geographical horizon, which indicate some important changes in material life, they will have to be used with great discrimination. To give a few instances, BK X of the *RV* will have to be placed either towards the close of the Ṛgvedic period or perhaps after it, and the last 22 chapters of the *Vajasaneyi Sarnhita* will have to be dated about 700 BC. Some Brāhmaṇ as such as the *Jaimini*, and particularly the *Sāmavidhāna*, cannot be used for describing material life before 600 BC. The latest study of the Upanishads and later Vedic texts show that their composition may well have continued down to 500 BC. Enough work has been done by Vedic scholars to prepare the basis for an adequate study of material culture in chronological and geographical order by historians and archaeologists. Vedic texts can surely help the archaeologist to map out his programme and to check some of his results, but once a solid archaeological sequence has been established, the dating of the texts may have to be revised in its light.

The problem of using the *Mahābhārata* is still more complex. What the critical edition has done is to weed out insertions that may have been made into the great epic after the fourth century AD. But since the epic is actually an encyclopaedia containing narrative, descriptive and didactic portions applicable to the period roughly from the tenth century BC to the fourth century AD it is difficult to utilize it for any historical purpose unless a quick attempt is made by means of computer to salvage the original 2400 *slokās* submerged in the sea of 100,000 *slokās* to which the text came to be expanded by Gupta times. Even the oldest stratum of the present critical edition, the *Śabhā Parvan*, as shown by Edgerton, cannot be dated earlier than the second or the first century BC; the *Virata Parvan* seems to have been composed a century later, and the *Santi Parvan* still later in the early centuries of the Christian era. We face a similar difficulty in settling the date of the Rāmāyaṇa of which 1200 verses were inflated to 24000 verses by Gupta times. Hence in terms of social, economic or material history the Epic period becomes a misnomer, and Dr Singh has rightly placed the early Pali texts first and the epics next. But it is doubtful whether descriptions of weapons or rules of war in the epics hold true even of the three centuries preceding the Christian era. Ethics of war as known from the Great Epic would rather reflect the early centuries of the Christian era than Vedic times. Of course, some elements might be traced back to Vedic times, but those of change should always receive more attention.

From methodology we turn to the contents of the present study Dr Singh has carefully sifted and arranged the archaeological and linguistic evidence (both Aryan and non-Aryan) pertaining to the introduction of the horse in India. The ingenious theory that the horse was known to the pre-Aryans independently of the Aryans, as a separate word is used for it in Dravidian languages, has been developed by Dr Singh, but cannot apply to the Indus culture unless archaeologists discover clear evidence of the horse before 2000 BC. In spite of the discovery of horse bones at Rana Ghundai in north Baluchistan in pre-Harappa levels, it is difficult to think of any wide use of the horse in the Indus basin on the basis of the available positive evidence; the absence of the horse on Harappa seals is in sharp contrast to the portrayal of other different animals on them. Clearly the horse was not used on any considerable scale in India before 1500 BC not even by the Harappans.

Dr Singh supplements the material on the Vedic chariot collected by Stuart Piggott. Piggott points out that the number of spokes in the wheel is nowhere mentioned (*Pre-historic India,* p. 277), but a passage in the first book of the *Ṛgveda* (1.164.11) shows that it might have twelve spokes *(dūādaś)*. This would favourably compare with Homeric chariots which had eight spokes and the Celtic which had from four to ten or twelve spokes, and would show that towards the end of the Ṛgvedic period the Aryan chariot was very effective. It is a pity that so far no chariot or chariot fittings have been discovered in India. Nor is there much hope for their recovery in future, because wooden objects can hardly survive in tropical climate. But if chariots were used on the scale suggested by the *Ṛgveda*, we may someday discover their metal fittings; terracotta representations of wheels from Rangpur ascribable to 1500–800 BC. Do not show any spokes.

It is a sensible hypothesis that chariots could be used only by the aristocracy, obviously the *rājanyas*, while ordinary soldiers would have to content themselves with horse riding. The view that riding was not known to the Vedic people has been rightly questioned. It was known outside India as early as the fourteenth century BC, and it would be expected that it should be practised there also.

Dr Singh shows that the trained elephant was known to the Vedic people, who surely adopted it from the pre-Aryans. However, it is doubtful whether without the use of iron goods they were domesticated in any good numbers before the rise of the Magadhan empire in the sixth century BC. Elephants loom large in the army organization of *Mahābhārata* and the accounts of the Greek writers, which reflect the state of affairs after 400 BC.

The question of arms and weapons in ancient India involves a consideration of the use of various types of metal in pre-Vedic, Vedic and post-Vedic times. The Harappan weapons, characterized by the absence of shields, helmets and armour, were made of low-tin bronze and were without any ribs or sockets. Whatever weapons of the latter type have been found on the Harappan sites have been attributed to intruders or foreigners from western Asia, but it would be wrong to think that the Aryans owed their success to socketed axes, for these are not generally found in India before the beginning of the Christian era; the only exception is a socketed copper cell from Kurukshetra. Why they were not adopted for such a long period in India is a problem to which the archaeologists should address themselves. But surely swords were known to the Ṛgvedic people, as Dr Singh has shown on the linguistic basis. Archaeologically we know of at least one sword from the eastern border of Afghanistan, which can be associated with the newcomers. If we carefully examine the copper hoards of the Ganga basin it would appear that copper-swords with ribs were known in later Vedic times, but whether they were used by the Vedic people is debatable. Dr Singh approvingly quotes the opinion of B.B. Lal, with whom Stuart Piggott, Childe, Haimendorf, and others agree that the copper-hoards need no longer be attributed to the Aryans. But even those who hold this view do not ignore the similarity between the Fatehgarh antennae sword and the one from Koban culture in south Russia assignable to 800 BC. Gordon, although not willing to associate the copper-hoards with the Aryans, takes special notice of the Manpur dirk from Bulandshahar in western UP and derives it remotely from dirks found in late Harappan levels. Since these are similar to objects in western Asia they have to be associated with the newcomers in some form or the other. With this background we can take a close look at the problem of copper-hoards. Since as many as 18 of the 34 copper-hoards have been found in the Kuru-Pañcāla area of western UP, and since the lowest chronological bracket for them is not lower than 800 BC, it seems likely that they were manufactured under Aryan patronage and were evidently used by people living in western UP in later Vedic times. The absence of intermediate links between the Upper Ganga basin on the one hand and Koban culture on the other should not worry us so much as the fact that bronze weapons were used in Ṛgvedic times. In this respect there is a striking contrast between India and Iran. Bronze objects have been found in good numbers in central and western Iran before 1000 BC, which marks the advent of the Iron Age there. Iron tools facilitated the production of bronze objects, and in the period from 1000 to 700 BC we find numerous bronze axes, swords and daggers, none of which have their counterpart in India during that period. Archaeological probings in India have been insufficient, but not so little as to explain away the rarity of bronze objects. A few bronze weapons, discovered in Punjab and Afghanistan might be attributed to the Ṛgvedic people. But if such weapons were used there, why were they not found in later Vedic times in UP?

This possibly may be explained by the isolation of the later Vedic people from the areas such as Iran and Afghanistan which supplied tin. But all this remains conjectural for the moment. So far as definite archaeological evidence is concerned only a few copper objects in stratification belong to later Vedic times; these are copper-rods and beads from Hastinapura. Obviously the description of arms and weapons in Vedic texts will not be placed on a firm footing unless it is corroborated by archaeological discoveries.

Dr Singh's book provides an excellent assemblage of evidence on the discovery of iron objects at various north Indian sites during the fifteen years or so, though the inference that iron appeared in India as early as 1000 BC seems to be rather ambitious at the moment. Recent discoveries of iron objects from excavations at Atranjikhera might push back wheeler's date (500 BC) by four hundred years. The suggestion that iron weapons were necessary to clear the thick jungles in the Ganga basin would apply only to the area east of Allahabad or more particularly east of Banaras which has a rainfall of over 40 inches. In the later Vedic period, upto 600 BC, Aryan activities were mainly confined to western UP with a rainfall between 25 to 40 inches, and hence comparatively thinner vegetation could be cleared with the help of copper weapons. The occurrence of iron slag in association with Painted Grey Ware in later levels is certainly significant, but Carbon-14 datings for Hastinapura have now brought down its dating to *c*.500 BC. This perhaps should hold good of all the other north Indian sites where iron has been found in such a context. Carbon-14 datings for the iron objects from Atranjikhera push back their date to the ninth-eighth centuries BC, but this isolated instance does not enable us to make out a strong case for their widespread use in India, as was the position in western Iran in the corresponding period. Surely the situation may be altered by future discoveries.

Literary evidence should not be ignored, but where the dates of texts cannot be fixed in absolute terms, it is safer to place more reliance on archaeological discoveries. The term *syama* occurs in the *Vajasaneyi Samhita* in Chapter Eighteenth, but has no parallel in the *Tattiriya Samhita* which is older. The former is so recent that it was not known to Panini in around 400 BC, although the grammarian knew the latter composed in western and the *Maitrayani Samhita* composed in southern India.

Much cannot be built on the basis of the eastward expansion of Videgha Mathava given in the *Satapatha Brāhmaṇa*, for it is one of the youngest Brāhmaṇas, and cannot be placed much earlier than 600 BC. In any case the term *krsna ayas*, which seems to stand for iron, does not occur in that text. On the other hand it occurs in the *Jaimini Brāhmaṇa* which, as its prose shows, is still younger. Recent discoveries, especially those of iron objects, seem to confirm some of the dates assigned to later Vedic texts independently on the basis of linguistic studies.

The author clearly brings out the military character of the different Vedic bodies, mostly tribal, which were preoccupied with war. He pointedly draws attention to the link between the warrior aristocracy and the possession of chariots, as is found in Shang China. Indeed military needs led to the disintegration of tribal groups based on a sense of equality. We may add that in the age of *Ṛgveda* the spoils from war worked as the most potent solvent of tribal society. Gradually priests and warriors came to have the major share of the spoils and emerged as upper classes in society. Thus the surplus which helped maintain the ruling class in early Vedic times did not consist of regular taxes collected from the peasants but of booty and tributes, mainly in cattle derived from defeated parties, Aryan or non-Aryan.

Horse, elephant, chariot, copper and iron are subjects which have to be tackled properly if we want to understand the material background of early Indian warfare. Dr Singh's book goes a long way in doing this, and undoubtedly he has something new to say on each one of these points. What is further important is that he links up military technology with social organization and by implication ascribes the Aryan success to their superior equipment. This line of inquiry has to be pursued further in relation to the success of the Greeks, Persians, Bactrian Greeks, Ṡākās and Kuṣāṇas, and finally the Muslim Turks. Recently, there has been a reaction against the study of military history, but, as Wheeler suggests in his Foreword to Dr Singh's work, 'economic' and 'cultural' history cannot be studied in isolation from military history; on the other hand, a detailed account of the campaigns of Alexander in India, as has been given by V.A. Smith, will not help us much. An examination of the impact of military equipment and technology on social structure is a welcome feature of Dr Singh's book, and the subject can be followed up by also considering the impact of society on the military system.

Not the least merit of the present book is the eminently readable and elegant style and the concise manner in which it has been written. The tendency to load the thesis with the opinions of too many authorities has been scrupulously avoided, but not at the cost of essential points. The book has been handsomely produced and is provided with a fine index. An up to date and thorough study, it takes account of military developments in western Asia and pre-Vedic India and considerably adds to our knowledge of the military equipment and organization in the Vedic period. Without doubt it is an impressive piece of historical writing and shows Dr Singh as a historian of great promise.

CHAPTER 2

Stages in Ancient Indian Economy

I

The economic history of India can be traced back to 3500 BC, which marks the birth of an urban civilization, based on the surplus produced by the peasants. This civilization became fully urban by 2600 BC. Although the two well-known centres of Harappa culture were Harappa and Mohenjo-Daro, several other sites, including some towns, have been recently discovered, extending the outposts of the culture into eastern Punjab, Rajasthan and the Narmada estuary in the Kathiawar peninsula; it is reported that Harappa pottery has also been unearthed at Kausambi near Allahabad. The means of transport was nothing better than the cart drawn on uncharted roads, but there does not seem to be any doubt about the close connection between the different Harappa areas, which are characterized by uniformity in several aspects of material life such as the use of the same chalcolithic implements, pottery, and weights and measures. The period of this civilization extends from *c.*2500 to 1900 BC.

There is no doubt that thickly populated and congested nuclei of houses, which can be rightly designated as towns, were populated by the rulers (possibly priests), traders and craftsmen, who lived on the surplus produced by the peasant communities inhabiting the villages situated in the suburbs. Agriculture and domestication of animals such as bulls, dogs, elephants, etc., were practised, but the archaeological evidence suggests that the means of production were primitive. It was neither plough nor hoe agriculture, but cultivation was probably carried on by means of the cell, the use of which cannot be definitely attested on account of the difficulty of identification. It is suggested by Gordon that wooden ploughs may have been used,[1] but perhaps they were drawn by men and not by oxen. Of such cutting implements as could extend the area of cultivation, we hear of the stone axe, which could not be as effective as the socketed axe. The latter first appears in cemetery H, ascribed variously to the Aryans or to a still unidentified people known as the Ravi people. In spite of such primitive implements the peasants produced sufficient grain, owing to their hard work and the efficiency of the economic organization. The excess over and above their needs, could be diverted to meet the needs of the people living in towns and engaged in trade and commerce. Perhaps a part of the grains was received as taxes, which were stored in the two huge granaries at Harappa and Mohenjo-Daro.

We have no evidence of trade in grains, although a part of the excess grain may have been exported to the neighbouring backward semi-nomadic people. Cotton cloth and raw cotton in bales may also have been exported. There are good reasons to suppose the existence of commerce in copper, lead and tin, which were wanting in the area covered by the Harappa sites and probably imported by traders from Iran, perhaps by way of the sea. Trade in tin might not have been as brisk as that in copper, for the proportion of tin found in the Harappa bronze is less than that used in contemporary Mesopotamia. Besides these two metals of common use, the Harappa people also traded in several precious metals such as lapis lazuli, amazonite, jade, etc. These were apparently used as objects of ornamentation and refinement by the higher class people. In commerce the Harappa culture gravitated more towards the West than the East, for the Harappa seals belonging to the period between 2500 and 1900 BC, especially after 2400 BC, have been found in some quantity in Sumer or Lower Mesopotamia. Trade between Sumer and the Indus Valley seems to have been particularly thriving between 2400 and 2150 BC. Whether the Harappa traders set-up their regular trading

[1] D.H. Gordon, *The Pre-historic Background of Indian Culture*, Bombay: 1958, p. 71.

agency in Sumer, just as the Semites did in Asia Minor, is not known; in any case there must have been certain well-defined laws to regulate such brisk commercial relations.

Unless the Indus Valley scripts are deciphered the nature of the organization, which made urban life possible on a scale incomparable in ancient India from the point of view of a limited area, will remain a matter of speculation. Obviously the laying out of towns with streets and perfect drainage system, and the erection of houses all made of burnt bricks, must have required a huge staff of bricklayers, masons, woodcutters, charcoal burners, smiths, surveyors, engineers and carters, a fact which bears testimony to the great organizing feat of the Indus Valley people. The industry of bricklaying and building was far more important and developed in the Indus Valley than in the land of the Euphrates and Tigris, where the bricklayers specialized in bricks baked in the sun. It is suggested that all economic activities were directed by some central authority, but the theory that slave labour was an important part of the economy and daily life of the Harappa civilization has not much evidence to commend it. Judged from Indian standards, the two-room tenements should not necessarily be taken as coolie lines, for even now the average family cannot boast of more than two rooms, which are sufficient to serve the needs of an Indian household of five, mostly working outdoors.

From the material point of view the chief cause of the disappearance of Harappa culture seems to have been the stagnation which is evident throughout its existence. On its first appearance about 2500 BC it strikes us as a chalcolithic culture with static maturity, which perpetuates its monotonous, uniform character, with some minor local variations, for about a decade. At the end of this period it goes out of history practically unwept and unsung. During this long period the Indus people do not make any creative or original contribution to the further progress of material life. Their ultimate fall is ascribed to climatic enervation and lack of external stimulus. But when the Harappa culture came into contact with external elements, instead of getting invigorated it died an ingnominious death. The theory that the Aryans destroyed the sites of Harappa culture looks plausible, and is becoming increasingly popular.

II

Evidently the Aryans possessed certain technological and material advantages, which enabled them to overcome their opponents in India.

The widespread use of the horse yoked to their chariots was a potent cause of the military success of the Aryans, who combined it with the knowledge of cultivation by the plough. Although the *Ṛgvedic* Aryans do not seem to have been acquainted with bronze weapons, for *ayās* means pure dark copper, this was more than compensated by their use of horses and chariots, which made them formidable from the military point of view. The Vedic period which can be called the period of *Plough Cultivation* extended from *c.*1000 to 500 BC.

The striking contrast between the material life of the Aryans and the Harappa people does not lie in the use of metals, but in the almost complete absence of towns in the *Ṛgvedic* period. If we rationalize the exploits of Indra recorded in the earliest Indian hymns, the Aryans appear as the destroyers of towns and not their builders. At best the *Ṛgvedic* Aryans lived in fortified places protected by mud walls, mostly in times of flood, and these cannot be regarded as towns in the Harappa sense. Perhaps the absence of urban life among the *Aryans* should be ascribed more to their early migratory habits and the predominance of cattle rearing than to any other weakness in the material basis of their culture. Besides, in the first phase of their expansion when they were surrounded by hostile aborigines, commonly known as Dasas and Dasyus, they could not afford to lead a settled life in towns.

But the destructive exploits of their hero-god Indra should not make us blind to the great constructive role of the Aryans in the economic history of India. Literary evidence shows that their chief contribution was the introduction of cultivation by means of the plough drawn by bulls, evidently not known to the Harappa people. In the later Vedic texts, while the Vratyas are described as not cultivating the soil, the Vedic Aryans are frequently credited with practising agriculture. That the non-Aryans, with whose practices the Vratyas were supposed to have been tainted, knew agriculture is beyond any doubt. Hence the condemnation of the Vratyas as non-agriculturists only imply that the non-Aryans did not practise the art of ploughing in the Aryan manner. The Vedic Aryans yoked the oxen to their plough, in contrast the Harappa people who seem to have dug the fields themselves. Another factor which promoted agriculture was the knowledge of seasons. Five seasons are mentioned in the *Ṛgveda*. The various operations connected with ploughing, sowing, cutting of the corn with the sickle, threshing and winnowing are found in the first and tenth book of the *Ṛgveda*, which suggests that agrarian economy became more stable towards the end of the *Ṛgvedic* period. References in the tenth book of the *Ṛgveda* also suggest that the Aryans used fire for clearing the forests and thus making the land fit for cultivation.

Despite their practise of ploughing the Aryans are known to have had only one variety of grain known as ýavā, which may be taken either as a generic name for the various kinds of grain or in its later meaning barley. Perhaps cattle raising was a more important occupation, especially in the beginning of the *Ṛgvedic* period. Its importance can be inferred from the fact that 'the search for cows', *gavisti*, was another name for war, that constant prayers were made for line; and that the daughter was known as *duhitr*, which literally meant the milker of the cow. In addition to cows, goats, sheep and horses were domesticated, since common words for these animals are found in Indo-European languages. Of these kine and horses are mentioned in the *Ṛgveda* in the context of agricultural operations, although the exact use of the latter in agriculture cannot be determined. At any rate, horses were not yoked to the plough, although they may well have been used as pack animals for carrying grain and fodder. Cattle were tended by common herdsmen, thus suggesting common ownership of some kind, but this cannot be said of the ownership of land with the same certainty. Common ownership of land in the *Ṛgveda* is an arguable proposition. Several words for fields and the practice of measuring land suggest that at least in actual practice there was private ownership of land. But this was of a very limited nature, for even in the later books of the *Ṛgveda* we have no evidence of the sale, transfer, mortgage or gift of land of its disposal by an individual in any other way. We do not know whether the German analogy of Tacitus, who refers to the communal ownership of land distributed periodically among individuals, holds good of the Ṛgvedic Aryans, but clearly private ownership of land had not become effective during this period.

Among the arts and crafts the most important seem to have been those of weavers, wheelwrights and smiths. Weaving seems to have been mainly confined to wool, which was derived from the sheep. Cotton attested by archaeological evidence in the case of Harappa people, is not known to the *Ṛgveda*. On account of the importance of chariots in war the *rathakaras* (wheelwrights) performed an important function; so also seems to have been the case with the smiths, who made tools, implements and weapons of *ayas*. How far they inherited and carried on the craft traditions of the Harappans, whom they succeeded, cannot be said. The Ṛgvedic word for potter, *kúlāla*, has no parallels in other Indo-European languages, which might suggest that the Aryans adopted the local traditions in pottery. R.L. Twinar considers it a Dravidian word. The tentative results of recent excavations at Hastinapura credit them with the introduction of Painted Grey Ware.

Since the Ṛgvedic Aryans were mainly occupied with war, they hardly had any time to produce the necessary surplus for purposes of trade. Although literary evidence testifies to their comparatively advanced knowledge of agriculture, their migratory habits and preoccupation with cattle raising were serious handicaps in the development of trade. The cow being the medium of exchange, internal transactions of sale and purchase were mostly in barter, although at one place the price of what appears to be an image of Indra is stated in terms of an unspecified unit, suggesting an incipient money economy. It is reasonable to suppose that the Ṛgvedic Aryans did not possess any knowledge of the sea, and the word *samudra* is used in the sense of collection of waters lying at the mouth of the Indus River.

III

The later Vedic period (*c.* 1000–500 BC) witnessed the expansion of the Aryans from the Punjab and western UP into eastern UP and northern Bihar. The texts of the period give some clue to the material basis of this expansion. The *Satapatha Brāhmaṇa* states how Videgha Mathava went on burning the forests till he reached the Sadanira in north Bihar, an event which probably took place towards the end of the Vedic period. Burning, which was now adopted on a considerable scale, seems to have been supplemented by the use of the axe for cutting forests and of the iron ploughshare for bringing virgin land under cultivation. Although, according to one source the plough was made of *udumbara (Ficus Glomerala) wood, the khadira (Acacia Catechu)* ploughshare had now given way to the iron ploughshare. We have references to the yoking of six, eight, twelve and even twenty-four oxen to the plough, indicating deep ploughing which could be rendered possible only by the use of iron ploughshare. Literary texts indicate the advent of iron about 800 BC, for we have references to the iron smelter and blacksmith in the *Yajus* collection, but archaeological evidence about 1000 BC is more likely better. The presence of iron slag in a Hastinapura layer is attributed to about 800 BC. At several places iron appears.

Although the *Atharvaveda* contains innumerable prayers for the increase of cattle, agriculture had come to be the chief means of the livelihood of the people, cattle remaining the principal form of their movable property. The *Satapatha Brāhmaṇa* devotes one whole Brāhmaṇa (VII.2.2) to rites in connection with ploughing. In addition to barley, the chief crop produced during this period was wheat, which still continues to be the staple food of the people in the Punjab and UP. But it is for the first time during this period that rice, known as *urihi*, makes its appearance. Remains of rice, ascribable to about the eighth century BC, have been found at Hastinapura. At this stage, however, rice seems to have been a crop of secondary importance. Sugarcane, which is mentioned in the *Atharvaveda* (1.34.–5), may have been valued as a wild product.

In this period we have clear evidence of the private ownership of land. It is stated that a person who has a dispute about a field or with his neighbours should make an offering to Indra and Agni on eleven potsherds. For the first time we hear of attempts at grants of land. We learn that the Kṣhatriya can grant a settlement to a man with the consent of the clan (SB, VH.1.4). This implies the existence of separate holdings under the general control of the ruling tribe, at the head of which stood the king. But we have no cases of actual grants, for when in one case land was granted to a Brāhmaṇa, the goddess of the Earth refused to be transferred.

The Vedic economic organization was closely related to the varṇā-divided social organization, which had been firmly established during this period. The priests, who headed the social order, officiated at the various rituals, sacrifices and festivals associated with agricultural operations, and offered prayers for the success of their patron chiefs in war. The Ksatriyas earned their livelihood by means of war and government. To the Vaiṣyas was assigned agriculture, and to the Śūdrā service of the three higher varṇas. Thus the priests and warriors had hardly any connection with the primary aspect of production. It is not clear whether they owned large areas of land during this period. Keith holds that during the period of the Brāhmaṇas there had emerged large estates worked by slaves and serfs. But there does not seem to be any basis for such a theory, for we have hardly any instance of slaves being employed in production. Inequalities of wealth did not result so much from the direct exploitation of slave labour as from the collection of a part of the produce from the peasants in the form of axes by the king and his officers. In the *Atharvaveda* prayer is made to Indra for the grant of a share in villages, kine and horses to the king (TV22.2). The share in villages perhaps implies a share in the crops produced by peasants, who paid this to the *bhagadugha*, after which it was perhaps deposited with the *samgrahitr*.

An important development in the later Vedic economy was the rise of diverse arts and crafts, which are enumerated in the list of the sacrificers at the *purusha-medha* (human sacrifice). This indicates considerable progress in the differentiation of functions but not any qualitative change in economy. We hear of smelter (*dhmatṛ*) and smith or carpenter (*karmara*), but we are not quite sure whether they had anything to do with iron working, which had just begun. Numerous copper-hoards found in Bihar and UP, ascribable to this period, indicate the predominance of copper working, copper tools and implements. General words for weaving suggested that this craft was mainly confined to women and practised on a wide scale. Leather work, pottery and carpenter's work, probably connected with building activities, had also made some progress. We also hear of jewel workers, who probably catered for the needs of people living in towns. The presence of towns during this period is attested by the use of such words as town (*nagara*), town-dweller (*nagarin*), and the mention of Kausambi, Kosala and Vidarbha as great towns. Excavations prove the existence of at least two great towns Kausambi and Hastinapura, the origins of which can be attributed to this period. It is doubtful whether arts and crafts contributed in any substantial measure to the rise of these towns, as they seem to have been rather seats of political power.

The texts of the period make distinct references to the sea and to sea voyages, which may have been made for the purpose of carrying on commerce, stimulated by the rise of new arts and crafts.

IV

The period from *c.*500–322 BC may be taken as marking a significant change in the economy, which was strengthened by the widespread use of iron, the extensive cultivation of rice, sugar and cotton, the rise and growth of numerous towns in north eastern India, the further diversification of crafts and their organization into guilds, and last but not the least the brisk inland and foreign trade.

The technological basis of the economic progress was the growing knowledge of the use of iron, which was further facilitated by the use of bellows. Although in one text it is stated by way of simile that a ploughshare is heated throughout the day, suggesting thereby that the bellows was not in use, several texts of the period clearly refer to the use of bellows.[2] The importance of its introduction has to be emphasized. It made possible production of iron tools and implements on a large scale, and this hastened the process of the clearance of jungles in Bihar. Various kinds of rice, known as *sāli* during this period, and especially the cultivation of sugarcane, required deep ploughing, which in turn needed the periodical sharpening of the ploughshare by means of bellows. The evidence from Panini shows that fields were ploughed twice or thrice; they were also divided according to crops. Thus an improved knowledge of cultivation and the use of effective implements enabled the peasants to produce more surplus, which could be used in feeding the people of about sixty towns that are mentioned during this period, and also for promoting trade. Trade received further impetus from improvement in means of transport. A later Jātaḳa (iv, 210) informs us that a sheath of iron, two inches wide, was put round the outer edge of the wheel to make it very strong. It seems that by this time iron products themselves had become an important item in trade. Herodotus, who flourished in the fifth century BC, refers to the iron-tipped arrows carried by Indian soldiers of the army of the Persian ruler Xerxes. Similarly his contemporary Ktesias pays tribute to the excellence of the two swords of Indian steel presented to Artaxerxes Mnemon. Thus it is rightly suggested that trade in Indian iron and steel had already commenced from this time. At any rate, in spite of less archaeological evidence, it is fair to infer that the use of iron in pre-Mauryā times made an important contribution to the overall development of economy.

It seems that the Buddhist ideology of non-injury to living beings and reaction against Vedic sacrifices helped to protect the cattle wealth, which was indispensable for the progress of agriculture. A Buddhist text (*Sutta-Nipata*, PTS, 296-7, cf. 309) states that cattle constitute the source of grain, strength, beauty and happiness, and hence they should not be slaughtered. This value was also emphasized by a brāhmaṇical law book, which lays down the difficult penance of *-candrayāṇa* for slaying a milch-cow or a draught ox (*Baudhayana*, I.10.4). In view of many references to cow-slaughter in Vedic texts[3], this must be regarded as a very healthy development from the economic point of view. Cattle were probably owned individually, but, as in the Vedic period, a grassland or woodland was owned in common.

[2] *Panini*, VII.3.47; A.F. Rudolf Hoernle, ed., *Uvasagadasao*, Calcutta: 1890, p. 108.

[3] Das, S.K., *The Economic History of Ancient India*, Calcutta: 1944, pp. 110–11.

Efforts for the extension of the arable land by clearing woodland continued in pre-Mauryā times. It is laid down by a lawgiver that the king may injure trees that bear fruits or flowers in order to extend cultivation and for sacrifices.[4] There prevailed the practice of burning forests for this purpose, as can be inferred from the comment of Abhayasuri on a passage of a Jain canonical text.[5] Initiative for bringing virgin soil under cultivation was obviously taken by the state or the community, to the pioneering or collective efforts of which can be ascribed the rise of plots of 500 or 1000 *karisas*, cultivated by slaves and hired labourers. But individuals did not lack such initiative. We have the instance of sale of forest land cleared by the proprietor or his ancestors.[6] It seems that in eastern India a considerable portion of hind lay in the hands of the two upper varṇās, who were free from taxes, but perhaps a greater part of the land was in possession of *gahapatīs* (peasant proprietors) or *kutumbikās* (well-to-do peasants). The number of such independent peasants was substantial, and their holdings were just sufficient to maintain them. According to Baudhayana a lawgiver of about the fifth century BC, an ideal economic holding, necessary to support a family, seems to have been a holding of land measuring six *nivartanas*. This may have been the average size of a holding with regional variations. In any case the holdings of individuals were well-demarcated, for Panini refers to a systematic survey of agricultural land undertaken by special officers called *kṣetrakārās*, corresponding to the *rajjugahaka-amaccas* of Buddhist sources. We have no idea of the rate of tithe, which may have varied from one-sixth to one-twelfth, but in cases of emergency taxes in cash were also levied upon the people.[7] In spite of individual ownership two things are very clear about the land system of pre-Mauryā times. First, although land revenues were assigned to the brāhmiaṇas, there was no sizeable class of intermediaries between the king and the tillers of the soil. The peasants paid taxes directly to the king and were sometimes compelled to perform corvee. Second, there was a definite anti-alienating and communal feeling, subsisting from old tribal days, which did not allow free and easy disposal of land by way of sale, gift (or) mortgage.

[4] *Vasistha*, XIX, 12.

[5] *Uvasaga*, 51.

[6] Rhys Davids, *Buddhist India*, pp. 46–7.

[7] V.S. Agarwala, *India as Known to Panini*, Lucknow: 1953, pp. 414–15.

The distinctive feature of pre-Mauryā times is the development of urban economy, which reappears in India after a lapse of about one thousand years. In connection with the begging round of a monk the Jain canonical texts mention different kinds of urban settlements such as a scot-free town, a town with an earthen wall, a town with a small wall, an isolated town, a large town, a sea town and a capital.[8] We further learn that Aristobulus, when sent on a commission by Alexander to a region left a desert by a shifting of the Indus to the east, saw the remains of over a thousand towns and villages once full of men. Unfortunately, these towns of the Indus valley have not been excavated so far. Taking the country as a whole, to this period are assigned sixty well-known towns, spreading from Campa in the east to Bhrgukaccha in the west, from Kaveripattana in the south to Kapilavastu in the north.[9] Big cities such as Sravasti were twenty in number, and six of them were considered sufficiently important to be the scene of Buddha's passage. These were Campa, Rajagrha, Saketa, Kausambi, Banaras and Kusinara; the greatness of Pataliputra was still to come. The towns owed their importance to arts and crafts. Thus in the case of Rajagrha, later texts refer to the existence of eighteen guilds. Of the conventional eighteen guilds referred to in the Buddhist texts only the names of four, viz., woodworkers, smiths, leather-workers and painters are mentioned. Every guild was presided over by a head, and had its own laws to observe. In two Buddhist birth stories, the royal procession on two important occasions is said to have included the eighteen guilds, which implies that the kings exercised some general control over them. Probably the *bhandagarika*, who held the office of the treasurer at Banaras, exercised such a supervision over all the guilds on behalf of the king. Industry and trade were handled by *setthis*, who generally lived in towns but also maintained connections with their counterparts living in the countryside. There were different grads of *setthis*, high and low, and the title of the setthi was conferred as a mark of distinction by the king. Such *setthis* were also granted *bhogagamas* of revenues of the villages for their upkeep. But we are not sure whether the *setthis* had any connection with the guild. At any rate, the king's supervision did not destroy the initiative of the guilds, for while administering justice he was required to take

[8] *Anlagada-Dasao* (Tr. L.D. Bamett), pp. 44–5; *Ayaranga Sidta* (Fl'S), 1.7.6.4; H. Jacobi, ed., *Kalpasutra*, p. 89; P.L. Vaidya, ed., *Suyagadam*, II.2.6.

[9] S.K. Das, op. cit., pp. 175–83. Kaveripattana is mentioned in a past story injat., iv. 238.

into account the laws of the prevalence of the guilds, they did not suffer from lack of mobility. We know the story of a whole village of carpenters who emigrated overnight to a different place because they found it impossible to comply with thc wishes of the king.

We do not know the exact relation between the village and the town. Villages, owing to better means of production, produced seven kinds of grain and seven kinds of pulses, obviously supplied surplus food for the large number of artisans, merchants and soldiers and for the household establishments of the king and nobles living in the town. Panini indicates that the king[10] and richer sections of people employed as many as a dozen varieties of attendants to look to their personal comforts too. Whereas the king collected his taxes in kind, some *setthis* collected grain from their *bhogagamas* in the countryside, which enabled them to live comfortably. In return for surplus grain the towns probably supplied cloth to villages, for we hear of the cultivation of cotton in the neighbourhood of Banaras which manufactured cloth from it.

Like town life, trade revived on a considerable scale after a lapse of 1200 years. Cloth seems to have been an important article of trade, for the early Pali texts suggest that cotton came into general use in the age of the Buddha, but trade was mainly confined to luxury articles. Nevertheless, traders laden with commodities frequented the distant and difficult trade routes in the country. We have frequent references to caravans of 500 carts each in the Buddhist birth stories. Traders also visited such distant countries as Babylon. Shore-sighting birds were employed to facilitate navigation.

Trade was facilitated by the advent of money economy, which was ushered in by the use of punch-marked coins. Vedic evidence for the prevalence of coins is not corroborated by any finds belonging to that period. Our earliest finds of coins cannot be dated beyond the age of the Buddha, when they were used by groups of merchants who punched their marks on them. During this period money economy had become so important that even the price of a dead mouse is staled in terms of money. We repeatedly hear of *setthis* or others possessing eighty kotis (crores) of wealth living in towns. Moneylending was practised, and although it was not encouraged by Buddhism, as by Calvinism, those who had not cleared off their debts were not permitted to join the Buddhist *Sangha*.

[10] V.S. Agrawala, op. cit., pp. 97–8.

It would be fair to conclude that in pre-Mauryā times urban and rural economy developed on even lines in north-eastern India, although the precise role of the state in this connection cannot be indicated. Coins first appear in the north-west. But in the Ganga region, it has been suggested that the punch-marked coins were issued by the ruling dynasties of Magadha and Kośala; the possibility cannot be ignored, but identification of coins with particular rulers still awaits final solution. The rulers showed interest in other economic activities such as the clearance of forests, regulation of the land system and supervision of guilds.

V

In Mauryā times we witness an unprecedented expansion of the economic activities of the state. The distinguishing feature of Mauryā economy *c*.322–200 BC is the state control of agriculture, industry and trade, and the levy of all varieties of taxes on the people. Evidently the state was in dire need of a great amount of surplus in kind and cash, which had been rendered necessary because of several factors. No other state in ancient India, either earlier or later, maintained such a huge standing army as the Mauryās did. The process had begun with the Nandas (354–324 BC), who had raised their army from 5,000 elephants, 20,000 cavalry and 50,000 foot soldiers to 60,000 elephants, 100,000 cavalry and 200,000 foot soldiers. Perhaps these figures accord well with the traditions about the enormous wealth of the Nandas. But by the time of Chandragupta Mauryā this figure multiplied almost twice, for Plutarch and Justin inform us that this first Mauryā emperor overran the whole of India with 600,000 men. Megasthenes puts the total number of Mauryan army at 400,000. To maintain this large army, which was essential to defend the different parts of the far-flung empire, must have meant terrific economic strain, which could not be met without finding new sources of income. Secondly, the Mauryās followed the policy of maintaining sufficient surplus in the treasury for emergencies. The normal taxes were not considered sufficient to meet all the needs of the state, and hence the state undertook and regulated numerous economic activities, which formed a profitable source of income to it. These enterprises necessitated the employment of a vast, numerous bureaucracy consisting of the superintendents and subordinate staff in some thirty departments; this further burdened the state exchequer, which had to be replenished by new sources of taxes.

The Mauryās made an important contribution to the development of rural economy by founding new settlements *janapadanivesa* and rehabilitating the decaying ones by drafting surplus settlers from overpopulated areas. The Śudrā, who were hitherto regarded as the collective property of the three higher varṇās, meant for their sender as slaves and hired labourers, were encouraged to settle down as farmers in these settlements, made possible by the aid granted to them by the state. In order to bring virgin soil under cultivation, they were allowed remissions of taxes and other concessions by way of supply of cattle, seeds and money in the hope that they would repay when they were in a position to do so. In the new settlements land was granted to retired village officials and priests, but such land could not be sold, mortgaged or inherited. Even the ordinary peasants could not pass on their land to the non-taxpaying peasants. If the farmers failed to cultivate the plots allotted to them, these were transferred to others for better use. Although the extent of these new settlements is not known, it would be reasonable to suppose that by means of Śūdrā labour a considerable portion of the Ganga basin was brought under cultivation.

The state farms working under the supervision of the *sītādhyakṣa*, or superintendent of agriculture, formed a major source of income to the state. We do not know the origin of these farms, but they seem to have been the natural culmination of the large scale farming with units of 500 or 1,000 *kāriśas* earned on by the kulaks in pre-Mauryā times. Magasthenes refers to the absence of slavery but under Chandragupta a considerable number of slaves and hired labourers were employed in working these farms. Besides, the superintendent made use of an advanced knowledge of agriculture; thus Kauṭilya refers to six seasons, whereas we find only five seasons in the earlier period.

What helped agriculture most was the provision of irrigation facilities by the state and the regulation of water supply for the benefit of the agriculturists. Megasthenes informs us that in the Mauryā empire the officer measured the land as in Egypt, and inspected sluices by which water was distributed into the branch channels, so that everybody might enjoy his fair share of the benefit. We learn from Kauṭilya that irrigation cess amounted to a fifth, a fourth or a third of the produce of the irrigated soil. As in Egypt, the regulation of irrigation may have contributed to the centralization of the state power, especially in western Bihar, UP and Punjab where only a regular supply of water could ensure the normal yield of crops.

The Mauryā states regulated trade and industry by means of a number of superintendents. The superintendent of commerce (*panyādhyak-sa*) corresponded to Megasthenes' 'great officers of state of whom some held the charge of the market'. The superintendent of weights and measures (*pāütavadhȳak-sa*) was responsible for enforcing correct weights and measures. The superintendent of ships regulated communications by water and realized ferry dues. But the customs on commodities for internal and external commerce were mainly collected by the superintendent of tolls (*sūlkadhyak-sa*), who realized customs varying from 1/5 to 1/25) according to the nature of commodities. The state derived further profit from the supervision of several industries. The superintendent of weaving (*sūtradhyak-sa*) looked after the weaving industry, which was mainly run by women labour. The superintendent of liquor managed the breweries and state wine shops, which flourished at the cost of private breweries, encumbered with the payment of heavy duties to the state. Thus the state enjoyed almost unrestricted monopoly in trade in liquor, as in salt.

In my opinion the main base of royal power, and all agriculture, trade and industry, was mining and metallurgy. Speaking of the Kathaians in the time of Alexander. Strabo states that the Indians are unacquainted with the mining and the smelting of ores and hence do not know their wealth and traffic with simplicity[11] but this can apply to the Kathaians and not to the Indians as a whole. In the Mauryā period Kauṭilya provides for the superintendent of mines (*aḳāradhyak-sā*), who was expected to possess a thorough knowledge of the technical aspects of mining, including metallurgy. He was to prospect for new mines and discover old and disused ones by various signs. The literary evidence suggests that gold, silver, copper, lead, tin, iron and bitumen were worked. But except for the mining of copper and gold the archaeological evidence is scanty. It has been suggested that the copper and gold mines in Dhalbhum in Chotanagpur were worked from the time of Chandragupta Mauryā. The nearest copper mines to the Mauryā capital Pataliputra are those of Baragunda in the Hazaribagh district and Singhbhum, and probably they furnished at least some copper vessels, used at the court.[12] Since numerous small heaps of iron slag are to be found scattered all over the iron belt in south Bihar, these may have been the refuse of local

[11] McCrindle, *Ancient India as described in Classical Literature*, p. 86.

[12] Murray, *JRASB*, 3rd series, vi, 101.

iron smelters.[13] But whether these workings are as old as the Mauryā period cannot be stated. Literary evidence, however, does not leave any doubt about the working of iron, for lolia (iron) in its various forms is mentioned far more frequently in the *Artha-sastra* than tamra (copper). The *lohāḍhyaksa* seems to have been the officer-in-charge of iron working. Other officers employed in connection with mining and metal work were the superintendent of digging (*khanyāḍhyaksa*), the officer who distinguished between different elements (*lāksanāḍhyaksa*) and the superintendent of salt (*lavanāḍhyaksa*). Thus the state enjoyed a monopoly in the working of mines and in trade in mineral products. This was not only a source of great income but was also of great help in strengthening the central power for only the state could equip the soldiers with metal arms and furnish agriculture and industry with necessary tools and implements. Kauṭilya was fully conscious of the importance of metals and mining. He points out that the treasury has its origin in mining, and force (*daṇḍā*) in the treasury, and it is by means of the treasury and force that earth is acquired (II.2).

The income derived from economic undertakings was supplemented by a large number of customary and new taxes. The chief tax was the royal share in the produce of the peasants, amounting to perhaps one-sixth. But the Greek accounts suggest that this was levied at the rate of one-fourth of the produce. One Greek source indicates that the levy amounted to one-fourth, whereas the other states that the peasants received one-fourth of the produce as their share. Perhaps the second is due to some confusion, and both mean the same thing. However, we hear of sharecroppers, who were supplied with seed, oxen, etc., by the state and received arable land for cultivation. Those who were in a position to invest their own capital in the land allotted to them by the state received hardly the crop share. Thus the state derived income from both the fixed royal share of the one-sixth of the produce as well as from sharecropping. Besides the regular *bhāga* (royal share of one-sixth), the peasants were require to pay the *pindakara*, which was lump assessment made on the groups of villages. We do not know the nature of another tax, known as *bāli*, which was as old as Vedic times but may have been a religious tax during Mauryā times. *Kara* was probably a part of the produce from the fruit and flower gardens paid to the state. *Señabhakṭa* probably involved an obligation on the part of the villagers to supply provisions to the royal army when it passed through their

[13] Ibid., 79.

territories. *Hiranya* seems to have been a payment in cash. In addition to these the peasants had to pay irrigation cesses, to which reference has already been made.

We have seen how customs and ferry dues constituted important sources of income to the state. Taxes were also levied on the guilds of artisans living in the capital (or *durga*), which may imply that the artisans living in the countryside, enjoyed exemption. Thus the list of taxes in Mauryā times is impressive, and reveals a deliberate attempt on the part of the state to extract as much surplus produce from the people as possible. What is more remarkable than even these numerous taxes levied normally, is that it could not meet the mounting expenditure of the state. And hence, although we hear of emergency tax in Paniṇi, for the first time the *Artha-sāstra* provides such taxation measures on a large scale. One such measure was the imposition of *pranạyā*, which has been interpreted as the gift of affection, but this meaning seems to be as illusory as that of the term bait in the sense of voluntary offering in Mauryā times. *Pranạyā*, however, could be levied only once and amounted to one-third or one-fourth of the produce according to the nature of soil. Another extraordinary measure laid down by the *Artha-sāstra* is the compulsory raising of a second crop by the cultivators. We learn from Patanjali that the Mauryā rulers also derived income from the images of gods. This may have been done either by selling them or establishing them for worship. The latter device was recommended by the *Artha-sāstra*. According to the Jain tradition, Chanakya issued eight hundred million debased silver coins called *karsapāṇas* to fill the treasury. All these were emergency measures to meet extraordinary situations in Mauryā times. Moreover, a major portion of the ordinary taxes seem to have been set apart for this purpose, for the Mauryā policy was to deposit half the income as an insurance against emergencies. Had they not followed this policy, the incidence of normal taxation on the people would have been lower. But as it is, the numerous ordinary and extraordinary taxes, and the undertaking and control of important economic activities of the country, show that the whole economy of the country was geared to the financial needs of the state.

Perhaps most of these taxes were realized in kind and deposited in the central storehouse under the supervision of its superintendent (*kös-thagaradhyaḳ-sa*). But as would appear from payment to government employees in cash (their highest salary being 48,000 panas and the lowest 60 panas) and from the duties of the superintendent of the mint, money economy had made considerable headway. This can be also inferred from several hoards of the punch-marked silver coins, certain types of which are specifically ascribed to Mauryā rulers. Nevertheless, further development of money economy was thwarted by the Mauryā policy of freezing half of the collected taxes in die treasury and not putting them to any productive use. Besides, the irksome customs levied on all varieties of commodities may have acted as another deterrent to the progress of money economy. In spite of this the country registered substantial economic progress in the Mauryā age, which witnessed giant strides in the development of agriculture and the mining industry.

VI

The state control over all sectors of economy established by the Mauryās did not last for more than a century. In post-Mauryā times (*c*.200 BC–AD 200) we no longer hear of state farms worked by slaves and hired labourers under the supervision of the superintendent of agriculture. But land seems to have been mainly in possession of individual farmers. As regards the extension of the area of cultivation, state efforts seem to have been replaced by individual efforts. The *Milinda-panha* refers to the individual who clears the forest and takes other steps for making the land fit for cultivation. And because he brings the land under use, he is called the owner of the land.[14] This is also corroborated by Manu, according to whom sages declare a field to belong to that particular person who cleared away the timber, and a deer to him who first wounded it (IX. 44). Thus, theoretically the investment of physical labour in a piece of unclaimed property was supposed to confer on the individual the title to that property. The principle was probably enunciated to give a fillip to the extension of cultivation. This can be also inferred from a passage of Manu according to which the acceptance of an untilled field by a brāhmaṇa is less blamable than that of a tilled one (X. I 14). Although, as we shall see presently, the practice of making grants of cultivated land had already come into vogue, the underlying idea of making grants of untilled land to the Brāhmaṇas was to make it arable. Gautama and Manu[15] encourage separate households for brothers on the ground that it increases religious merit; this implies promotion

[14] Milinda, Trenckner's edn., p. 219.

[15] XXVIII, 4 and IX. 111 respy.

of individual ownership of land. The *Divyavadana* refers to individual farmers in large numbers working hard and engaged in cultivation.[16]

This period provides us the first epigraphic evidence for the grant of land by merchants, lay worshippers and rulers to Buddhist monks for their support and allied religious purposes[17] in the *Sātavāhana* dominions. Grants made by the rulers tarried freedom from taxation and full and unrestricted enjoyment of the resources of the village which was granted. Some inscriptions refer to the size of plots of 2, 3, 4, 8, 12, and 25 *nivartanas*[18] one *nivartana* being roughly equal to an acre and a half. These plots do not necessarily give any idea of the fragmentation of land, except suggesting that there also existed smaller plots of land. We have, however, also a reference to a grant of 100 *nivartanas* of land of a royal field.[19] Remarkably enough none of the inscriptions from northern India refer to the grant of land during this period, although the epigraphic reference to the *aksayanivi* (perpetual endowment) system in connection with money donations may suggest that the grant of land according to this tenure, which became fashionable in Gupta times, had already begun during the first two centuries of the Christian era.

Stringent punishments, including death, laid down by the law books for those who cause any harm to water reservoirs and destroy embankments, and the glorification of the virtues of constructing wells and tanks, indicate that the importance of irrigation was fully realized. Irrigation facilities continued to be provided by some rulers on regional basis. Thus Kharavela not only repaired and enclosed a tank in Kalinganagari but also extended an old canal, opened by King Nanda, at the cost of a hundred thousand panus. The work of similar importance was undertaken in Sauratra by Rudradaman (AD 150), who repaired a major breach in the dam of the lake, by spending enormous wealth out of his own pocket, without burdening his subjects with taxes, forced labour and emergency impositions. The happy tradition of constructing tanks in western India was maintained by the successors of Rudradaman. Tanks seem to have been constructed by Śākā and Kuṣāṇa chiefs in north-western India. Evidence of the popularity of tanks in this part as well as UP, during the first two centuries of the Christian era, is furnished by the practice of offering ritual tanks, which have been discovered at

[16] Cowell's edn., p. 463.

[17] *Lüder's List* Nos. 1000., 1024, 1030, 1053.

[18] *Arch. Suru. Western India*, iv, 97.

[19] Ibid., p. 160.

Taxila, Hastinapura, Udaipur, Anicchalra (in Bareily), Kausambi and Bhita near Allahabad. Whereas tanks may have been constructed by rulers, initiative for such undertaking was also shown by individuals, whose houses, tanks, orchards and fields were protected against seizure by others.[20] Tanks were also dug by co-operative efforts made by the villagers. There is however not much evidence for the use of canals in the first two centuries of the Christian era. This might suggest that comparatively smaller plots of land had come to be the order of the day, and irrigation by wells or tanks may have been employed as an aid to the intensive cultivation of these plots.

Although the state did not undertake agricultural operations as it did in the Mauryā period, it probably enforced laws to protect agriculture, which was apparently disturbed by repeated foreign invasions. Thus Manu enjoins the king to punish people for the theft of agricultural implements (IX. 293) and provides mutilation for selling false seed corn, for taking up seed already sown, and for destroying boundary marks (IX. 291). Perhaps this was one of the most tangible economic benefits, in return for which the state levied taxes on the agriculturists. The *Milinda-panha* refers to the village headman (*gāma-samika*), who summoned all the village householders through his messenger to the front of his house for the purpose of levying taxes on them on the king's behalf (p. 147).

The state hardly exercised any control over arts and crafts, which witnessed a remarkable growth during this period. We do not come across so many kinds of artisans in the earlier Buddhist texts or the *Artha-sāstra*, as during this period. The *Digha Nikaya* mentions about two dozen trades,[21] but the *Mahāvastu* gives a list of thirty-six kinds of workers living in the town of Rajagrha.[22] The list is not exhaustive, for it is said at the end of it that there are others besides these mentioned. The *Milinda-panha* enumerates as many as seventy-five occupations (p. 331), about sixty of which were connected with various kinds of crafts. Of these eight crafts were associated with the working of mineral products, such as gold, silver, lead, tin, copper, brass, iron and precious stones or jewels (p. 331). A variety of brass (*prakuta*), zinc, antimony and red arsenic are also mentioned.[23] All this betokens considerable

[20] Manu, VIII. 264.
[21] PTS. ii, 50.
[22] Senarl's edn. iii, 442–3.
[23] *Mahāvastu*, ii, 106.

advance and specialization in the working metals. In particular, technological knowledge about the working of iron had made considerable progress.[24] It is because of this that Indian iron and steel are mentioned in the *Periplus* as imports into the Abyssinian ports.

Cloth-making, silk-weaving and the making of arms and luxury articles[25] seem to have made progress during this period. Five processes of cloth manufacture were undertaken by Gotami, the aunt of the Buddha.[26] Mathura had acquired special celebrity for its manufacture of *sātaḳā*, a special kind of cloth.[27] Manu levies taxes on the produce of the weavers, who probably owed their affluence to trade in textiles produced in Mathura. We do not know whether there was any special progress in the manufacture of oil, but the *táilkachaḳrá* or oil wheel is mentioned in the *Ďivyavädaña* (p. 70). In the inscriptions of the period weavers, goldsmiths, dyers, workers in metal and ivory, jewellers, sculptors, fishermen, smiths and more frequently perfumers, figure as donors of caves, pillars, tablets, cisterns, etc., to the Buddhist monks, which suggest that their crafts were in a flourishing condition.

In post-Mauryā times we get the earliest epigraphic evidence regarding the existence of the guilds of artisans. Artisans were organized under their headmen, who probably enjoyed the favour of the king.[28] During the second century AD in the Sātavāhana territory, money (in silver *panas*) was deposited by the lay devotees of Buddhism with the potters, the oil millers and the weavers for the purpose of providing robes and other necessities for the monks.[29] In the same century a sum of money was deposited by a chief with the guild of flour makers at Mathura, out of the monthly interest of which a hundred brāhrnaṇas were to be served daily.[30] Thus the craftsmen organized in guilds could function independently. Evidently they could purchase raw materials and implements with money deposited with them and could pay interest on it out of the proceeds from the sale of their commodities. Literary evidence indicates that the number of guilds had increased during this period. Besides the traditional eighteen guilds the *Mahāvastu* (iii, 442f.)

[24] It is stated that even when beaten, black iron carries weight and that it does not vomit up the water it has once soaked in *Milinda* (p. 415).

[25] *Milinda*, p. 331.

[26] Ibid., p. 240.

[27] Pataniali. I. 1 .2: Kielhnrn i, 19.

[28] *Lüders'* List, No. 346.

[29] Ibid., Nos. 1133, 1137.

[30] *EI*, xxi, Incr. No. 10.

mentions eleven kinds of artisans, all working under their respective heads (ii, 463–78). A comparison of the two lists of this text attests the existence of at least two dozen guilds of artisans during this period. Many of these artisans functioned both as producers and small traders. Although the Buddhist texts refer to Rajagrha and Sakala as centres of arts and crafts, most artisans known from inscriptions were confined to the Mathura region and to the western Deccan where their prosperity was stimulated by the growing trade with Rome.

From the economic point of view the most important development of the period was the thriving trade between southern India and the Roman Empire. In the beginning the major part of this trade seems to have been by land. But the movement of the śākās, Parthians and Kuṣāṇas which followed from the first century BC, put an end to this trade. The Parthians of Iran, however, imported iron and steel possibly from China or India. But from the first century AD, trade was carried on mainly by sea. The discovery of monsoons by Hippalus in AD 46 gave a great impetus to this trade, which may have existed in driblets in earlier times. The sailors now became armed with better knowledge of navigation, which enabled them to call at the Indian ports of Bhrgukaccha (Broach), Arikamedu (Pondicherry) and Tamralipti. But the trade between India and Rome was not carried on in articles of daily or common use. The details show a brisk commerce in luxury goods but no extensive production by large industries.[31] It seems that the Romans mainly imported spices for which southern India was famous. They also imported muslins, pearls and jewel-stones from central and southern India. All this may be taken as constituting 'terminal trade', for these products were directly supplied by India.[32] Besides, some 'transit trade', especially in silk, which diverted by Parthian hostility from the more direct continental routes, sometimes found its way from China via the east coast of India to the ports of the Malabar coast from where it went to die West. In return the Romans exported to India wine-amphorae and red-glazed Arretine ware, which have been discovered in recent excavations at Arikamedu. But what is more important, the Romans exported to India large number of coins that were invariably of gold and silver. Sixty-eight hoards of Roman coins of the first century AD have been unearthed in the subcontinent, and no fewer than fifty-seven come

[31] K.H. Warmington, *Commerce between India and the Roman Empire*, Cambridge: 1928, p. 300.

[32] Wheeler, *Rome beyond the Imperial Frontiers*, Pelican, p. 164.

from south of the Vindhyas.[33] This justifies the complaint of Pliny who bewails the fact that Rome was being drained of gold on account of her trade with India.

It has been suggested that the Indians in peninsular India did not know the use of gold or silver currency,[34] and that, for the most part, the imported coins can only have been used as bullion. But we have some silver coins ascribable to the Andhras, and the epigraphic evidence suggests the use of silver *panas*. Hence Roman gold coins may have been valued for their intrinsic worth, but may also have circulated in big transactions. In the north, the Greek rulers issued a few gold coins, but the Kuṣāṇas issued them in considerable numbers. It is difficult to subscribe to the theory that all Kuṣāṇa gold coins were minted out of the Roman gold. As early as the fifth century BC, the Indian satrapy paid a tribute of 320 talents of gold annually to the Persian empire. The source of the metal may have been the gold mines, reported to have existed in Sind in the time of Alexander.[35] This territory and the gold mines of Dhalbhum lay under the sway of the Kuṣāṇas who enjoyed the benefit of the knowledge of melting and mining transmitted by the Mauryās. But on account of contact with Rome they began to issue the dinara type of gold coins, which became abundant under the Gupta rule. Nevertheless, in day-to-day transactions silver, and especially gold coins, could hardly be used by the people, *Patanjaii* refers to payment in *niṣkās* to the wage earners (*karmakārās*), but these do not seem to have been gold coins at this stage. In this connection, the issue of lead or potin coins by the Andhras is significant, for it indicates that in the Deccan and in the coastal area money economy had come to be prevalent. The same inference can be drawn in respect of northern and north-western India from the coinage of the Kuṣāṇas, who perhaps issued the largest number of copper coins. Copper coins were also issued in large quantities by the Naga rulers, especially Ganapati Naga, and by several indigenous dynasties such as those of the Yaudhevas and the Mitra rulers of Kausambi, Mathura, Avanti and Ahicchatra and other dynasties. This would suggest that perhaps in no other period had money economy penetrated so deeply into the life of the common people of the towns and suburbs as during this period, a development which fits well with the growth of arts and crafts and the country's flourishing trade with the

[33] Ibid., p. 165.

[34] Ibid., p. 167.

[35] Strabo. XV 1.34 in Hamilton and Falconer, iii 96.

Roman Empire. In spite of this progress of money economy, if we rely on Manu it would appear that royal officers were not paid in cash. Revenue officials, who were in-charge of one, ten, twenty, a hundred or a thousand villages, were remunerated by grants of land,[36] which indicates the dominance of natural economy in rural areas.

VII

The main interest of the economic history of Gupta age (*c.* AD 200–500) lies not so much in its foreign trade and money economy as in the partial feudalization of the land system and the rise of local units of production. An important development was the grant of cultivated land to temples and Brāhmaṇas in northern and eastern Bengal, and in the eastern part of modern Madhya Pradesh. But the land grants in Madhya Pradesh differed from those in Bengal in two important respects. The Bengal grants were the results of sale transactions effected by individuals and involved the transfer of land, but the central India grants were made by feudatories who gave away villages. The Bengal grants were made with the consent of the officers of the central government and carried immunity from taxes only, but the central India grants provided administrative immunities as well. Nevertheless, in the case of both these regions, terms denoting uncultivated land were used in a conventional sense. The same seems to have been true of the grants dated in the Kalacuri-Cedi era, found in Gujarat and Maharashtra during the fifth to the seventh century AD. The usual phraseology in most of such grants is that villages and plots of land were granted together with *údranġā* and *upaṇkārā*, inclusive of all dues and exempt from all gifts, forced labour and special lights, and not to be entered by soldiers and policemen, which indicates that those areas were settled areas. It has been suggested that the practice of granting land in Bengal and other parts of India extended the area under cultivation and rural settlement. This may have been true of some plots of land in northern and eastern Bengal, but generally in Madhya Pradesh, Gujarat and Maharashtra, settled villages and cultivated plots of land were the objects of gifts. In some cases the order regarding the grant of a village to the Brāhmaṇas was conveyed to the Brāhmaṇas and other inhabitants of the village, which shows that the Brāhmaṇas were not introduced into the village as pioneering cultivators.

[36] Manu, VII. 115–20.

The terms of transfer indicate that generally plots of land were cultivated not by the Brāhmaṇas but by temporary peasants. It seems that the number of independent and permanent peasant proprietors paying land tax directly to the king was falling off. Fa-hsien states that 'only those who till the king's land pay a land tax' and that they are free to go or stay as they please.[37] This probably excludes a large number of other people, who did not pay land taxes to the state but to priests, temples, monasteries and other intermediaries. For in the succeeding paragraph Fa-hsien clarifies the position by stating that monasteries are given fields and gardens with husbandmen and cattle to cultivate them.[38] Land grants from the fourth to the sixth century AD in Maharashtra and Gujarat clearly establish that the recipient was given the right of enjoying the land, cultivating it or getting it cultivated on lease.[39] The number of the Brāhmaṇas who were actual cultivators may not have been insubstantial, for the law books of the period provided that Brāhmaṇas might legitimately take to cultivation. But the Brāhmaṇas and temples often got their lands cultivated by others.

The law books show that similar arrangements were made in relation to secular holdings, with the difference that the owner of the land had to make some payment to the state. Kauṭilya provides that in new settlement land fit for cultivation should be given to the peasants by the king,[40] but Yajnavalkya lays down that land should be assigned to the cultivator by the landowner (*kshetrasvāmi*), who, of course, was entitled to the fruits of improvement made on the land in the case of the absence of the owner (11.157). In the organization of the land system Yajnavalkya (11.158) introduces three stages, viz., *mahipaṭī* (king) *kshetrasvāmi* (landowner) and *karshakā* (cultivator), which is roughly corroborated by Bṛhaspati (XIX. 54–5). The intermediaries leased out land to cultivators, who were liable to penalties if they neglected cultivation.[41] So these cultivators were in the nature of temporary peasants. The same seems to have been true of the peasants under donees, who could replace old peasants by new and thus might oust their tenants.[42] Besides, the economic advantages, which hitherto accrued to the state, were completely transferred to the donees, thus cutting asunder the ties

[37] *Legge*, A Record of Buddhistic Kingdoms, pp. 42–3.
[38] Ibid., p. 43.
[39] *CII*, iv, No. 2. line 6; No. 11. line 13, etc.
[40] *AS*, II.1.
[41] Yaj.II.157-8; Br., XIX.19. 53–5.
[42] *CII*, iv, Introd., p. clxxi.

between the central government and the peasants. The state, however, maintained its control over the free peasants through the imposition of taxes. The villagers had to make not only various kinds of contributions to royal troops and officials when they passed through their areas, but they were also subjected to forced labour of all varieties (*sarua-visti*), probably for military purposes. Local officers were gradually assuming economic power. Vatsyayana informs us that peasant women were compelled to fill up the granaries of the village headman, take things into or out of his house, clear or decorate his residence, work in his fields, and spin yarn of cotton, wool, flax or hemp for his clothes (V5.5), so that clothes might be supplied to him locally. Some of the commodities thus produced were also put on sale, apparently to cater for the simple needs of the villagers. The Mauryā states regulation of trade and industries was giving way to the management of these affairs by the chiefs of local economic units, independent of the central control.

There is further evidence to show that an important development in Gupta times was the rise of local units of production. Irrigation tended to be a local responsibility. In the Gupta period we have a reference to the repair of the famous Sudarsana takes in Saurastra, carried out by the local provincial government. But already from the beginning of the Christian era the local population had begun to take initiative in irrigation. The law books of Bṛhaspati lay down that the guilds should look after irrigation dams (XVII. 11–12).

Elaborate laws about corporate activities can also be linked with the rise of local and 'autonomous' units of production. The law books of Gupta times lay down detailed rules regarding partnerships in business and functioning of guilds. These corporate bodies not only performed important economic functions such as carrying out joint contracts, plying trade and receiving money deposits, but also performed judicial and executive functions in relation to their members. Epigraphic evidence of the period shows that the guilds not only issued coins and seals, but also maintained their militia, which according to the Kalacuri inscriptions, was known as *śrēnibāla*. The increasingly autonomous character of the guilds, as virtually independent units of production and political power, can be inferred from the rules which govern the relation between the guilds and the state. Whereas the earlier texts enjoin the king to pay respect to the customs of the guilds (*śrénidhárma*),[43] those of the Gupta period instruct the king to enforce the usages

[43] Gaut., XI. 21–2; Manu, VIII. 41 and 46.

prevalent in the guilds.[44] Bṛhaspati lays down that whatever is done by the heads of guilds towards other people, in accordance with prescribed regulations, must be approved by the king, for they are declared to be the appointed managers of affairs (XVII.18). He also warns that if the usages of localities, castes and families (*kulās*) are not maintained, the people will get discontended and wealth will suffer thereby (I.126). Thus it seems that the guilds were free to act in whatever way they liked, and the king was bound to accept their decision.[45] It is true that on certain occasions the king could interfere in the affairs of the guilds. Narada ordains that the king should prevent a combination of different guilds probably of a hostile nature, the arming of these corporations without sufficient grounds, etc. He should also prevent them from embarking on anti-state or immoral or criminal actions (X. 4-7). But these regulations clearly show that during this period the guilds were considered capable of threatening the authority of the state. Probably some of these guilds dominated the economic life of the towns such as Vaisali and Mandasor, and thus functioned as independent units of production.

That local units of production were coming into existence can also be inferred from the paucity of coins of common use from the Gupta period onwards. Whereas the Indo-Bactrians, and especially the Kuṣāṇas, issued a considerable number of copper coins, which were evidently in common use in Punjab, and occasionally are found even as far east as Buxar in Bihar, the Gupta emperors, other than Kumaragupta, hardly issued any copper coins. Thus Fa-hsien seems to have been correct when he stated that cowries formed the common medium of exchange. Even allowing for the fact that copper is more susceptible to corrosion than more precious metals, the comparative rarity of Gupta copper coins suggest that money economy was becoming weaker at this time. Coins in general become still rarer from the time of Harsavardhana onwards, which leads us to the conclusion that from the seventh century AD onwards trade suffered a decline and urban life began to disappear, a feature which can be compared with a similar development in Iran.

Reference has been made to the issue of copper coins by several indigenous dynasties of northern India in post-Mauryā times. There also began the practice of issuing coins by the *nigamas* during the post-Mauryā and Gupta periods, which seems to provide further

[44] Yaj., II. 192. I. 361; Narada, X. 2.

[45] R.C. Majumdar, *Corporate Life in Ancient India*, Calcutta: 1918, p. 62.

evidence of the rise of self-sufficient economic unit. This accelerated the process of political disintegration, for issuing coins was an important function of the sovereign power. Besides, the issue of the seals by Nalanda villages, which glorify themselves as *janapadas* even in Gupta times, indicates that they were emerging not only as politically independent but as economically self-sufficient units. At least four such seals were issued from villages, some of which were issued by the *nigamas*, but not by rural units as we find in post-Gupta times.

The rise of the local units of production undermined central authority, but some allied developments such as the strengthening of guilds helped to improve the position of artisans, who, instead of working a day in a month for the king, were now required to pay taxes. This was obviously an indication of further progress in arts and crafts. As in the previous period, during this period also the basis of economic progress lay in the extended and better technical use of metals. The *Amarakōsa* furnishes us a long list of commonly used metals. We get two names for bell-metal (*píltạla*) (11.9.96), four names for lead (II.9.105), three names for mica, four names for antimony (II.9.100), four names for blue vitriol (II.9.101), three names for vitriol of copper (*ŕasanjanā*) (ibid., 102), four names for calx of brass (II.9.103), five names for yellow orpiment (*hariṭalā*) (ibid.), five names for red chalk (*śilaiatü*) (ibid., 104), seven names for red arsenic (ibid., 108), three names for nitre or saltpetre (ibid., 108), and five names for natron or alkali (ibid., 109). Thus these furnish us not only the names of metals, natural and artificial, but also various kinds of ingredients used in making alloys. Copper, mica, manganese or glass, and mines of which the king was regarded as the owner, are mentioned in the works of Kalidasa.

From the point of view of common use the most important metal was iron, for according to a Mahayanist text the yogi was permitted the use of earthen or iron pots, but not of gold, silver, bronze or copper pots. The *Amarakōsa* gives seven names for iron and two for iron rust.[46] The same text provides five names for ploughshare (II. 9.13) which shows it to be the most important agricultural implement and indicates more cultivation of land. It seems that during this period some improvement in the ploughshare also took place. In connection with the performance of the ordeal ceremony it is stated that the ploughshare, in weight and eight angulus or four inches in breadth, was used in cultivation.[47] The

[46] II. 9. 98. 9.

[47] Brhaspati, IX. 79-80.

weight seems to be reasonable, although the breadth may have been actually less. At any rate this indicates the use of a heavy ploughshare intended for deep ploughing or brining virgin soil under cultivation. As is evident from the Mehrauli Iron Pillar of Chandra, the technical knowledge in iron working had reached its high watermark during this period. The manufacture of bronze articles, which became more abundant from this period onwards, became widespread on account of the increasing and easy use of iron implements. Metal workers formed an important and sizeable class of artisans, but hardly owned metals. It was laid down that a metal worker in iron, copper, lead, tin, silver or gold, has to pay to the metal owner, who gives these to him to prepare utensils, for the loss in smelting which exceeds the usual loss.[48]

Besides metal workers, we learn of the presence of garland makers, washermen, potters, bricklayers, weavers, tailors, painters, armourers, leather workers, blacksmiths and shell-cutters, for each of whom Amara gives two names (II. 10.5.10). He, however, gives four names for goldsmiths and five for carpenters (II. 10. 8-9), which shows that their crafts were considered more important in society. The inscriptions show that in central and western India the crafts of silk-weavers and oilmen flourished well, for they were organized in guilds, made endowments for religious purposes, and especially the silk-weavers of Malwa showed considerable mobility and initiative.

Despite flourishing arts and crafts foreign trade does not seem to have been as extensive as in post-Mauryā times. Trade with Rome, which was the main source of earning bullion for India, was undermined by the Roman reaction against the drain of gold, and was completely stopped because of the barbarian invasions of the Roman and Gupta empires. Trade was revived between India and the Byzantine Empire as we learn from Procopius and the balance was in favour of India. As usual the chief article of import for traders was spices, to which we may add silk produced and manufactured in India. Chinese silk was probably obtained by the Byzantium directly from China rather than through India. The coastal people of southern India carried on trade with the countries of South-East Asia, where they had planted colonies, but this did not seriously affect the economy of the interior of the country. Really the comparative absence of copper coins issued by the central authority during this period shows that there was hardly any medium

[48] Jolly, *Hindu Law and Custom*, p. 236.

through which the ordinary folk of one town could enter into exchange relations with those of the other. The gold coins issued by the Gupta rulers could be useful only for big transactions such as the sale and purchase of land, in which dinars were used. Smaller transactions were evidently conducted through the barter system or cowries. It will be therefore fair to hold that Indian economy in Gupta times was based on self-sufficient units of production in villages and towns. The bond of state control which kept these units together in Mauryā times and that of copper currency which unified it in post-Mauryā times or longer operated during this period. This is, however, not to suggest that production declined. On the other hand, it seems to have shown a substantial rise, causing some improvement in the position of the lower order.[49]

The above survey of the economic history of ancient India, covering a period of about 3,000 years, would show that changes in economic life were not as swift and rapid as in political life, but they were not altogether absent. We can mark certain well-defined stages in this long history, namely the urban economy of the Harappa culture; the pastoral and plough-cultivation economy of Vedic times; the wider use of iron, the extensive cultivation of rice, sugarcane and cotton, and the rise of towns in pre-Mauryā times; the Mauryā state control of all sectors of economy; expansion of mono economy and thriving trade with the Roman Empire in post-Mauryā times; and the partial feudalization of land system and the rise of local units of production in Gupta times. Many of these changes could not have been rendered possible without periodical improvements in the tools, implements and knowledge of production. It has been held that in India there has been practically no change in the means of economic production for more than 2,000 years,[50] but as far as ancient India is concerned there can be no basis for such a view.

The French version of the article was published in the *Journal of World History*, vol. VI, No. 2.

[49] R.S. Sharma, *Śudrās in Ancient India*, Delhi: 1958, pp. 234–41.

[50] S.N. Dasgupta, *A History of Sanskrit Literature*, Calcutta: 1947, Introd., p. xciv.

CHAPTER 3

Peasant Production in Ancient India*

In the Marxist view the mode of production includes the various types of resources which generate production; these are called means of production. It also includes relations of production which are established as a result of the distribution of the production resources or because of

* For the earlier studies see Bhupendranath Datt, *Studies in Indian Polity*, Calcutta: 1944; S.A. Dange, *India from Primitive Communism to Slavery,* People's Publishing House, Bombay: 1949; and R.S. Sharma, *Some Economic Aspects of the Caste System in Ancient India,* Patna: 1952. D.D. Kosambi, *An Introduction to the Study of Indian History*, Popular Prakashan, Bombay: 1956, was a pathbreaking work. Dev Raj Chanana, *Enclavage dans Í Inde ancienne dé aprs les Texts Palis at Sanskrit,* Pondicherry: 1957, was the first well-researched work on slavery; it appeared in English version as *Slavery in Ancient India*, People's Publishing House, Delhi: 1960. My own books include *Śudrās in Ancient India,* Motilal Banarsidass, 1958, 3rd edn. 1990; *Aspects of Political Ideas and Institutions in Ancient India,* Motilal Banarsidass, 1959, 5th edn., 2004; *Material Culture and Social Formations in Ancient India,* Macmillan, First published 1983, reprinted nine times (1985-2005), 2nd edn., Delhi 2007; *Perspective in Social and Economic History of Early India,* Munshiram Manoharlal, New Delhi, 1983, 2nd edn., 1995 and *Origin of the State in India,* Department of History, Bombay: University of Bombay, 1989. Also see Romila Thapar, *From Lineage to State: Social Formation in the Mid-First Millennium* BC, Delhi: Oxford University Press, 1984. The best book on the subject is Brendan O' Leary, *The Asiastic Mode of Production,* Oxford: Basil Blackwell, 1989.

the sharing of the fruits of production. Means of production in the context of ancient India comprise land, water, pastures, labour power and tools used for artisanal and agriculture operations. Those who possess the means of production form the dominant class, and those who are dispossessed of these form the dominated class. Further distinction is caused by the sharing of the surplus.

The concept of surplus plays a vital role in the Marxist theory. If producers consisting of peasants, artisans and others produce something over and above their day-to-day needs, this extra produce is called surplus. In ancient India it is given to the state as taxes and tributes and to the priests and religious bodies as gifts, tithes, etc. Basically those who live on the surplus and do not take part in primary production constitute the ruling class or its allies, and those who are deprived of the surplus form the ruled class. The same applies to the possession of the means of production. However, in ancient India we notice the peculiar phenomenon of entitlement to surplus without much control over the means of production. The differences over the sharing of the production resources and the surplus lead to class conflict. Some Marxists consider 'ideology' to be a part of the mode of production. Whereas the significant role of ideology in influencing production cannot be denied, it is best studied as a byproduct of the operation of the productive forces.

We may review the application of the Marxist theory to the period from Ṛgvedic times to Mauryā times. The Ṛgvedic people were confined to Afghanistan, Pakistan (mainly Punjab), and to Punjab and Haryana in India, especially in the upland or hilly areas in 1500–1000 BC. They practiced both agriculture and stock raising. *Yava* mentioned in the *Ṛgveda* means cereals though they are not specified. But the general impression created by the *Ṛgveda* in one of pastoralism. Animals served not only as a source of food but also of dairy products. The verbal term for milking occurs in most Indo-European languages. It seems that agriculture provides fodder which led to the expansion of pastoralism. Numerous terms indicating non-cattle institutions are derived from cattle. They are *gavesana* (search for cows), *gavisti* (battle on the issue of cows), *gavyuti* (measurement of distance), *gopa* and *gopati* (head of cattle—and therefore, of people).

There is very little indication of private ownership of land. More than land, pastures such as *vrjana* provided free access to all, though chiefs seem to have possessed far more cattle than ordinary clansmen. This may have been the result of distribution of booty acquired from perpetual wars that were fought between tribes for possession of cattle.

Horses may have been largely owned by the chiefs. The importance and ownership of the horse can be inferred from many horse-based names of the Vedic chiefs.

Unequal distribution of horses and cattle brought inequality in the early Vedic society. The *Purāṇas* indicate grossly unequal distribution of cattle, which are shown in the possession of members of the two higher varṇās, but such references are lacking in the Vedic texts. The Vedic chiefs claimed larger shares in booty as reward for their physical and mental qualities. Clansmen surrendered to the chief all the booty they captured. Occasional *báli̅* or voluntary tribute given by clansmen and defeated chiefs may also have generated inequality.

The early Vedic society was neither fully egalitarian nor class divided. The Brāhmaṇas and Kṣatriyas are mentioned only a few times in the *Ṛgveda* and only an interpolated passage suggests the varṇā system. Basically it was a kin-based society in which close kin groups were engaged in cattle rearing, agriculture and war. The frequency of the terms *jana, vish,* etc., indicate the tribal or the kin-based character of society.

In 1000–500 BC the Vedic people moved to preponderantly alluvial tracts lying in the Indo-Gangetic divide, and in the land lying in between the Ganga and Yamuna. Though stock-raising continued to be important, the settlement marked by the use of the diagnostic pottery called 'painted grey ware' shows that agriculture became far more important with the production of wheat, rice and lentils. The appearance of iron probably helped the chief in wars, as tribal analogies suggest the control of the head of the tribe over the mines. Though initially iron was not used on any large scale in agriculture, the peasants produced a modest amount of surplus to enable the chief to perform ostentations sacrifices. However, there is no archaeological evidence of urban settlements prior to 500 BC in the later Vedic zone.

Land, the principal means of production, could not be alienated by the chief without the consent of his clansmen, but the chiefs certainly owned far numerous heads of cattle. Possibly they received regular *báli̅* though it had not been converted into taxes. Differentiation between the prince and the peasant had started, but it was not so wide and sharp. They ate from the same plate and used the same weapons though horses may have probably been used only by the chiefs.

Towards the end of the later Vedic period (500 BC), the varṇā system had become a reality. This was linked with production relations. The Brāhmaṇas who received gifts and the Kṣatriyas who received voluntary payments had come to the forefront. The Vaiśyas were mainly peasants and the Śūdrās were a small serving community. Certain groups of families took to war and administration, and received shares without working in fields and pasture grounds. Similarly, other groups became confined to priestly functions and received gifts which they did not have to return. Although progress in agriculture made this possible, how and why the priests and warriors claimed a larger share in the surplus needs to be investigated. Differentiation is attributed to the difference between the senior and junior lineage, but why and how such lineages were formed needs to be explained. In our view the earliest social division may have been in the form of male dominance caused by plough agriculture and the use of horse. In the male society further differentiation may have arisen because of differences in age and experience coupled with mental and physical qualities. Whatsoever be the precise cause, the relations of production appearing at the end of the Vedic period were legalized as varṇā system when iron came to be used substantially in the upper and middle Ganga plains in artisanal and agricultural production.

The society that emerges in post-Vedic times in the middle Ganga plains can be called a peasant society in the sense that free peasants dominated it numerically. If the 'peasant mode of production' means a mode in which the peasant meets the subsistence needs of his household and then provides sufficient surplus for the support of priests, warriors, administrators, artisans, merchants and urban people, this term can be used to describe and analyse the system of production that prevailed in pre-Mauryā times. In this system priests and administrators act as managers of production, and merchants function as economic mediators between the peasants and artisans on the one hand, and the ruling groups on the other. Like peasants, artisans, slaves and agricultural labourers are also directly engaged in production and work for their subsistence.

The 'peasant mode of production' arose in the thickly forested but extremely fertile alluvial plains of the middle Ganga. The use of iron in clearing vegetation and breaking the hard soil of the new alluvium led to an enormous increase in the production of food grains. The beginning of paddy transplantation increased its yield nearly twofold or more. This scenario explains the burgeoning of settlements in the period of the Northern Black Polished Ware from 600 to 200 BC.

No doubt cereals were produced in part of the middle Ganga plains around 200 BC and in other parts from 1500 BC onwards. But the Neolithic-Chalcolithic settlements are much fewer in comparison with the NBPW settlements. It is wrong to think that the intensive use of bone and stone tools together with the practice of double cropping produced surplus. Double cropping was not practiced in the middle Ganga plains till the 1930s or so, and there is no evidence of intensive use of bone and stone tools in promoting agriculture in the middle Ganga plains.

Archaeological findings leave no doubt that iron acted as a catalyst in transforming the agricultural and artisanal scene. Its increasing use multiplied not only the iron tools but also the objects made of copper, bone, stone, semi-precious stone, woods and glass. Iron tools facilitated the fabrication of metal money which boosted petty commodity production and long-distance exchange. But the most important consequence of the use of iron was the production of agriculture surplus which enabled the peasant to pay taxes to the state and provide gifts for the priests. According to the Sanskritist P.V. Kane, the Vaiśyas were the principal taxpayers, and according to the Pali scholar Richard Fick Brāhmaṇas and Kṣatriyas were exempted from payment of taxes. Thus the two higher orders formed privileged varṇās. The Śūdrās acted as domestic slaves, hired labours and artisans, but they were not engaged in production as slaves on any large scale. The relations of production formed towards the end of the Vedic period were formalized in the law books or the Dharmasutraṣ between 500 and 200 BC.

Kauṭilya's model of the state visualizes state control of production. Whether centralization applies to the Mauryā state has been under debate.[1] His *Arthaśātra* may not be Mauryā but it is not much later than the third century AD. The Mauryā model may have continued modification under the Śatavāhaṇās and the Kuṣāṇas.

There is no way to measure the effectiveness of the state control of production. We do not know whether it was real or symbolic. But if palace economies could be practiced in Egypt and Mesopotamia in the Bronze Age, state control of production could be possible in the Iron Age. The effective jurisdiction of the Mauryā state may have been confined to the middle Ganga plains. These plans had four to six million people, if we calculate on the basis of the figures of soldiers given by classical writers. If the East India Company controlled the Ganga plains from Allahabad to Calcutta, the Mauryā state could also do it in pre-

[1] I.W. Mabbett, *Truth, Myth and Politics in Ancient India,* New Delhi: 1972; J.C. Heesterman, *Inner Conflict of Indian Tradition,* Delhi: Oxford University Press, 1985, pp. 16–18, 129, 132–3, 139–40, 142–3, 260 with fns 20–1; Romila Thaper, *The Mauryans Revisited,* Calcutta: 1987.

industrial times. By river and land route the A-sokan pillars could be transported from Chunar to Allahabad, Meerut and Ambala and also to Śānchi and Amaravati, not to speak of Patna and other places in Bihar.

Production relations seem to have been upset towards the end of the third and beginning of the fourth centuries AD. The earliest Purāṇic descriptions of the Kali age assigned to these centuries by the Sanskritist R.C. Hazra speak of the chaotic conditions created by the refusal of the Vaiśyas and Śūdrās to perform the functions prescribed for them.[2] The rulers are called tyrannical and grabbers of property (*vittapiharinah*) and the Brāhmaṇas are shown as behaving like Śūdrās. The state tried to cope with the situation by using force which is lauded in many texts. They also seem to have adopted the practice of land grants which led to unequal distribution of land and eventually to the contraction of the area covered by the ancient mode of production.

We cannot apply any single label to the ancient mode of production. The Asiatic mode applied to the economic systems of both ancient and medieval India by Karl Marx has lost its relevance because of the material and methods available to us 150 years after his study of India. Marxism certainly helps us understand better the economic and other aspects of ancient history, but the specific historical findings of Marx may not be always useful. The attempt to place the ancient Indian economy in the straitjacket of the slave and hired labourers on state farms, but neither the number of farms nor that of the slaves are known. A-soka's claim to have brought 100,000 captives from Kalinga to Pataliputra may be an empty boast, for the term one hundred thousand or *sata sahasa,* repeatedly mentioned in his inscriptions, is a cliché. The law books state that the Śūdrā must be reduced to slavery, for which they are created by the Creator Himself. But the ancient texts mostly suggest domestic slavery and not slaves engaged in artisanal and agricultural production. Ancient Indian society can be called a slave owning society in the sense that people employed domestic slaves, but it cannot be characterized as a society based on the slave mode of production.

The Marxists speak of the Asiatic mode of production, and some of them also apply it to pre-modern India.

The Asiatic mode of production stresses not only the role of the slaves in production, but also oriental despotism which regards the king

[2] Sharma, R.S., 'The Kali Age: A Period of Social Crises' in, *India: History and Thoughts—Essays in Honour of Basham,* ed. S.N. Mukherjee, Calcutta: A.L., 1982, pp. 186–203.

as an untrammeled agrarian emperor. But in ancient India and in later times the rules of the Dharmasastras and the continuity of tradition controlled the king. Thereby neither the theory of slavery nor that of the despotic agrarian emperor can be applied to the pre-modern history of India. Therefore the Asiatic mode of production has no place in Indian history.

The early mode of production could be called a peasant mode, though such a generalization ignores the Śudrā labour employed in production; the Vaiśyas were mainly peasant producers who paid taxes in ancient India.

We have no idea about the number of members of various varṇās. Though some Śūdrās were used as slaves, they did not outnumber the Vaiśyas in ancient times. Bharatratna P.V. Kane, who wrote five volumes of the history from the Dharmasastras,[3] state that the Vaiśyas were the principal taxpayers in ancient times. This suggests that they were mainly peasants who produced and paid taxes. Hence it would be wrong to think that the Śūdrās were mainly used as slaves in the mode of production. It seems that the mode of production was far more managed by the Vaiśyas than by the Śūdrās who could only be reduced to slavery according to Manu.

In developing the idea of the Asiatic mode of production some scholars stress the role of slaves in the mode of production and also emphasize the presence of oriental despotism. Some Marxists apply this mode of production to pre-modern India. But the historical sources do not show that the agricultural production was mainly carried on by the slaves. Similarly the country did not experience the rule of an untrammeled agrarian emperor.

It is said that the king controlled both land and water. Control of water or hydraulic despotism does not appear in early India. The rules of the law books or the Dharmasastras governed the connections of the different castes with the management of production as well as the functioning of the raja on the basis of Dharma. Further, the tribal traditions of equality did not completely disappear from society even when it was divided into castes. Only the Śūdrās were considered slaves. On the other hand the Ksaṭriyas represented the varṇā of rulers. But the kings ruled with the support of the Brāhmaṇas who created an ideological atmosphere through their teachings and various social and religious rituals and festivals.

[3] R.S. Sharma, *India's Ancient Past,* New Delhi: OUP: 2005, p. 324.

Chapter 4

Economic Life of Northern India in the Gupta Period

The successive lists of these on South Asian history in progress in various universities, compiled by the Department of History, School of Oriental and African Studies, University of London, show that of recent years the study of economic and social history of India is engaging the serious attention of scholars. Dr Maity, like many other, tries to make amends for the neglect of 'the activities of common men' (p.1) by the historians of earlier generations. He has set himself the task of reconstructing the economic history of the Gupta period, on which he has produced a very competent Ph.D. thesis for the University of London, prepared under the able supervision of Professor A.L. Basham, who graciously contributed a scholarly foreword to the book. A welcome feature of the book is the wealth of epigraphic and numismatic material which has been brought to bear on it. Dr Maity also made full use of the relevant foreign sources, which have been hardly utilized hitherto for the purpose of the economic history of this period. Further, he has laid under contribution, works on lexicography and astrology such as those of Amara Simha and Varahamihira. Recent archaeological excavations at Gupta site have also not been ignored.

Although the much used Dharmaśātra literature supplies considerable matter to this study, the picture that emerges from an examination of supplementary sources mentioned above is refreshing. The obvious merit of Dr Maity's study is the integration of diverse sources in reconstructing the economic life of a precisely defined period. While much has been written on the economic life of the earlier periods, except in the case of the Mauryā period they are piecemeal studies based exclusively either on the Buddhist, or Brāhmaṇical or Jain sources. As a result, these pictures, though adequate in some cases, are incomplete in every case. Dr Bose's *Social and Rural Economy of Northern India* takes into account the important sources, but treats the period 600 BC–AD 200 as if it marks one well-defined phase in the economic history of India. But Dr Maity's work does not lend itself to this criticism. The chief limitation with regard to the use of sources is his inclusion of Manu and omission of Kātyāyanā. It is well-known that in many respects the law-codes of Narada and Brhaspati are the elaborations of the provisions laid down by Manu, and hence, except for extracting supplementary information or for following the developments that had begun in the post-Mauryā period, Manu cannot be utilized for the period *c.* AD 300–550. Kātyāyanā throws considerable light on money lending and property suits, but in other respects the omission of this source by the author does not substantially affect the picture he has outlined. One wonders whether the commentaries to the Pali canons, written and compiled in Ceylon during this period, can be made to yield corroborative information about the economic life of Gupta times. It must, however, be said to the credit of Dr Maity that he has taken great pains and care to scrutinize his references. He makes use of his own grandmother's tales (p. 165, fn. 4; p. 173, fn. 5), but in a true historical spirit.

In my opinion the most important and valuable part in the book is the Chapter Two which deals with land system in the Gupta period. It discusses the various aspects of the land problem—such as ownership of land, types of tenure, land survey and measurement, grants and sale of land. Dr Maity's section on land measurement throws new light on the various units of measure. The *kulyāvapa* being the most frequent measurement in the Gupta inscriptions of Bengal, the author enters into a detailed discussion of the meaning of this term and concludes, that a *kulyāvapa* measures a little more than 14 acres (p. 41).[1] Dr Maity makes certain important points about the sale of land. On the basis of the available epigraphic material he notes that land was sold only for religious purposes; there are no cases of secular sales, a point which we might elucidate. It is true that in the Gupta period secular sales are as conspicuously absent as those of grants of land for secular purpose. But secular land transactions, as is evident from the elaborate rules regarding sale of land in the *AS* (III. 9-19), were conducted as early as the Mauryā period. The provision that tax-paying peasants (III. 10) should sell their land only to similar peasants clearly presupposes secular sales. In all such cases the king was entitled to some sort of registration fee (III. 9), a practice which continued into the Gupta period. The fact that land transactions even for religious purpose were not exempt from such fees in the Gupta period might indicate the existence of secular sales on which such impositions were regularly made. If the account of Fa-hsien is to be given credence, in the Gupta period some officers were assigned land revenues, but we have no charters for such grants. In all likelihood charters relating to land grants and sales for secular purposes were inscribed on brittle and perishable materials, and therefore have not survived. Since such acts did not have commemorative value in the public eye, no attempts were made to inscribe them on permanent and durable materials. As regards the motives underlying these land grants, Dr Maity states that feelings of piety and benevolence finds expression in religious and charitable gifts (p. 43). But gifts were probably also inspired by the necessity of keeping the Brāhmaṇas in good humour and observing the social customs, and thus had became almost obligatory.

The third chapter discusses the sources of revenue mainly on the basis of inscriptions. While discussing the import of technical revenue terms such as *upārikāra* and *úḍrāṅgā* Dr Maity takes into account the interpretations of other scholars but offers his own suggestions. As regards *upārikāra*, he accepts the suggestion of Dr D.C. Sircar that it means extra cess (p. 62). But the writer makes two ingenious interpretations of the term *úḍrāṅgā;* first, that the term is derived from *ḍráṅgā* and is therefore a police tax levied on the district for the maintenance of the local police stations; secondly that the term is derived from the Sanskrit word *údaka*, and may be a water tax. Dr Maity, however,

[1] These conclusions were first published in *JESHO,* I, pp. 98–107.

leaves the question open, and does not state his preference for either of the two alternative suggestions. As the to term *úḍrāṅgā,* there is no doubt that it was a tax collected by an officer called *audrangika* (Sircar, *sel, Inscrs.,* 360, fn. 9). We suspect that similarly *upāriḳārạ* was a tax collected by the *upārika.* Our view is supported by the joint mention of the two officers *upārika* and audrangika in a list which mentions several other revenue and police offices (ibid., 360, 1.4). Linguistically the connection of *upāriḳārạ* with *upārika* does not seem to be untenable, for the former may be abbreviated into the latter with consequent change in meaning. Thus if *upārika* is taken in the sense of an overlord, *upāriḳārạ* may have been an extra tax paid to him and to the state.

The fourth chapter provides a readable and solid account of agriculture, famine, irrigation, forestry, gardening and animal husbandry. The author introduces a small, but very interesting, section on the effects of the principle of *áhimśa* on animal life. The fifth chapter introduces us to the various industries of the Gupta period and closes with a note on the general condition of industry and industrial workers. Maity finds it strange that Varahamihira is almost silent about industries, and explains it by stating that his profession was more favoured by the agricultural and commercial interests than the industrial (p. 5). We do not know whether the absence of references indicates slackness in industries, which incidentally may be taken as a presage of feudalism, but in this case we shall have to account for the astrologer's references to trade and commerce.

The sixth chapter, which is devoted to trade and commerce, gives us much new material about the overseas trade of the Gupta period on the basis of foreign records, including those of Cosmos, Procopius and Justinian. We learn that the Gupta age was specially noted for the flourishing condition of trade in Indian silk products. Just as in the first century AD the Roman empire was being drained of gold bullion by the Persian merchants, who functioned as go between in silk trade with India. The drain was so heavy that Justinian had to adopt stringent measures of price control to stop this. He enacted that one pound of silk should not cost more than eight pieces of gold, and that he would confiscate the wealth of one who violated this law (p. 137). The use of silk was obviously confined to richer sections of society. But whether trade in general served only their needs is a question worth investigation. Information on the comparative volume of trade in the Gupta period and on trade routes would have been welcome additions to the study of its economic life.

Two other chapters, which discuss the position of labour and corporate economic life, are based chiefly on Brāhmaṇical law books and serve to bring together at one place the relevant material on these subjects. Dr Maity is not dazzled by the 'golden' trappings of the Gupta period, and candidly concludes that hired labourers probably suffered perpetual discontent and poverty under the superstructure of material progress and prosperity (p. 152). Nevertheless, there are reasons to suppose that during this period the slave system, especially as far as it is related to the system of production, was in a state of decline. Although the classification of slaves into sixteen categories by Narada apparently suggests that the slaves had increased in number, the provision of Yajnavalkya that nobody can be reduced to slavery against his wishes shows that the Śūdrās could not be degraded to servile condition. Besides, the reference of the period hardly supply us with any information regarding slaves employed in productive work.

Dr Maity rightly prefaces his chapter on currency, exchange and moneylending with the remark that so far Ideologists have studied Gupta coins mainly for the sake of political history, ignoring their value for economic history (p. 165). The author therefore makes a fresh examination of coins from this angle, and his appendix relating to the gravity and gold content of Gupta coins is a major contribution not only to the economic history of the Gupta period, but also to the political relations of the Guptas with the Kuṡānas to the former's political history after Kumaragupta I. But at places the author cannot resist the temptation of switching on the political history; for instance he gives much attention to the identity of the Kumaradevi Chandragupta type of coins (pp. 174–78). We think there is some further scope for discussing the bearing of coins on the economic history of the Gupta period. Why are copper coins comparatively rare and gold coins so abundant in the Gupta period? Does the latter fact indicate restricted use of money? Most hoards of gold coins have been found in Uttar Pradesh and in the neighbouring area of Bharatpur, which shows that these coins were more current in the heart of the Gupta empire. We wonder whether the provenance of gold coin throws any special light on the money economy of this area. Dr Maity rightly suggests that gold coins may have been used in big sale transactions and not paid as taxes by ordinary peasants, but in our opinion revenues from big landed proprietors or taxpayers may have been collected in gold coins, which may indicate the rise of big taxpayers in the countryside during this period. Perhaps the term *bīranýa* in inscriptions refer to the payment of tributes in gold not by the peasants in general but by certain rich persons in the village. Has all this anything to do with the shrinkage of money economy and the consequent rise of local units of production?

We may also make one observation relating to the section on moneylending. Dr Maity points out that the general rate of interest on secured loans was 15 per cent per annum (p. 183), but adds that on unsecured loans Brāhmaṇas, Ksaṭriyas, Vaiśyas and Śūdrās paid per annum 24, 36 48 and 60 per cent respectively (p.183). He does not explain the difference in the rates of interest on such loans according to varṇas. It appears that the lawgivers of the Gupta Period (Viṣṇu. VI. 2., Yaj, II, 37) uncritically take over the older rules (M., VIII. 42, Vas., II. 48, p. 183, fn. 9), which may have been operative in the earlier period and superseded by a more equalitarian law of 15 per cent (nr., I. 99; B., X. 22), which is first mentioned in the *Artha-sāstra* of Kauṭilya (*sapadapana dharmya masavrddhih panasatasya,* III, 11).

There is no doubt that Dr Maity's work is a pioneer monograph in several respects. But there is some room for further research on several other economic problems of the Gupta period. One of these is the organization of agrarian economy, with special reference to the economic pattern of village. One wonders how far the self-sufficient village economy, potters, carpenters, barbers, physicians, weavers, etc., attending to the needs of the village on the basis of a fixed share of produce at the time of harvest and rent-free land for building purposes that became typical of India in subsequent times, had its origins in the Gupta period. We also require some information about the nature and organization of urban economy. It has also to be determined whether tools and implements used by agriculturists and artisans underwent any changes, leading to consequent increase in production and rise in standards of life.

Dr Maity does not say anything about the population problem in the Gupta period. In the appendix he refers to some passages from the *Brhat Samhita* which allude to the decline of population (p. 196), but he does not follow this up in the body of the text. Reference to famines, plagues, pestilence, etc., in astronomical and literary works coupled with an examination of the village sites of the Gupta period may yield some material on this point. The author refers to the non-availability of land in north Bengal, which indicates increase in population in that part of the country. But we do not know whether there was any definite rise in material standards during this period and, if so, whether this led to a rise in population. Finally, although Dr Maity's book is the first work on the economic life of a restricted period in ancient India, it fails to bring out the specific features of economic developments of this period as compared to the post-Mauryā or post-Gupta periods. These criticisms are merely intended to give space for further study for Dr Maity could not possibly have covered more ground than he has in a Ph.D. thesis. We are grateful to the author for what he has done, but we have posed these problems because his work has roused great expectations for the future.

Sometimes it is contended that those who work on economic history should have a good grounding in economics; our author gives sufficient proof of this equipment. From the historian's point of view, to find out the nature of the correlation between economic phenomena and other developments is a fruitful study. But such a line of enquiry can be rendered possible only by a thorough analysis of the economic conditions existing in a particular period, and in this the author has succeeded amply. We hope that he will zealously pursue his investigations further.

Chapter 5

Some Economic Aspects of the Caste System in Ancient India

I

In as far as the caste system is occupational and is based on the division of labour, its rise is connected with the emergence of a stable economy. The Vedic and Dharma-sātra literature do not throw any light on this question. What has been said on their basis does not explain the early stage leading to the rise of classes.[1] The Brāhmaṇical and Jain traditions supplemented by the Buddhist source can be made to yield some information on this aspect of the earlier social history. Their account of the pre-varṇā society and the origin of the varṇās enables us to have

[1] A summary of some of the theories of the origin caste can be found in K.P. Chattopadhyaya's article in *Visvabharati Quarterly,* 1924–25, vol. II. Hutton has quoted the theories of two dozen writers on the origin of the caste in his book *Caste in India* (latest edition) on pp. 170–6. His own conclusion are found on pp. 189–90.

some idea about the precarious economy of the primitive man and the beginning of its stability with the rise of agriculture.[2]

Anthropological studies have established that the earlier society was a food gathering society. Its main sources of livelihood were plucking the fruits and roots, and hunting the animals. Speaking of the primitive people Morgan says, 'In the means of subsistence, they advanced from natural fruits in a restricted habitat to scale and shell fish on the coasts of the sea and finally to bread roots and garnes.'[3] Although the Buddhist, Jaina and Brāhmaṇical accounts do not mention anything about fishing and hunting but from the deception of the impotence of the *kalpabṛkṣa* in the Kṛta age, it is clear that in the early stages people mainly lived on fruits. Their's was a food-gathering economy. The trees did not provide them only with food but also dress and shelter.[4] Therefore when later on house came to be built on the model of *śakhā*, the came to be known as *sālā*.[5] In course of time people were overtaken by the greed and the *kalpabṛkṣa* perished.[6] This was followed by the discovery of another source of livelihood—growth of plants and beginning of natural cultivation.[7] According to the Brāhmaṇical and Jaina sources this was in the Treta age.[8] Till the advent of the Treta age there was no case-division and nothing like greed or the tendency to steal.[9] But all the same the earliest economy rested on a very precarious footing. Repeated mention is made of the destruction of the means of livelihood in the early stages.[10] It shows an unstable economic base. It is only after the rise of agriculture by means of labour that we cease to hear about such frequent destruction of the means of livelihood. It would be reasonable to hold that in the pre-agriculture

[2] This account is found in the important Brāhmaṇical Purāṇa, viz., Markandeya (Chapter 49), Vaya (Chapter 8), Kurma (Chapter 29), Brahma (Chap. 4), Brahmanda (Chs. 29 to 31), Viśṇu P. (Bk. I. Ch. VI) and Jaina Purāṇa, Padma Charista Ch. 3. The picture of the pre-varṇā society in this articles has been mainly drawn on the basis of the Vāyu Purnana which contains the longest description.

[3] Lewis H. MoṚgan, *Ancient Society,* p. 526, (N.Y. 1878).

[4] Vāyu Purāṇa, VIII-86 and 87.

[5] एवँ प्रसिद्धाः शाखाभ्यः शालाश्चै व ग हाणिच। V.P. VIII-121 and 80.
तस्मात्ता वै स्म ताः शालाः शालत्व चैव तासतत्।। Ibid., VIII-84.

[6] प्रणश्यन्ति ततः सर्वे वृक्षास्ते ग हसंस्थिताः। Ibid., VIII-84.

[7] अफालककृटाष्टाचानप्ताः . . . Ibid., VIII-128.

[8] Padmacharita, chap. 29–65.

[9] वर्णाश्रमव्यवस्थाश्च न तदासन्न सङ्करः
नलिप्सन्ति हि ता योन्ननुग्र न्ति चैयहि V.P. VIII-60 & 49.

[10] V.P. III 137–9.

economy, technique being too low, there could be hardly any surplus above what the people required for consumption, and therefore there could be hardly any scope for social inequality based on wealth. But once agriculture was firmly established, labour was found more productive and surplus could be accumulated. Gradually the individuals began to appropriate the surplus to themselves and to their kins and near relatives. As the Purāṇas say: 'They, then, appropriated to themselves by force and violence rivers, fields, hills, trees, shrubs and plants.'[11] In other words the stability of the agrarian economy led to the rise of the private property. The next step was the institution of the division of labour leading to social inequalities and their gradual crystallization in the form of vàrnās. To quote from the Vāyu Purānā again: 'The means of subsistence having been provided Svayambhu established divisions among the people according to their tendencies. Rapacious and destructive men were made Kṣatriya. Truth-speaking and men of sacred knowledge were made Brāhmaṇas. Cultivators and husbandmen were made Vaiśyas and those who grieved and ran, and were addicted to manual tasks, and were inglorious and feeble were made śudrās.'[12] Such a division of the caste pre-supposes a society where some fought and prayed while others produced for them. This is a state of affair which may not be relished by the conscious producers, and they may refuse to perform the tasks assigned to them. Therefore, the Purāṇas further say that their duties (that is the duties of the caste) were settled but they did not fulfil their several duties and came into mutual conflict.[13] There arose the class struggle. Having become aware of this fact the Lord Brahma prescribed (daṇḍā) criminal justice and war as the profession of the Kṣatriya.[14]

The Buddhist sources present more or less the same picture of the economic condition of the pre-caste society. They refer to the rise of the varṇās according to their occupations just after the rise of the private property. According to them the rise of agriculture and private property is followed by the rise of the Kṣatriya or the protecting class who constituted the state and then appeared the other varṇā like the

[11] V.P. VIII-131.

[12] V.P. VIII-155-9.

[13] पुनः प्रजास्तु ता मोहात् तान धर्मान्तान पलायन्। वर्णधमैंरजीवन्त्यो व्यरुध्यन्त परस्परम्।
V.P. VIII-160.

[14] ब्रह्मा तमर्थ बुद्धवा तु याथातथ्येन वै प्रभुः
क्षत्रियाणां बलं दण्डं युद्धमाजीवमादिशत्। V.P. VIII-161.

Brāhmaṇas, Vaiśyas and the Śūdrās.[15] The only difference between the Brāhmaṇcial and Buddhist account is that while the former makes Kṣatriya the protector of the castes, the latter makes him the protector of private property. Hence if these traditional accounts of the origin of the caste are considered in the light of the rise of classes among the primitive tribes, it would be clear that the rise of varṇās in India was intimately connected with the beginning of a stable economy and the rise of private property.

II

An analysis of the function of the different varṇas would reveal that while the Brāhmaṇas and Kṣatriyas were engaged in non-productive activities like praying and conquering, the other two castes were engaged in the primary task of production. The main functions of the Brāhmaṇas were teaching, praying and sacrificing, and as a class they had practically nothing to do with manual labour.[16] Economically they enjoyed a privileged position in the society. According to the Śānti Parva, it was considered an ordinance of religion that fruits and roots constitute the property of the Brāhmaṇas. They would have the first claim over their use and only when their needs have been satisfied, the surplus should go to the other people. It was not proper for anybody to use them at the cost of the Brāhmaṇas.[17] This is also corroborated by Kauṭilya who wants the state to provide the Brāhmaṇas with forests for *soma* plantation, for religious learning and for the performance of penance.[18] Probably the greatest source of their income was as it is even today–gift and presents received from the religious-ridden people. Almost each and every lawmaker in ancient India enjoins on the king to make gift to the Brāhmaṇas.[19] The epic and Purāṇic injunctions on the virtues of making

[15] Digha Nikaya–Aggannasutta; Mahāvastu, vol. I, pp. 340–8 and Tibatan Dulva, vol. V, quoted in Rockhill's *Life of Buddha,* pp. 2–9.

[16] Vāyu P. ch. VIII-162; ch. 54-111; Markandeya P. Chap. 28-8; and Brahma P. Ch. 22-3 and 4.

[17] वद्धनस्पतीन्भक्ष्यफलान्नच्छिन्द्युर्विषयेतव
ब्राह्मणानां मूलफलं धर्म माहुर्मनीषिण:
ब्राह्मणेभ्यो तिरिक्तंच भु जीरन्नितरेजना:
न ब्राह्मणापरायेन हरेदन्य कर्थेचन: Śānti Parva, Ch. 89-1 and 2.

[18] AS Bk. 2, Ch. 1, sec. 20.

[19] Gautama X-9; Ap. II. 10.26. I; Visnumrti III-81 and 84; Manu VII-82; Vajn I-133 and 315; Brahaspati XVII-2 & 3.

gifts to the Brāhmaṇas are too numerous to mention here. It was laid down that the kine taken from the enemy by force should be given away to the Brāhmaṇas so that they may drink their milk.[20] The practice of making gifts to the Brāhmaṇas was sanctioned not only by religion and society but in some cases it was enforced by law. According to Katyayana-smriti, if a man did not carry out his promise of gifts to Brāhmaṇas, he was made to pay it as a debt and was liable to receive the lowest amercement.[21] As the custodians of the gods in the temples the Brāhmaṇas enjoyed certain other economic advantages. It has been an age-old practice in India to grant lands and villages to the gods. While explaining *Jaimini* ix.19, Sabara makes it clear that a field or village cannot be used by a deity, but is used to maintain its attendants. Medhatithi (on Manu xi. 26 and ii. 189) expresses the same view. There were special provisions for the protection of the temple property. Law makers provide stern punishment, in some case, amounting to death against encroachment on temple property.[22] Kauṭilya provides for the office of Devtadhyaka.[23] So enormous was the temple wealth that it could be used by the king when the royal treasury was empty. But a later authority Paithinasi quoted by Aprarka ordains that the king should not deprive temples and corporations of their properties.[24] Although there is very little to contradict the statements of the *Dharmasūtrā* and the Smṛitis about the status of the Brāhmaṇas, it is possible that the picture presented by the Brāhmaṇical writers might be a bit exaggerated. But even the 'non-sectarian character.'[25] of Kauṭilya's *Arthaśāstra* makes no basic difference in the privileged economic position of the Brāhamaṇas. According to Kauṭilya, the Srotriyas were granted *brahmadēyạ* lands which were free from taxes.[26] Besides they enjoyed the other economic privileges like consumption of salt free from duty,[27] appropriation of ripe fruits and flowers for the worship of gods and rise can barley for the performance of *agrayan* sacrifice.[28] More substantial

[20] नतुबध्यधनोतिष्ठेत्पिवेयुर्ब्राह्मणाः पयः S.P. Chap., 96-6.

[21] स्वेचछया यः प्रतिश्रुत्य ब्राह्मणाय प्रतिग्रहम्
नददयाद णवद्दाप्यः प्राप्तयात्पूर्वसाहसम। KS 642 (Kane's Edition).

[22] Yaj II-228; A.S. Bk. II. 9 and Manu IX-280.

[23] A.S. Bk. V. Ch. 2.

[24] Kane, *History of Dharmasastra* Vol. II, p. 212.

[25] Proceedings of the Second Oriental Conference, p. 389.

[26] A.S. Bk. II. Ch. 1, sec. 19.

[27] A.S. Bk. II. Ch. 12, sec. 30.

[28] A.S. Bk. III. Ch. 24, sec. 41.

economic concessions made to the *Srotriyas* were immunity of property escheat,[29] and its exemption from additional taxation or confiscation by the state in times of financial trouble.[30] They also enjoyed claim of receiving back their goods in preference to everyone else except the king.[31] How far the *Srotriyas* covered the Brāhmaṇa class as a whole is a question which needs consideration. Probably there might have been very few Brāhmaṇas who might not be acquainted with the literature and hence these privileges might benefit the whole Brāhmaṇa class. But Kauṭilya also recommends two economic privileges for the Brāhmaṇas as a class. These were provision of free passes[32] to cross rivers and freedom from the payment of dues while passing by military stations.[33]

The fact that the Brāhmaṇas were the recipients of numerous favours is amply demonstrated by the countless tales about giving thousands of cows and slaves to the Brāhmaṇas. Such instances can be cited from the Vedic, Buddhist, Purāṇic and general literature.[34] The Jatākas, which are regarded as representing the actual state of affairs mention Brāhmaṇa landowners, in some cases possessing as many as 1000 *karisas* of land. The *ḿahāsāla* (wealthy) Brāhmaṇa has been mentioned very often in the *Jatāka* stories,[35] and also of Brāhmaṇas possessing eighty *kōṭis.* A law code of about the sixth century AD provides that the ruler should bestow on the Brāhmaṇas, houses and landed property, exempt them from taxation, declaring in a written grant that the revenue is remitted.[36] And this is what we find in a large number of inscriptions. Although there are many inscriptional evidences of even earlier grants but from the seventh century AD onwards the overwhelming number of epigraphic grant records are grants made to the Brāhmaṇas.[37] What is more

[29] A.S. Bk. III. Ch. 16, sec. 71.

[30] A.S. Bk. IV. Ch. 2, sec. 90.

[31] A.S. Bk. III. Ch. II, sec. 63.

[32] A.S. Bk. II. Ch. 28, sec. 45.

[33] A.S. Bk. III. Ch. 20, sec. 75.

[34] As we learn from the Somadatta Jatāka a Brāhmaṇa was given sixteen decorated oxen, much wealth and a village for his residence by a king. Many examples of such gifts have been cited by P.V. Kane in his *History of Dharma-sāstra*, vol. IV, p. 276.

[35] Jatāka, vol. I, p. 140; vol. II, p. 272; vol. IV. pp. 237 and 325; vol. V. pp. 193 and 227 and vol. V, p. 32.

[36] Bṛhaspati XVII-3.

[37] Although no exact figures can be given but that is the impression one gets after a perusal of the contents of the inscriptions.

striking—from the very early times the Brāhmaṇas enjoyed exemption of their property from taxation. Their property was considered the most sacrosanct object. Evidences of this can be traced as early as the times of the *Atharvaveda*. According to it 'the dreadful evil befalls the kingdom of one who eats a Brāhmaṇa's cow or desires to devour him or claims his wealth.'[38] According to *Satapatha Brāhmaṇa* one of the important privileges of the Brāhmaṇa was the freedom from oppression.[39] Probably it was this which led to his freedom from taxation in the *Dharmasūtrās* and even in the comparatively 'secular' state of Kauṭilya.[40] According to Kauṭilya, while settling a tract of country the king was required to grant revenue free lands to various classes of Brāhmaṇas.[41] Mention is made of tax-free villages in Kauṭilya. Obviously they refer to the entire villages that were granted by the king in favour of temples or Brāhmaṇas with complete immunity from taxation.[42] At least so far as the Vedic Brāhmaṇas were concerned it seems almost certain that they were not liable to taxation.[43] Many actual instances of such immunity can be furnished from the inscriptions.[44] Such is the force of the old tradition that even in modern times there are some villages where the local assessors exempt the Brāhmaṇas from the imposition of the *chaukidārī* tax.[45]

According to certain sources nobody enjoyed greater security of property than Brāhmaṇa. It is repeatedly stated in the *Mahābhārata* that the king is the master of the property of all except the Brāhmaṇas and hence he cannot touch their property so long as they continued to perform their duties.[46] The *Mahābhārata* cites the famous example of King Nabhaga, who, after his conquests, gave away whole kingdoms along with their rulers as sacrificial presents to the Brāhmaṇas. The only exception was made in the case of wealth of learned Brāhmaṇas and ascetics.[47] The Śānti Parva makes it obligatory on the king to provide

[38] A.V.V. 19. 35. S.B. II. 5-6, 36. Vaisistha I. 42–45.

[39] A.S. Bk. 2. Chap. 2. Sec. 19.

[40] Ghoshal, *Agrarian System in Ancient India.* P. 22.

[41] S.P. Ch. 76-5 and Manu VII-138.

[42] S.P. D.C. Sarkar *Select Inscriptions,* vol. 1, pp. 266, 361, 404, 410–11, 414–15 and 417.

[43] In my own village Barauni in the District of Monghyr in Bihar till very recent times, say 15 yeas back the brāhmaṇas were not charged chaukidārī tax.

[44] S.P. Ch. 76-10 & Ibid.: Ch. 77-2.

[45] S.P. Cha. 89-3 & 6.41. S.P. Ch. 130-20.

[46] Katyayana-smrti, Vers 8245.

[47] S.P. Ch. 98-27 and 28.

means of sustenance for the Brāhmaṇas who was afflicted for want of support.[48] According to it even in times of distress the Kṣatriya was forbidden to take the wealth of the Brāhmaṇas and ascetics.[49] This gives the impression that in times of emergency also the Brāhmaṇa could not be deprived of the wealth. According to Kāṭyāyana, however, in case a Brāhmaṇa was guilty of theft and his crime was proved, the king could deprive him of all his wealth.[50] It was believed that protection of Brāhmaṇa's property brought great religious merit. It was said that he who dies in defence of the property of a Brāhmaṇa acquires the merit of a sacrifice with infinite presents.[51]

Debt law made special concession to the Brāhmaṇas. In case of inability to pay the debt, the creditor could make all others work for him and even get them imprisoned except the Brāhmaṇa.[52] It was also ordained that the king should make a Brāhmaṇa return debt due to the creditor by conciliatory words, make their return a debt according to the usage of the country and should make others repay their debt by means of physical pain that is imprisonment, etc.[53] According to one source the Brāhmaṇas enjoyed another socio-economic privilege, that is, while other castes including even the Kṣatriyas could be reduced to slavery, the Brāhmaṇas could not be enslaved on any account.[54] Obviously such a law was meant to secure their exemption from direct participation in the work of production.

It will appear from what has been said about the economic position of the Brāhmaṇas that like the priests of other ancient societies, they enjoyed a privileged status. There is no doubt that in some cases the ideal of poverty was held before the Brāhmaṇas but probably this had been more realized in modern times than in ancient times. Both the legal rules and actual examples in ancient India established that the Brāhmaṇas received not only huge gifts but also enjoyed freedom from taxation. In view of these economic privileges enjoyed by the Brāhmaṇas

48 Kāṭyāyana 478-9; Manu VII-177 and IX-229.

49 Kāṭyāyana 477-78 cf. Manu VIII-49. Such practices continue in our villages to this day. In the realization of debt some concession is shown to the Brāhmaṇas but the people of the lower castes are put to great hardships.

50 Katyayanta 715-18.

51 Beni Prasaad in 'Age of Imperial Unity', p. 311, Bombay, 1957.

52 Hopkins, 'Positions of the Ruling Caste', *J.A. O.S.*, vol. XIII, p. 89.

53 Fick, *Social Organization of N.E. India,* p. 119.

54 S.B. VII. 7.1 and V. 2.1.17.

it would be difficult to sustain the statement that 'they enjoyed high prestige of birth but were mostly poor'.[55]

III

The Kṣatriyas constituted the members of the ruling class and like the brāhmaṇas they also enjoyed the privilege of exemption from taxation. Speaking of the warrior castes in the epics, Hopkins states that they were as a matter of fact free from taxes.[56] Similarly on the basis of the study of the economic condition of the sixth century BC in the eastern lands, Fick observes: 'It seems that even in the eastern lands the Khattiyas and the Brāhmaṇas—this in spite of their wealth and in spite of the undisputed fact that the greater portion of the land was in their hands—were free from taxes'.[57] While they had not to pay any revenues to the state, as members of the ruling class the Kṣatriyas had a large share in the taxes realized from the people. In the *Śatapatha Brāhmaṇa* the nobility or Kṣatriya class has been described as the either among the peasantry and the peasants have been described as the food of the nobility.[58] Besides numerous other taxes, the king received land tax which varied from one-sixth to one-fourth of the produce. The principle underlying taxation was that the people should be left at the subsistence level and the surplus should be extracted out of them.[59] The revenues were spent mainly on the military needs of the state. As the *Mahābhārata* says, 'In the treasury again is the root of the army. This is also repeated by Kauṭilya who says that 'out of revenue arises the army and the territory is acquired by means of the revenue and the army. According to Śukra, a later authority, out of the three purposes for which the *kosa* was to be accumulated, the two were the upkeep of the army and the performance of sacrifices.[60] If Megasthenes' statement about the cash payment of the soldiers be correct, at least in the Mauryan times the maintenance of the army must have accounted for a large amount of cash revenue. *Śukranitisāra* clearly states that half of the income of the

[55] Manu X-118; Agni Purāṇa Ch. 222-26 an Hiuentsiang, translated by Watters, vol. I, p. 176.

[56] S.P. Ch. 87-18-21 and Manu VII-127; Śukra IV. 2. II.

[57] S.P. Ch. 130-35.

[58] A.S. Bk. II. Chap. 6.

[59] Śukra IV. 2.3.

[60] Śukra I-316 & 17.

feudatory king should be spent on the army.[61] It is clear that since the Kṣatriyas made up the overwhelming mass of the soldiers, they consumed the greater part of the state revenue. The chief means of their livelihood was warfare. It was a regular industry and one of the main sources of their wealth. One of the three modes of acquiring wealth for the Kṣatriya was by means of conquest.[62] War, says Clauswitz, is a continuation of politics by other means. It can be said as well that in ancient times it was a continuation of economics by other means. The political history of ancient India is mainly a history of war between the ruling classes of different states. By means of it the Kṣatriyas appropriated to themselves the surplus of the conquered peoples. Organized plunder of the foreign states was an integral part of the state policy. Thus out of seven distinct classes of the state troops mentioned in the *Arthaśāstra* two classes were required to be maintained by means of raw materials or by the plunder of foreign states.[63] Similarly Śukra[64] sanctions the king's exaction of wealth from foreign state by forces or fraud or robbery. The distribution of spoils was a great material advantage to the army men. According to Kauṭilya, the soldiers who participated in the work of beheading the enemy, received double salary and obtained possession over the spoils of the enemy.[65] Gautama rules that except horse or elephant whatever is acquired by a soldier by his individual effort should be given to the king by him.[66] Kamandakā and Śukra also say that the man who conquers money, gold or raw materials is their owner.[67] Manu goes further and prescribes that the soldiers could take as booty chariot, horse, elephant, umbrella, wealth, grains, animals and women except jewels, gold and silver. In his view the king should gather all the spoils and distribute them among the loyal warriors.[68] Kāṭyāyana also considered pillage a regular and legitimate source of income and prescribed specific rules for the distribution of spoils. Thus it was provided that the booty would be divided into ten shares; out of them

[61] V.P. VII-161; Ibid., Chap. 45-83; Kurma P. Ch. 49 and Ch. 2, Markandeya P. Ch. 26-29; Brahma P. Ch. 19-19 and Ibid., Chap 222-8; Brahannardiya P. Ch. 23-24; Garuda P. Ch. 19-3 and Ibid., Chap. 205-18.

[62] शुद्धाथलब्धकरजेदण्डाप्तंजयजंतया। Caruda P. Chap. 205-89.

[63] A.S. Bk. IX. Chap. 2.

[64] Śukra IV. 2. 7.

[65] A.S. Bk. X. Chap. 3.

[66] Gautama X-20-23.

[67] Kamandakā X X-21 and 22; Śukra IV. 7, 372.

[68] Manu VII-96 and 97.

one would go to the king, four would go to the head of the pillagers, three would go to the specially intrepid among them, two would go to the capable fighters of the party and the rest would each get one share.[69] Pillaging must have involved fighting and hence could not be done without Kṣatriyas. Therefore it will be seen that warfare was a paying occupation and a source of great income to the Kṣatriyas.

IV

As regards Vaiśyas, in all sources they have been described as performing their important occupation, viz., cultivation, tending cattle and trade,[70] and it was admitted that these are the three things which provide all men with the means of living.[71] There is an impression that the Vaiśyas were generally the owners of cattle and land. They might be in the nature of small independent peasant proprietors or *ǵah-apatīs* as described in the Buddhist literature. As independent tax-paying peasant proprietors of who were entirely devoted to the work production, they constituted the backbone of the society and government. It's probably because of their importance as taxpayers, that the Mahābhārata enjoins on the king to always conciliate and protect the Vaiśyas (*gominah*) and ensure them the security of their property.[72] It is expressly stated there that the king should always act in such a way towards the Vaiśyas that their productive powers may be enhanced because the Vaiśyas increase the strength of a kingdom, improve its agriculture and develop its trade.[73] This might give the impression that the Vaiśyas were independent peasant proprietors and traders. But the Mahābhārata also informs us that a large number of the Vaiśyas earned their livelihood by tending the cattle and cultivating the land of the non-Vaiśyas, who were obviously members of the higher castes. Thus while emphasizing that the main duty of the Vaiśyas was the rearing of the domestic animals,[74] *Śānti Parva* throws light on the actual ways by which the Vaiśya is to earn the means of his sustenance.[75] It was provided that if he keeps (for others)

69 Kat 633-35.

70 *Manu* I-90 and V-480.

71 कृषिगारक्ष्यवाणिज्यंलोकानामिहजीवनम् । S.P. Ch. 89-7.

72 S.P. Ch. 82-35 to 37.

73 S.P. Ch. 87-38.

74 S.P. Ch. 60-22 and 23.

75 S.P. Ch. 60-24.

six kine, he may take the milk of one cow as remuneration; if he keeps for others a hundred kine, he may take a single pair as fee. Further, if he is engaged in cultivation with seeds supplied by others, he may take a seventh part of the yield which would be his annual remuneration.[76] These rules regarding wages of the Vaiśya labourers may be compared to those given in kauṭilya. According to him ordinarily the cultivator shall get one-tenth of the crops grown and a herdsman one-tenth of the butter clarified.[77] An exactly similar rule is given in *Kāṭyāyana smriti*,[78] regarding the wages to be paid to cultivator and herdsmen. It is not clearly stated in these three sources whether the wages-earners were Vaiśyas but since *kṛṣī* and *pasupālya* constituted the main business of the Vaiśya, it is much likely that most of such people were Vaiśyas.[79] It is difficult to say whether the Vaiśya acted as independent traders with their own capital or ordinary peasant middlemen who like the serfs of the medieval European feudal lords took their products to the weekly 'hats' (markets). The *Mahābhārata* says that if the Vaiśya trades with others' wealth, he may get a seventh part of the profits as his share. A seventh also is his share in the profits arising from the trade in horns; but he should get a sixteenth if the trade be in hoofs.[80] This may again be compared with kauṭilya who ordains that trader would be entitled to get one tenth in the commodities in which he is asked to deal.[81] It can be presumed that ordinarily the trader (Vaidehaka) belonged to the Vaiśya caste. Such remuneration as is provided in the Mahābhārata and Kauṭilya for trading in articles and produces owned by others could only provide the wherewithal for the trader and could not help him in amassing fortunes. Of the three occupations of the Vaiśya namely agriculture, tending cattle and trading only the last may be regarded as a sort of secondary production—otherwise the rest two were the prevalent forms of primary production. There are instances to show that on account of thriving trade and commerce some of the Vaiśyas rose to be wealthy merchants in ancient times. During the sixth century BC we hear of many *setthis* of eighty *kotis* worth being associated with the Buddha both in

[76] S.P. Ch. 60-25 and 26.
[77] A.S. Bk. III. Chap. 13.
[78] Kāṭyāyana smrti-656.
[79] A.S. Bk. I. Chap. 3.
[80] S.P. Chap. 60-25.
[81] A.S. Bk. III. Chap. 13.

his previous birth stories and in his later career as Gautama Buddha.[82] It may be misleading, however, to regard the Vaiśya as a wealthy class. Some individual Vaiśya might be rich but in the pre-industrial self-sufficient economy in which trade was confined to the luxury articles and did not touch the day-to-day needs of the people, they could not grow as wealthy as their modern representatives are.

Like the Vaiśyas, the Śūdrās also tended cattle, lived by trade and carried on agriculture.[83] In addition to these occupation the Śūdrā's sphere of activity included not only the various mechanical crafts but it embraced all branches of art such as painting, music, dancing and other fine arts.[84] Ordinarily the Śūdrā's service was reserved for procuring the comforts of the twice-born people and thus for securing his own livelihood but in times of adversity he could also support himself by means of mechanical arts and buying and sellings.[85] Therefore, strictly speaking here was no fundamental difference between the economic activities of the Vaiśya and Śūdrā. But compared to the Vaiśyas the Śūdrās suffered from some economic disabilities. The Śūdrā mechanics and artisans who subsisted by manual labour were subject to forced labour. They could be compelled by king to work for him one day in a month.[86] Gautama ordains that the Śūdrā's accumulation of wealth should be for the support and benefit of other varṇās.[87] And a law which does little credit to the ancient champions of private property is that the Śūdrā was not permitted to amass wealth because it would do harm to the Brāhmaṇas and other high caste people; and hence his property could be confiscated.[88] As to the material condition of the Śūdrās there is some information about the domestic servants. They could be allotted

[82] For instance in the Nidana Katha of the Jatākas besides the well known munificence of Seth Anatha. Pindaka, there is the mention of half a dozen *setthis* who built monasteries for the Buddhists.

[83] Baudhayana I. 5. 10-24; Vajn I-66 and Garuda P. Ch. 96-65.

[84] Viśṇu II-5 and II-14; Gautama X-60 and Manu X-100 and V-120.

[85] द्विजाति संश्रितं कर्म तादर्थ्य तेन पोषणम्
क्रयविक्रयजैर्वापि धनैः कारूदभवेन वा।
Viśṇu P. Bk. III Ch. 8-32. Gita Press Edition.

[86] Gautama X-31.

[87] Gautama X-64 and 65.

[88] संचयांश्च न कुर्वीत जातु शूद्रः कथ वन
पापी यान्हि धनं लब्ध्वा वशे कुर्यादगरीयसः।
S.P. Chap. 60-30 cf, Manu X-129.

a maintenance out of the family property of the master according to their ability, industry and the number of their dependant.[89] Generally the domestic servants would be given by their masters their remnants of food, old clothes, the refuse of their grain and their household furniture.[90] Especially the living conditions of the lower classes of Śūdrā like the *Nisadas, Ayogavas, Medas, Andhras, Chunchus Magus, Ksattris, Ugras, Pukkasas, Dhigvanas* and *Venas* were very miserable. They were distinguished by certain marks and subsisted by their peculiar occupations of 'low' type.[91] Dogs and donkeys constituted the only wealth of the *chandalas* and the *Svapakas* who used the garments of the dead as their dress, took their food from broken dishes and had their only ornaments made of black iron.[92]

Without much difference in their respective occupation the Vaiśyas and Śūdrās made up the producing masses. It appears that they were employed in more or less the primary task of production and by doing so, they supplied the material basis for the existence of the whole social order. The job of the Śūdrās together with that of the Vaiśya was of such enormous importance in the society that probably the entire social fabric rested on their producing and procuring activities. For it was laid down that the king should carefully compel the Vaiśyas and Śūdrās to perform the work prescribed for them, since if these two castes swerved from their duties, they would throw the whole world into cofusion.[93] It meant that if they would go on strike the whole social structure would be upset. As a matter of fact, either by means of providing a share of their produce or by their service, the Vaiśyas and Śūdrās supported the nobility and priestly class. On the basis of *Śānti Parva* 71.10, Śukra IV. 2-13 and Manu X, 119-20, it has been rightly pointed out by Kane that the principal taxpayers were agriculturists, traders, manual workers and artisans.[94] This means that at every stage the Vaiśya and Śūdrā were made to work and pay. Vaistha says that the Vaiśya and Śūdrā could overcome their misfortunes by their property, and not by prayers and the strength of arms as in the case of Brāhmaṇas and Ksatriyas.[95]

[89] *Manu* X-124.
[90] *Ibid.*, X-125 and Gautama X-58.
[91] *Manu* X-50.
[92] *Ibid.*, X-51 and 52.
[93] *Manu* VIII-418.
[94] *History of Dharmasāstra,* Vol. III, pp. 190–1.
[95] Vasistha XXVI-16.

V

The caste was organized as an institution to provide livelihood to the people. It was ordained that everybody should earn his living according to his caste.[96] But the varṇā system also served as an instrument to solidify the economic distinction existing between various classes. Thus except Kauṭilya the law books do not provide for the same rate of interest for all classes of people. The interest charged on the Brāhmaṇa was 2 per cent, on the Kṣatriya 3 per cent, on the Vaiśya 4 per cent and on the Śūdrā it was 5 per cent.[97] The same disparity can be seen in matters of what can be described as a sort of crude income tax, According to Kauṭilya, the finder of the mines, precious stones and treasure was to get one-sixth. If he was a labourer, he would get one-twelfth. In this connection all the authorities Gautama, Vasistha, Manu, Yajnavalkya and *Agni Purāṇa* prescribe that if the Brāhmaṇa finds the treasure, he may take whole of it.[98] Except the last two authorities others do not state the position if the treasure is found by the members of the other three castes. According to them, Kṣatriya had to give away one-fourth to the king, another fourth to the Brāhmaṇa and keep half of it for his own use.[99] In case of a Vaiśya, it was necessary to give one-fourth of it to the king, one-half of it to Brāhmaṇa, and the remaining amount he could keep himself.[100] If a Śūdrā got a treasure, he had to divide it into twelve part, and give five parts to the king and five parts to the Brāhmaṇa. He could keep only two parts that is one-sixth to himself.[101] It is an example of naked class-taxation which taxes the poor and exempts the rich. Such a notion is entirely opposed to the modern income-tax law which professes to exempt the poor and to tax the rich.

Again, in matters of inheritance the share in property was determined on the caste-basis. If the Brāhmaṇa had four sons from his four wives of Brāhmaṇa, Kṣatriya, Vaiśya, and Śūdrā caste, the property would be divided into ten parts. The son of Brāhmaṇa wife would get four shares,

[96] Vishnu Purāṇa, Bk. III, Chap. 11–22 (p. 230) and Ibid., Chap. 13-22 (p. 244). Gita Press.

[97] Manu VIII-142; Yasjn II-37; Visistha II-48; Vishnu VI-15 and A.P. Chap. 253-63.

[98] Gautama X-43 to 45; Vaistha II-13-14; Manu VIII 35-39 Vajn II-34-35; Narada VII-6-7; Viśṇu II-58.

[99] Viśṇu III-59.

[100] Ibid., III-60.

[101] Ibid., III-61; Agni Purāṇa, Chap 255-12.

that of Kṣatriya wife would get three shares, the son of Vaiśya wife would get two shares and the son of Śūdrā wife would get one share.[102] In joint undertakings on the death of a partner the legitimate claimant had to pay a sort of inheritance tax to the king and here also taxes varied from caste to caste. The king was entitled to sixth, a ninth, a twelfth and a twentieth part respectively of the property of a Śūdrā, a Vaiśya, a Kṣatriya and a Brāhmaṇa.[103]

The caste system also affected the pay of the people engaged in public services. Higher posts which carried high salaries were not open to the lower classes particularly the Śūdrās.[104] While ministers, commanders, judges and important state officials were recruited generally from the Brāhmaṇas and Kṣatriyas, and sometimes from the Vaiśyas, the artisans and carpenters employed in the service of the sate belonged to the Śūdrā caste and there was a wide gap between the salaries of the higher and the lower employees. Thus the *rtvik* (priest), the teacher, the minister, the priest (*purohita*) and the commander-in-chief of the army, etc., each received 48,000 panas (either monthly or yearly) but the paltry sum of 120 panas was considered sufficient for the maintenance of the artisans and the carpenters.[105] Others received still less wages. For example, the servants in charge of the quadripeds and bipeds, and workmen engaged in miscellaneous work got only 60 panas.[106] In view of such disparities it may not be correct to hold the view that 'in India caste forbade a combination of the power of wealth with that of office'.[107]

One of the evidence of difference in the economic status of the different castes is to be found in the housing arrangement. In the *brhat Samhitā* it is stated that the Brāhmaṇa should have five houses and the area of his main house should be 32 x 35, the Kṣatriyas should have four houses and the area of his main house should be 28 x 31, the Vaiśya should have three houses and the area of this main room should be 24 x 28, and the Śūdrās should have two houses, and the area of the main room should be 20 x 25. The breadth of the house of the people

[102] Baudhayana II. 2.3.10; Vasistha XVIII-48 to 50; Viśṇu III-32; Gautama X-31.
[103] Brhaspati XIV.13.
[104] Śukra II-426-27; Nitiviakyamrta, p. 108 and Manu VIII-20.
[105] A.S. Bk. V. Chap. III.
[106] Ibid.
[107] *Age of Imperial Unity,* p. 311.

lower in status than the Śūdrā should be even less than sixteen cubits.[108] There is nothing to show how far this planning system actually worked but it is obvious that the higher castes, being more well-to-do, could provide for more living accommodation while the Śūdrā could afford to build only two houses. Another important example of the economic status of the different castes is to be found in the laws regarding slavery. Slaves were an important source of labour power. But there were different grades of fines in case of the enslavement of the members of the different varṇās.

VI

The above discussion would show that compared to the Brāhmaṇas and the Kṣatriyas, the Vaiśyas specially the Śūdrās suffered from many economic disabilities. There might be factional quarrels between the priests and the warriors but ordinarily it lay in their mutual interest to maintain their class privileges by combining together against the members of the lower classes. Everywhere in ancient Indian literature—Vedic, Epic and Dharm-sāstra—the necessity for the concerted action of the Brāhmaṇas and the Kṣatriyas has been emphasized. For instance, in the *Kau-sika Sūtra* of A.V., the Brāhmaṇa says to the king: 'Common to us be the good deeds and common the evil deed', The king replies: 'let evil deeds belong to him who does them, but good deeds and common to us'.[109] Since Brāhmaṇas and Kṣatriyas were the two vital forces in the society, protection is sought for 'this our priesthood nobility' but not for the Vaiśya and Śūdrā.[110] The common formula used in the prayer is 'uphold thou the priesthood, uphold the nobility.'[111] It is also claimed that the Brāhmaṇa and Kṣatriya must live upon the Vaiśya.[112] In connection with one of the ceremonies (in the *Satpatha Brāhmaṇa* in the *Agnichayana*) it is stated that the sacrificer encloses the two castes (Vaiśya and Śūdrā), on both side by the priesthood and the nobility, and make them submissive.[113] Later on in the *upanī-shads* the nobility and the priesthood have been treated as having common interest at many

[108] Brhatsamhita, Chap. 53-12 and 13, Nawalkishore Press, Lucknow.
[109] Quoted in Ghosal's Public life, pt. I, p. 155.
[110] Satapatha Brāhmaṇa IX 4. 1.7. and 8.
[111] Ibid., III. 6.1.17 and III. 5.2.11.
[112] *Pancavimsa Brāhmaṇa* VI. 1. 10 (Caland's edition)
[113] S.B. VI. 4. 4. 13.

places.[114] The same thing is emphasized again and again in the *Dharm-sāstras*. There prevails the maxim that the Kṣatriyas cannot prosper without the co-operation of the Brāhmaṇas and the Brāhmaṇas cannot prosper without the co-operation of the Kṣatriyas. It is only by their mutual co-operation that they can prosper both in this world and in the next.[115] According to Hopkins the same is true of the epics. He puts the view of the epic writers in these words: 'The true basis of kingly power is the priests' power of priestly power the king's power. Their union is perfection.'[116] Even in the republic states the Brāhmaṇas and Kṣatriyas were the dominant classes. Thus those who were neither Brāhmaṇa nor Kṣatriya could not be regarded as malvas or Ksudrakas is the members of the ruling class.[117]

While discussing the duties of the respective castes, the *Mahābhārata* clearly states that all the people have been placed under the charge of the Brāhmaṇas and Kṣatriyas.[118] The one recurrent note running through the *Śanti-Parva* is the absolute necessity for close co-operation between the Brāhmaṇas and the Kṣatriyas for the sake of domination over the rest of the community.[119] It is said that if the friendship existing between the Brāhmaṇas and Kṣatriyas from the days of yore breaks, confusion takes over everything. It destroys the whole social system based on the fourfold varṇā and destruction overtakes all.[120] Further, it is expressly stated that between the Brāhmaṇas and the Kṣatriyas they are rightful owners of everything in the universe.[121] If these statements are taken literally it is clear that the Vaiśyas and Śūdrās were relegated to the position of the vast class of have nots who were meant to produce comfort for the enjoyment of the higher classes. It may be too much to take these evidences at face value but so many statements about the combination of the Brāhmaṇas and Kṣatriyas must contain some stratum of truth. There are not too many clear statements of the bracketing of the Vaiśyas and Śūdrās in the same category. A few significant evidences, however, point to this conclusion. Thus, while according to Manu,

114 Katha Up. 2 .2.5. and Prasna Up. 2. 6. (Hume's Thirteen Principal Upnishads).
115 Manu IX-322.
116 Hopkins, *J.A.O.S.*, vol. XII, p. 254.
117 Altekar, *State and Government in Ancient India,* p. 75, Banaras 1949.
118 ब्राह्मणायचराज्ञंचसर्वाः परिददे प्रजाः S.P. Chap. 60-24.
119 S.P. Chap. 73-4, 5, 11, 12, 13, 28, and 32, Ibid, Chap. 74-2, 3, 14 and 22.
120 Ibid. Chap. 73-12 & 13.
121 नित्योदकी ब्राह्मणः स्यान्नित्यशस्त्रश्चक्षत्रियः
तयोर्हि सर्वमायत्तं यत्किंचिज्जगतीगतम् – S.P. 74-22.

Vaiśyas and Śūdrās were to be kept engaged in their producing activities under compulsion, according to Gautama they could overcome their difficulties by means of their earnings.

VII

The greed of the members of the upper classes for the wealth produced by the lower classes could be paralleled only by their utter contempt for the manual labour which produced it. Normally the work of the Vaiśya and particularly that of the Śūdrā was regarded as reprehensible by the members of higher classes. Ordinarily it was not permissible for a Brāhmaṇa to earn his livelihood by means of agriculture and trade.[122] Such as Brāhmaṇa deserved treatment as Śūdrā.[123] It was only in distress that the Brāhmaṇas and Kṣatriyas were permitted to take to the occupations of the Vaiśyas but in no case were they permitted to adopt the manual service of the Śūdrā.[124] If the Brāhmaṇa did this, he could be treated as a Chandāla. Even when a Brāhmaṇa undertook agriculture and trade in distress, it was provided that he should get it done through other agencies.[125] It was laid down that even in distress, while carrying on trade the Brāhmaṇa could not sell certain specified articles.[126] The practices of selling salt, honey, oil, curd and milk was regarded as contemptible on the part of all castes except Śūdrā.[127] Those Brāhmaṇas who lived by the occupations of the Vaiśyas and Śūdrā were not considered fit for being fed at the *Ṣrdhā* ceremony.[128] But they were not held in division if they adopted the occupations of the Kṣatriyas and actually there are many instance of such Brāhmaṇas. It is significant to note that in the comparatively simple society of *Ṛgveda*, no stigma is attached to agriculture.[129] The Buddhist literature of the sixth century BC furnishes some examples of the Brāhmaṇas directly taking to agriculture as a means of livelihood.[130] But as the society became more

[122] S.P. Chap. 63-1 and 3; Chap. 76-4 and 6.

[123] Ibid., 63-5.

[124] Brahma P. Chap. 222-19. Brhannardiya Purāṇa Chap. 23. p. 297, Gardua P. Chap. 106-21.

[125] Gautama X-5 and 6.

[126] Gautama VII-14.

[127] Parasarasmrti 1–65; S.P. Chap. 78-2 to 5.

[128] Baraha P. Ch. 190-187 t 189.

[129] Ṛgveda, X-34.

[130] Mehta. R.N., *Pre-Buddhist India*, p. 252.

complex and class-distinction more rigid, from about the fifth century BC onwards there began the tendency to forbid agriculture specially for the brāhmaṇas. It was said that the Veda impedes agriculture and the agriculture impedes the Veda.[131] The curious reason why it could not be permitted for the priests was that it injures the creature in the earth and the yoke hurts the cattle.[132] As the Kṣatriya, if poor, he might become a farmer but only as a resource in need.[133] Even in that case, according to the *Mahābhārata*, a Kṣatriya who has become exceedingly humiliated due to the weakness of his treasury and army should not take to the profession of a Vaiśya or Śūdrā.[134] This is a clear evidence of disinclination to take to the menial and manual profession of the lower classes. It is because of an attitude of contempt that the occupation of the Vaiśya was called intermediate and that of the Śūdrā was called inferior.[135] Even in times of distress, the Viśṇū Purāṇa enjoins upon the Brāhmaṇas and Kṣatriyas not to take to the duties of the Śūdrās.[136] If such was the contemptuous attitude of the higher classes towards the occupations of the Vaiśyas and specially those of the Śūdrās, in abnormal times, it can be well imagined in ordinary times. Whether it was agriculture or mechanical arts, all such production activities were held in great contempt by the members of the upper classes. The *Jatākas*, which are *anti-brāhmaṇical* in their attitude, provide some instances of the Brāhmaṇas taking to non-brāhmaṇical occupation but even they make a distinction between 'high' (*ukkattah*) and 'low' (*hina*) labour. Thus the wood-workers and the potters, the barbers and sweepers, the hunters and the fisherman all are considered as belonging to the lower class and their professions were held in contempt.[137] The Jatākas show that together with the Brāhmaṇas and the Kṣatriyas, the *gahapatis* and the *setthis* who corresponded to the Vaiśya class had deep contempt for the low caste people.[138] It was obviously the stigma of the *hinasippas*

131 Baudhayāna 1. 5. 10. 28 Cf. Manu X-78-82.

132 MBH II 208-23; Manu X-83 and Gautama X-3.

133 Commenting on Manu X-99 and 100 work of the artisans and mechanics—*Mānavdharma-sāstra* edited by V.N. Mandalika, vol. II.

134 यस्यकोशबलगलान्या सर्वलोक पराभवः
भैक्ष्यचर्या न विहिता न च दिट्शूद्रजीविका। S.P. Chap. 130-23.

135 Sūkranītīsāra III-552-54.

136 क्षात्रं कर्म द्विजस्योक्तं वैश्यं कर्म तथापदि
राजन्यस्य च वैश्योक्तं शूद्रकर्म न चैतयोः। Viśṇu P. Bk. III. Chapo. 8-39, Gita Press Edn.

137 Fick, op. cit., p. 322.

138 Jatāka IV, p. 378.

associated with them which relegated certain people to the position of the low castes in the society.[139] Probably this contempt for manual labour was characteristic of the class-divided society. It is worthy of a remark that in Egypt there prevailed the famous formula that 'the scribe is exempt from all manual tasks; it is he who commands'. In ancient Greece the attitude of the higher classes towards manual labour can be summed up in the words of Xenophon (fifth century BC): 'What are called mechanical arts carry a social stigma and are rightly dishonoured in our cities, and in some cities especially in warlike ones, it is not legal for a citizen to ply a mechanical trade.'[140] It may be pointed that even now in our villages, the idea that the Brāhmaṇa and Kṣatriya can take to plough is detestable. It should be noted that the contempt the higher castes had for the manual labour produced an almost unique social phenomenon in the history of ancient India. Anthropological explanation apart, this was an important cause of the creation of the untouchable class (*antyājas*) which accounts for considerable section of the present Indian population.

VIII

Such was the nature of caste system in ancient India. The four castes of the society could be grouped in two main classes: warriors and priests on the one hand, and the common people on the other. The former were the organizers of production, the latter were the workers in production. Since the Brāhmaṇas and Kṣatriyas were mostly exempt from taxation, the Vaiśya has been described as 'bālīkṛt'[141] or payer of taxes. As it has been shown, the Vaiśyas and the Śūdrās were the principal taxpayers. On the basis of Kauṭilya, *Viṣṇu-smṛtī, Markandeya Purānā, Agni Purānā* and *Kamandakānītisāra*, it can be safely asserted that the Vaiśyas and Śūdrās formed the overwhelming majority of the population.[142] In the role of small traders, agricultural labourers, domestic slaves, craftsmen and artisans, they did all the productive work of the community. But in return they were blessed with various kinds of economic disabilities. The small ruling class of Brāhmaṇas and Kṣatriyas did no productive

139 Fick, op.cit., p. 315.

140 Quoted in Farrington, Greek Science Part I, pp. 23–24. 1949.

141 Ait. Brāhmaṇa 35-3.

142 A.S. Bk. VI-1; Viṣṇu II-4 and 5; Markendya Purāṇa. Chap. 49-47 and Agni Purāṇa Chap. 222-1 and 2.

work but enjoyed important economic privileges. This economic aspect on the caste system has been generally overlooked. Higher caste did not mean only high social status due to the prestige of birth but also better material prospects due to monopoly of the higher posts in the state. It may be that in some cases even the Śūdrās could rise to high offices but that involved a consequential change in their caste status. There are certain popular evidences to suggest that it was difficult to think of the caste of a person without the wealth he possessed. *Chāṇakyanītisāra*, *Pañchatantra* and *Bhrtṛhariśataka*, 'which should be regarded as giving expression to popular notions based on actual facts, confirm the intimate connection between wealth and caste. Thus the *Chāṇkyanītisāra* clearly states that wealth determined the caste.[143] According to it if a person is wealthy but outside the caste, the people of higher castes flatter him.[144] Therefore, the very fact that a higher caste person curries favour with the wealthy person, raises his social status. *Pañchatāntra* also states it clearly that wealth makes a man powerful, in other words, a Kṣatriya; it makes a man learned, in other words, a Brāhmaṇa.[145] Similarly, Bhartrhari says that it is the wealth which makes a man noble or learned.[146]

Taking the above evidence together it seems that while a higher caste meant a high economic and political status, wealth also determined the caste of a man. Such a study of the economic aspects of the caste system does not warrant the statement that in ancient India there was no concentration of the prestige of birth, influence of wealth, and political office which imparts an aristocratic tinge to social organization and sustain aristocratic government.[147] It is possible that 'there was no aristocracy in India in the Greek or European sense of the term.[148] But

[143] धनं जातिर्धनं रूपं धनं विद्या धनं यश।
कि धनेन विहीनानां याज्यो निजीवितैर्गुणैः।
Chāṇkyanītisāra, Chap. IV-13, Calcutta 1926.

[144] धनिनो जाि त्हीनस्य विलसत्यत्तमस्तथा। Ibid., Chap. IV-19.

[145] अर्थेन बलवान् सर्वो प्यर्थाद्भवति पण्डितः
पश्यैनं मूषकं पापं स्वजाति समतां गतम्।
Pañchatantra, p. 59, Poona I 30.

[146] यस्यास्ति वित्तस नरः कुलीन।
स पण्डितः स श्रुतवान् गुणज्ञः
स एव वक्ता स च दर्शनीयः
सर्व गुणाः का चन माश्रयन्ते Bhrtrharisataka.

[147] *Age of Imperial Unity,m* p. 311 and Beni Prasad, *The State in Ancient India,* pp. 7 and 8.

[148] Ibid., p. 311.

there is no denying the fact that there was some sort of aristocracy consisting mainly of the Brāhmaṇas and the Kṣatriyas,[149] which lived on the production activities of the Vaiśyas and Śūdrās.

It is natural that working as small traders, agriculturists, artisans and mechanics, the Vaiśyas and Śūdrās possessed the requisite technical knowledge and experience of production which the members of the higher class lacked. The difficulty was that they had neither any incentive in the shape of adequate rewards nor the facility of education to improve the technical methods and consequently the material well-being of the community.[150] This worked as a serious impediment on the technological and economic progress of the society. More than any other factor it is the caste-production system and the social relations resulting thereafter which explain the stagnation of the socio-economic life in India. It can be set as an important cause of what Toynbee calls the 'arrest of Indian civilization'. It is due to this that 'whatever might be the political aspect of India's history, its social condition has remained unaltered till the beginning of the nineteenth century'.

[149] R.G. Bhandarkar, *Collected Works,* vol. II, p. 446.

[150] The Śūdrā was not permitted to read the Vedic literature which constituted the mainstore of knowledge—Manu II-169 and 170; Yajan H-39 and 43 and Vasistha II-3.

BIBLIOGRAPHY

Unless otherwise mentioned the following editions of the original source have been consulted:

1.	Varāha Purāṇa	—	Bibliotheca Indica Series.
1a.	Brahma Purāṇa	—	Anandasrama Series.
2.	Brahmāṇḍa Purāṇa	—	Venkateswara Series.
3.	Kurma Purāṇa	—	Calcutta, 1890.
4.	markaṇḍeya Purāṇa	—	Bibiliotheca India.
5.	Vāyu Purāṇa	—	Calcutta, 1880.
6.	Viṣṇu Purāṇa	—	Wilson's Translation.
7.	Brhannārdiya Purāṇa	—	Calcutta, 1891.
8.	Padma Charita	—	Bombay, VS 1985.
9.	Śānti Parva	—	Chitrasala Press, Poona, 1939.
10.	Mānavadharmaśātra	—	Edited by V.N. Mandalika, Bombay 1886.
11.	Kauṭilya	—	Shama Sastry's Edition.
12.	Kāmandaka Nītisāra	—	Trivandrum Sansk. Series.
13.	Śukra Nītisara	—	Madras, 1882 & S.B.H., Allahabad.
14.	Kātyāyana Smṛti	—	Kane's Edition.
15.	Digha Nikāya	—	Pali Text Society, London, 1890-1911.
16.	Mahāvastu Vol. I.	—	Senart, Paris, 1882.
17.	Dharamasutra	—	Sacred Books of the East Service.
18.	Brāhmaṇas	—	Sacred Books of the East Service.
19.	Nārada and Bṛhaspati Smṛtis	—	Sacred Books of the East Service.
20.	Parāśara Smṛti	—	Banaras, 1907.
21.	Jātaka	—	Cowell's Translation.

CHAPTER 6

Early Medieval Land Grants: The Rāṣṭrakūṭa Case

The Rāṣṭrakūṭas, who ruled over the whole of Maharashtra, southern Gujarat and parts of Karnataka, seem to have made more grants of villages to temples and Brāhmaṇas than the Palas or the Pratiharas. Instance of these grants are available from the beginning of their rule. In AD 753–4, Dantidurga granted a settled village to a Brāhmaṇa in the Kolhapur region with the right to collect all the customary taxes, such as land-tax, occasional payments to officials, etc., and with the right to punish persons guilty of ten offence.[1] Similarly in AD 806–7, Govinda III allotted to a Brāhmaṇa a village in the Nasik area with the above mentioned rights, to which he added the right to forced labour, and exemption from molestation by regular and irregular soldiers and from the entry of all royal officials.[2] All these conclusions occur in his Paithan plates of 794,[3] and are repeated in a copper-plate grant of his in the Nasik district.[4]

[1] *IA*, xi, 112–3, 11. 29–44.
[2] Ibid., 156–9, 11. 34–50.
[3] *EI*, ii, no. 17, 11. 57–8.
[4] *IA*, vi, 67–8, 11. 12–13 of Plate II B.

In 871 a village was granted on similar terms to some Brāhmaṇas by Amoghavarṣa I.[5] Thus once increased under Govinda III, the fiscal and administrative concessions granted to religious donees were maintained on the same scale for about a century. A grant of a village made in 933-4 by Govinda V, however, omits the right to forced labour and exemption from the entry of royal officials.[6] In 972-3 a village was given in gift on these terms by Amoghavarṣa III in the Khandesh area[7] but not rendered free from the entry of regular and irregular soldiers. This shows that in spite of variations in terms the process of the grant of villages to priests continued for more than two hundred years under the Rāṣṭrakūṭas. All their copper plates have not been discovered, yet those found so far are not few. We learn that on his coronation in 915, Indra II granted 400 villages afresh resumed by previous rulers.[8] The Cambay plate of Govinda IV states that on a similar occasion he gave 600 villages for religious and educational purposes (agraharas) to Brāhmaṇas and 800 villages to temples (devakula).[9] These two alone would give a total of 1800 villages allotted to religious donees. We have no reasons to doubt the authenticity of these figures, for land grants were so frequent and common; in fact the total number of all such villages may have been far greater.

Religious grants were also made by the governors and feudatories of the Rāṣṭrakūṭas. In 821 Karkkaraja Suvarṇavarṣa of the Gujarat Rāṣṭrakūṭa branch made a perpetual grant of a field to a religious teacher free from taxes, not to be entered by regular and irregular soldiers and royal officers.[10] In 863 Dhruva III of the same branch granted to a Brāhmaṇa a village on similar terms; the donee was also authorized to punish the persons guilty of ten offences and to requisition forced labour from villagers.[11] These chief made grants independently of their overlord, but Bankeya, the governor of Banavasi under Amoghavarṣa, prevailed upon the latter to alienate a village and plots of land in several villages in favour of a Jain temple.[12] All told, the number of villages alienated

[5] *EI*, xviii, no. 26, 11, 66–7.
[6] *IA*, xii, 251 ff., 11. 50–53.
[7] Ibid., 266, 11. 43–53.
[8] A.S. Altekar, The Rāṣṭrakūṭa and their Times (Poona, 1934) p. 100.
[9] *El*, vii, no. 6, 11. 46–9.
[10] Ibid., xxi, no. 22, 11 . 48–51.
[11] *IA*, ii, 184–5, Plate II b, 11. 1–19.
[12] *El*, vi, no. 4, 11. 35–49.

by the Rāṣṭrakūṭas and their vassals in favour of learned Brāhmaṇas was considerable.[13]

The villages were granted in perpetuity, and the successors of the grantors were placed under the obligation of respecting these grants. Some grants survived even the overthrow of the family of the donor. Thus Indra II re-granted a village named Trena, formerly bestowed upon the donee's ancestors by Dhruva I and II of the Gujarat branch. The descendants were anxious for securing a re-grant of village, because the grantor's family no longer hold power in southern Gujarat.[14] Again, as shown earlier, Indra III renewed the grant of as many as 400 villages resumed by previous kings.

Administrative rights were distinctly made over to the beneficiaries both by the Palas and the Rāṣṭrakūṭas, although not by the Pratiharas. The Rāṣṭrakūṭas, however, gave the religious donees more coercive and administrative power than even the Palas did. Some Pala grants make gift-villages free from the entry of royal officials, other from that of regular and irregular soldiers and some from both; they also empower the donees to punish persons guilty of ten offences. But many Rāṣṭrakūṭa grants allow all these concessions together to the grantees. They do not, however, specifically mention the right to punish thieves, which is obviously covered by the right to punish ten offences. On the whole, we get the impression that the religious donees were not only larger in number under the Rāṣṭrakūṭas than under the Palas or the Pratiharas but stronger in administrative powers.

The Rāṣṭrakūṭa grants nowhere directly alienate villages in favour of officials and vassals, but Altekar, who has made a detailed study of their political system, holds that many state officers were paid by 'rent-free' (revenue-free) land.[15] We may better use the term revenue-free, for rent is something paid by the tenants to their landlords. Altekar adds that sometimes officers were remunerated by salaries, paid partly in cash and partly in kind.[16] In any case so far as revenue organization is concerned, villages in the Rāṣṭrakūṭa empire were grouped mainly in units of ten and its multiples[17] on the Dharma-sāstra pattern, according

[13] Altekar, op. cit., p. 189.

[14] Ibid., p, 98.

[15] Ibid., p. 245.

[16] Ibid., p. 189.

[17] A *bhukti* comprising 500 villages under the Rāṣṭrakūṭas is mentioned in *IA*, xi, 112-13, 1.32 Units of 12000, 500, 300, and 70 are also mentioned (Altekar, op. cit., p. 77).

to which officers in charge of such units should be paid by grants of land.[18] The arrangements seem to have been followed by the Rāṣṭrakūṭa kings, especially in payment to the district and village headen. Thus a *deśa-grāmakūṭa-kṣtra* or the revenue-free field of the district headman is twice mentioned in a spurious Ganga record.[19] Apparently the village headman, who was known as the *grāmkūṭa* in the Rāṣṭrakūṭa dominions, was remunerated similarly. It is definite that in the southern Maratha country the village headman enjoyed revenue-free land. A record of the *Rattas* of *Saundatti* informs us that the Gavuṇḍa. (village headman) of Kadole gave 200 *mattaras* of cultivable land, which was his revenue-free service land, situated in the circle of revenue-free service plots of the headman of the locality.[20] In such a case the fiscal officer would have to render account to his master for the area under his jurisdiction, except the portion of land or revenues set aside for his payment.

The dominions of the Gujarat Branch of the Rāṣṭrakūṭas presented a curious mixture to the decimal pattern and the Rajput system consisting of units of 12 and 84 villages. We know of a unit of 12 villages given as a grant,[21] forming a part of a group of 750 villages which in its turn was strangely enough divided into units of 10 village.'[22] A unit of 84 villages is also mentioned in another grant of the Gujarat branch.[23] Units of 12 villages or their multiples also prevailed in other parts of the Rāṣṭrakūṭa empire outside Gujarat. The Sanjan Plates of Amoghavarṣa I mention a group of 24 villages[24] and under Govinda II the *Pratiṣṭhāna-bhukti* contained several groups of 12 villages.[25] A unit of 12 villages is also known under Amoghavaraṣ III.[26] These all were obviously fiscal units, and, on the later analogy found under the Cāhamānas, they were given as fiefs to vassals or officials who were responsible for their administration.

We have some evidence to show that under the Rāṣṭrakūṭas military service was paid by land grants. Sometimes the Palava kings commemorated the victories of their general by renaming villages after

[18] *Manu*, VII. 19.
[19] Altekar, op. cit., p. 179.
[20] Ibid., p. 193.
[21] *EI*, iii, no. 9, 11. 15–16.
[22] Ibid., I, no. 8, 11. 35–6.
[23] *IA*, xii, 160, 11. 45–6.
[24] *EI*, xviii, 256–7.
[25] Altekar, op. cit., p. 137.
[26] *IA*, xii, 266.

him and granting them to Brāhmaṇas.[27] But Rāṣṭrakūṭa military officers were probably rewarded villages for their bravery. *Grāmabhoktṛs* serving the Śilāhāras,[28] appear to have been military captains enjoying villages. According to Altekar *grāmapatis* mentioned in Rāṣṭrakūṭa records were holders of *inam* (reward for service) village.[29] Since the village headman was known as *grāmakūṭa* in Maharashtra and was different from the *grāmapati*,[30] the latter may have been a military captain. If we rely on the account of the merchant Sulaiman it would appear that the contemporary kings did not pay their soldiers. He informs us that the troops of the kings of India are numerous, but they do not receive any pay. The king assembles them only in case of a religious war. They then come out and maintain themselves without receiving anything from the king.[31] This applies to the troops supplied by the vassals. The merchant also remarks that like the Arabs the Rāṣṭrakūṭa king gives regular pay to this soldiers,[32] but it is not clear whether,they were paid in cash or by grant of land. Altekar suggests that the families of the soldiers were supported by villages tenanted to them.[33] At any rate Sulaiman's statement probably refers to the standing army maintained by the Rāṣṭrakutas. But perhaps the troops supplied by the vassals outnumbered those maintained by the king.

Certain officials were paid by specified taxes. Taxes in kind imposed on foodstuff, vegetables, etc., formed part of the pay of local officers in the time of the Rāṣṭrkūṭas.[34] Altekar holes the *bhagakara*, substitute of *uparikara*. Implied taxes, normal of additional, in kind or cash, for the part payment of the salaries of the mofussil state officers.[35] This reminds us of a later, similar practice under the Candellas and the Gāhaḍavālas, and indicates partial feudalization, for under the feudal system the barons who carried on administration were not paid in cash or kind directly by the state but assigned certain revenues for their remuneration.

Vassals were assigned wide territories by their Rāṣṭrakūṭa overlord. New fiefs were created as a reward for military service. Most probably

[27] Ibid., vii, 270–80.

[28] *EI*, iii, no. 37, 1. 47.

[29] Altekar, op. cit., p. 189.

[30] Ibid.

[31] H.M. Eliot and J. Dowson (eds.), *History of India as told by its Historian* (London, 1867), i., 7.

[32] Ibid., 3.

[33] Altekar, op. cit., p. 251.

[34] Ibid., p. 181.

[35] Ibid., p. 216, cf. pp. 194–5.

Amoghavarṣa I granted the territory between the Narmada and the Tapi as a compensation for the loyal services of Karkka,[36] and the extensive dominion, which served as a bulwark against the Gurjar-pratiharas,[37] continued to be held by the Gujarat Rāṣṭrakuṭas till *c.* AD 862.[38] In their turn these chiefs allotted territories to their vassals. We learn from the inscription that a unit of 750 villages belonged to Karkka II.[39] Later the same source states that in this unit Chandragupta served as the general (*daṇḍnāyaka*) of the *mahāsāmanta* Pracanda.[40] It is natural to infer that this group of villages was held by Pracands as a fief from Karkka II, and perhaps the former's father Dhavalappa had received it as a reward for his bravery and loyalty.[41] Incidentally, it also shows that after having received fiefs the vassals made their own administrative arrangements. A further instance of grant made by the Gujarat line is found in the region of Govinda III (813) when the *mahāsāmanta* Budhavarsa, possibly of Cālukya extraction, was given feudal sway over a group of 12 villages.[42] Similarly, the Raṭṭas of Saundatti in the southern Maratha region, feudatories first of the Rāṣṭrakūṭas and then of later Cālukyas, had possibly created their own sub-feudatories, for they are described as the lord of the *desakāras*.[43] These powerful vassals practiced sub-infeudation without any reference to their overlord. But governors or lesser vassals either prevailed upon the sovereign to grant villages or did it with his permission. On the application of Bankeya, the governor of Banavasi, Amoghavarṣa I alienated a village in favour of a Jain temple.[44] Similarly, a Cālukya vassal of Govinda III had to obtain his sanction for giving a village to a Jain sage.[45] Again, Sankaragana, feudatory of Dhruva, took the latter's order for granting a village.[46] But whatever might be the difference between the bigger and smaller vassals, sub-infeudation was practiced widely under the Rāṣṭrakūṭas.

What distinguished the Rāṣṭrakūṭa polity was the right of sub-infeudation and ejection conferred on religious donees. They were

[36] Ibid., pp. 86–7.

[37] *IA*, xii, 158; the term *svāmī* is used for the overlord of Karkka.

[38] Altekar, op. cit., pp. 86–7.

[39] *EI*, I, no. 8, verse 20.

[40] Ibid., 11. 34–5.

[41] Hultzsch, ibid., p. 53.

[42] *tab-datta-siharakkhidvadasake prabhujyamane*. EI, iii, no. 9, 11. 15–9.

[43] *IA*, xiv, 24; cf. Altekar, op. cit., p. 263.

[44] *EI*, vi., no. 4, 1. 34.

[45] *IA*, xii, 18.

[46] *EI*, ix, no. 26, 11. 27–8.

given the right to enjoy the village or to get it enjoyed, to cultivate the land or get it cultivated.[47] This important concession is specified only in a few Pratihara charters in Gujarat and Rajsthan, and not found in Pala character. Under the Rāṣṭrakūṭa the practice seems to have been universal in Maharashtra, southern Gujarat and Karnataka. The privilege was fortified by the provision the royal officials were ordered not to cause any disturbance in the enjoyment of the village or getting it enjoyed by others, in its cultivation or getting it cultivated by other.[48] This left clear and ample scope for sub-infeudation by the donees. In such cases tenants would be mostly secular and be requisitioned by those temples and Brāhmaṇas who were given more villages than they could manage by themselves. Records of sub-infeudation by religious donees are wanting because they could not be recorded on copper-plates. But there is little doubt that the donees exercise this important privilege bestowed on them.

The administrative machinery of the Rāṣṭrakūṭas was a little more elaborate than that of the Pratiharas. A charter of 753-4 informs only three officers, *viṣayapati*, *rāṣtrapati* and *grāmakūṭa*, of the land grant.[49] A land grant of Krsna I (772) found in the Chanda District of Madhya Pradesh mentions only the first two officers and the *bhogapati*.[50] But a grant of 794 speaks of two new officials, *āyuktaka* and *niyuktaka*,[51] who usually appear in all later grants.[52] Thus we do not come across more than five regular officers. It may be argued that the other officers are not mentioned because they were not concerned with the grants.[53] But if this analogy is extended to Pala grant it would imply that two dozen Pala officials were connected with land grants, which does not seem to be reasonable. Really the Rāṣṭrakūṭa system did not provide for too many officers, for like the Pratiharas they mainly depended for their administration on their feudatories and vassals. This can be also inferred from the absence of the names of the police officials in the Rāṣṭrakūṭa records; only the Antroli-Charoli copper plates of Karkkaraja of Gujarat

[47] *IA*, xi, 159, 11. 49–50; xii 184-5, Plate II, 1. 19, Plate III, 1. 1; EI, xxii, no. 12, 11.54–5, etc.

[48] Ibid.

[49] *IA*, xi, 112–13, 11. 28–9.

[50] *EI*, xiv, no. 6, 1. 42.

[51] Ibid., iii, no. 17.

[52] *IA*, xi, 159, 11. 35–6; vi, 67-8, Plate IIB of Govinda III, 11. 4–5.

[53] Altekar, op. cit., p. 261.

mentions officials concerned with thieves (*corodharanikas*).[54] Again the argument that they need no mention in land grants,[55] does not seem to be tenable; probably in Maharashtra and Gujarat police functions were entrusted to local vassals, which dispensed with the necessity of employing regular officials for the purpose.

Feudalization of functionaries seems to have been a development of some importance under the Rāṣṭrakūṭas. Dalla, the chief foreign minister of Dhruva,[56] was a *sāmanta* (vassal) entitled to the use of five great musical instruments. Provincial governors were given the status of the *mahāsāmanta* or the *mahāmaṇḍaleśvara*[57] and often bore the title of *rāja* or *rasa* (Canerese).[58]

Some *viṣayapatis* (district officers) enjoyed feudatory status.[59] *Bhogikas* or *bhaogapatis*, officers in charge of *bhuktis* or *talukas*, sometimes possessed feudatory titles,[60] so also the governors of large towns. Kuppey, the governor of Soratur town in Karnataka, was a *mahāsāmanta* under Amoghavarsa I,[61] in the same manner as a governor of Siyadoni under the Pratiharas. Military officers were being equally feudalized; they were allowed to maintain feudal paraphernalia. As we learn from the case of the Brāhmaṇa *daṇḍanāyaka* Visottara under Govinda IV in 930, they were invested with the robes of their office, assigned distinctive parasols, and permitted to use elephants and chariots.[62] The Yuvaraja or the heir apparent was also given feudal titles.[63]

The association of feudal titles with officials may be interpreted in two ways; either the *sāmantas* or *mahāsāmantas* were appointed to different posts or else the officers were placed in the recognized feudal categories. The first does not seem to be possible for several reasons. Offices were older while feudal ranks were evolved later. Secondly, under the Pratiharas we know of officers who did not hold feudal titles in the beginning but received them only later. Thirdly, if we accept the

[54] Ibid.
[55] Ibid.
[56] *EI*, x, no. 20, 11. 56–6.
[57] Ibid., xix, no. 4 A, 1.4.
[58] Altekar, op. cit., p. 173.
[59] Ibid., p. 177.
[60] Ibid., p. 178.
[61] Ibid., p. 182.
[62] *EI*, xiii, 334 (verse 10).
[63] Altekar, op. cit., p. 152.

first alternative it would mean that even the Yuvaraja was first made a *mahāsāmanta* and then raised of the status of crown-prince. This lands us into an absurd position, for generally the eldest son was considered to be Yuvaraja by his birth. Hence the second alternative that officials were feudalized sounds more logical. The process of feudalization affected the whole social order, and in the Rāṣṭrakūṭa kingdom, besides feudatories, regular officers, civil and military, high and low, were placed in one feudal rank or the other. It seems that official posts by themselves did not carry sufficient weight unless they were given feudal recognition.

The Rāṣṭrakūṭa records give us the same idea of the powers and privileges as well as the obligations of the vassals. A measure of the high feudal rank enjoyed by some vassals was their investiture with the *pañcamahāśabda* by the Pratihara,[64] and Rāṣṭrakūṭa king.[65] The terms seem to have first become current in the first half of the seventh century; the Rāṣṭrakūṭa chief Nanaraja, a direct collateral ancestor of Dantidurga, claims in his grant of 631-2 that unlike his ancestors he was a ruler entitled to the dignity of the *pañcamahāśabda*, which he had personally won.[66] This implies that only certain remarkable service rendered by the vassal to his overlord enabled him to earn this privilege. Without doubt this was the highest feudal distinction that could be attained by a vassal, for even the Yuvaraja enjoyed no higher feudal privilege than this. Even when some feudatories had adopted such imperial titles as *paramabhaṭṭāraka-maharājā-dhirāja-parameśvara*, they continued to bear this epithet. Its meaning, however, is not quite clear. Most probably it signified the use of five musical instruments referred to by a Jain writer Ravakoṭyacary and enumerated by a Lingayat writer as *śṛṅga* (horn), *tammaṭa*, *śankha* (conch), *bheri* (drum), and *jayaghaṇṭā* (bellow victory.[67] This privilege was possibly confined to the paramount power in the beginning, but later allowed even to their vassals. It was, however, not known under the Palas although it was obtained in Orissa. Under the Rāṣṭrakūṭas, vassals were also permitted to use a feudal throne, flywhisk, planquins and elephants,[68] of which we have no clear indication under the Palas and Pratiharas. As shown earlier, an important right of the

[64] *EI*, iv, no. 44, 11. 1–10; ix, no. 1.3.

[65] Ibid., xxii, no. 12, 1.39; IA, xii, 184, Plate IIb, 1.1; the term used in these grants in *samadhigatā śesa mahāśabda*, but see the Antroli-chharoli record of Karkka Ii quoted in Altekar, op. cit., p. 42.

[66] Ibid., p. 7.

[67] *IA*, xii, 96.

[68] Altekar, op. cit., p. 263.

vassals was to create their sub-vassals, some of whom were given the privilege of using the five great musical instruments; we may quote here the examples of the *mahāsāmantā* Nimbadevarasa, a vassal of the Konkan *Śilāhāras*,[69] and of the *mahāsāmanta* Buddhavarsa, a vassal of the Gujarat Rāṣṭrakūṭas.[70] Subject to the payment of tribute the big vassals enjoyed full power over their revenues. They could assign taxes[71] and grant villages sometimes with and sometimes without the permission of the overlord. Under the Western Cālukyas, vassals could also sell villages without the sanction of the imperial power.[72]

The vassals bore both civil and military obligations towards their overlord. Their most important civil obligation was regular payment of tribute, which was sometimes personally realized by the overlord. The Rāṣṭrakūṭa King Govinda III went on tour in the southern parts of his empire for levying tributes from his feudatories.[73] A later text, the *Nitivākyāmrṭa*, refers to a special present made by vassals in the court on such festive occasions as the birth of a son or marriage.[74] Other obligations of a civil nature were compliance with imperial orders, and attendance at the imperial court on ceremonial occasions and at periodical intervals,[75] which took the form of rendering homage. The vassals were clearly not obliged to render any advice to the overlord or render him any administrative assistance at the centre.

Military obligation was more important, and consisted in rendering aid to the overlord in times of war. The vassals of the Rāṣṭrakūṭas had to supply a certain number of troops to their lord and participate in his imperial campaigns. The Cālukyas of Vengi had to furnish forces to the Rāṣṭrakūṭas in their wars against the Gangas.[76] Narasimha Cālukya, a feudatory of Indra !!!, took a successful part in the later's campaign against the Gurjara-Pratihara King Mahipala.[77] The Gujarat Rāṣṭrakūṭa viceroyalty, in practice a large fief, was created to serve as a shield against the Gurjara-Pratiharas for the protection of Malwa,[78] which was

[69] *EI*, xix, no. 4A, 11 . 4–5.
[70] Ibid., iii, no. 9. 11. 12–19.
[71] *IA*, xiii, 16011, 11. 45–54; xii, 136.
[72] *EI*, iii, 307.
[73] *IA*, xi, 127.
[74] XXX. 32 quoted in Altekar, op. cit., p. 265.
[75] Ibid., pp. 91–4.
[77] Naga Varmma, *Karṇāṭakabhāṣabhuṣaṇa*, ed. L. Rice, Bangalore: 1884, Introd., p. xiv.
[78] *IA*, xii, 158.

also a bone of contention between the Marathas and the Rajputs in the eighteenth century.

Just as the Rāṣṭrakūṭa rulers claimed military service from their vassals, so also their vassals claimed it from their sub-vassals. This can be inferred from the Kolhapur inscription of the Śilāhāras *mahāmaṇḍaleśvara* Gaṇḍarādityadeva. Although a record of 1135, it might be taken as a survival of the state of affairs when the Śilāhāras were the vassals of the Rāṣṭrakūṭas. It describes the relation of the *mahāsāmantā* Nimbadeverasa with various kinds of vassals, inimical and friendly probably to his overlord Gandaraditya. The *mahāsāmantā* is represented as 'a breaker of the hair-parting of the dames of hostile barons, a gallant dear to the courtesans of warriors, a wind dissipating the clouds of opponent barons, a furious elephant to *Nāgaldevi*, a time of world dissolution to enemy barons, a Gopāla to the worthiest of barons, an heroic Kumara to the demon Tara's rival barons, an awful rutting elephant to the beds of the lotuses the barons of Tondai, rod for the skilful right hand of King Gaṇḍaraditya . . . a crestgem of barons. . .'[79] This glowing account of the achievements of the great vassal may not be literally true, but it clearly indicates the obligation of a *mahāsāmanta* to suppress the inimical and protect the friendly *sāmantas*.

The overlord exercised control over his feudatories in various ways. Under the Rāṣṭrakūṭas feudatories had to entertain an ambassador from the imperial court. He exercised general supervision and control, similar to that of the Resident in British India. According to Sulaiman, he was received with profound respect due to the representative of the paramount power. He maintained numerous spies for obtaining information. Amoghavarsa I is known to have covered the courts of hostile kings with thousands of courtesans, who probably worked under the imperial ambassador.[80] The overlord made his power felt by alienating villages in the dominion of his vassals. Kṛṣṇa II allotted a village situated within the jurisdiction of the *mahāsāmanta* Pracanda.[81] Disloyal feudatories were kept under check by the fear of humiliation

[79] *vijay-Lakṣmīkāntaṃ, ripu-sāmanta-sīmantinī-sīmanta-bhaṅgaṃ, vīravārāṅganā-priya-bhujangam vairi-sāmanta-megha-vighaṭana-samīraṇam, nāgaladeviay gandha-vāraṇam, vidviṣṭa-sāmanta-viḷaya-kāḷaṃ sāmanta-gaṇḍa-gopālaṃ, dāyāda-sāmanta-tār-āsura-vīra-kumāraṃ, sāmanta-kedāraṃ, toṇḍa-sāmanta-puṇḍarīka-ṣaṇḍa-pracaṇḍa-madāvedaṇḍaṃ, gaṇḍarādityadeva dakṣiṇa-bhujādaṇḍaṃ . . . sāmanta-śiromaṇi . . .EI*, xix, no. 4 A, 11. 5–8, tr.

[80] Altekar, op. cit., p. 264.

[81] *EI*, I, no. 8, 11. 33–5.

and retribution that followed the failure of their rebellions. They were subjected to various indignities; the ruler of Vengi had to sweep the stables of his victor Govinda II.[82] Feudatories had to surrender their precious gems, treasures, dancing girls, horses and elephants to the imperial power as punishment for their disloyalty.[83] Even their wives were put into prison.[84] Sometimes the defeated feudatories were dispossessed of all their property and territories, out of which the king created livings for his dependents, as Kṛṣṇa III did in South Arcot district after having conquered the Chola territories.[85]

We have no clear idea of the royal machinery for dealing with the vassals. Perhaps the *mahāsandhivigrahika* was in charge of the *Rāṣṭrakmuṭā* royal policy towards the vassals both in times of war and peace. Altekar holds that this official drafted all the land charters because the foreign office possessed the most reliable and up-to-date information on the exploits and genealogy of the grantor to be incorporated in the grants.[86] But an equally, if not more, important portion of the charter related to the whereabouts of the grantor and grantee as well as of the village to be granted, and this could have been better recorded by the revenue office. However, this had to be done by the *sandhivigrahika*, because, in our opinion, he dealt with feudatories with whom peacetime relations were mainly governed by land grants. It may be on account of this that he drafted all secular charters and even those that related to land grants to Brāhmaṇas and temples.[87]

In spite of imperial control sometimes the vassals made their power felt in central politics. The feudatories of Govinda II rebelled against him and offered the crown to his uncle Amoghavarsa III, who was pressed by them to accept it to preserve the glory of the Rāṣṭrakūṭa kingdom. Altekar thinks that the phrase *sāmntai raha raṭṭārājya-mahim ālamba-āritham-abhyarthitaḷ*[88] which conveys this meaning, is figurative.[89] In view of the election of the king among the palas of Bengal and the Somavamsis of Orissa it would not be too much to take the phrase literally. The present instance therefore shows that the vassals

[82] Ibid., xviii, no. 26, verses 43–6.

[83] Altekar, op. cit., p. 267.

[84] Ibid.

[85] *EI*, iv, no. 40, verses, 34–5.

[86] Altekar, op. cit., p. 166.

[87] Mitaksara on aj., I. 319–20.

[88] *EI*, iv, no. 40 verse 21; v, no. 20, verse 19.

[89] Altekar, op. cit., p. 151.

could even depose and install kings, although such cases were rare and did not have the sanction of law.

The vassals and aristocratic elements occupied a fairly important position in local government, which was being gradually monopolized by narrow family circles. Supervisors over units of 10 or 12 villages were appointed by the district officers from amongst their relatives. In the Dharwar district an officer of Amoghavarsa I ruling over a unit of 300 villages had under him a relative in charge of 12 villages.[90] Bankeya, the governor of Banasvai, appointed his son Kundatta to administer the Nidgugundage twelve.[91] According to Altekar, the terms *rthika*, *rāṣṭriya*, *rāṣṭrapati* and *rāṣṭrakūṭa* were used to denote local chiefs, district officers and big landlords.[92] Some records mention *viṣayamahattaras* and *rāṣṭramahattaras*,[93] who seem to have been associated with the management of local affairs, but they probably represented aristocratic and hereditary rather than popular elements.

The mention of only the village elders in the grants indicates some social stratification in the rural area. In the Pala grants of Bengal and Bihar, all sectors of the village population right from the Brāhmaṇas down to the Cāṇḍālas are informed of the land grants. But they do not figure in the Rāṣṭrakūṭa grants in Maharashtra and Gujarat, on the other hand their place is taken by the *mahattaras* or the *mahattarādhikārins*.[94] Some of these rose further in status and acquired the rank of *rānaka*. The *mahattaka* Gogu-Rānaka, who acted as the executor of a grant of Amoghavarsa I, is an instance.[95] A *mahattarasarvādhikārin*, who held a similar position under Kṛṣṇa II,[96] is another example. Apparently, the *mahattaras* were elevated at the cost of the other sections of the rural population, and they provided suitable social base for the recruitment of higher functionaries and the growth of feudalism under the Rāṣṭrakūṭas.

Development of feudal relations between the state and the guilds also characterized the Rāṣṭrakūṭa polity. A guild of the merchants of Dambal was invested with umbrellas, *chowries* (ceremonial fans) and

[90] *EI*, vi, 107.
[91] Ibid., vii, 214.
[92] Altekar, op. cit., p. 26.
[93] Ibid., p. 158.
[94] *IA*, xii, 251, l. 41; 263, ll. 45–6.
[95] *EI*, xviii, 257.
[96] Altekar, op. cit., p. 160.

royal charters by the Cālukya king Jagadekamalla.[97] This seems to be true of the guilds under the Rāṣṭrakūṭas, for the Kolhapur[98] and Miraj[99] inscriptions of the Śilāhāras, the feudatories of the Rāṣṭrakūṭas, refer to the banner of the guild of the Vira-Balanjas (brave or true merchants) bearing the device of a' hill. Umbrellas, *chowries* and banners were symbols (ceremonial fans) and royal charters by the Cālukya king Jagadekamalla. This seems to be true of the guilds under the Rāṣṭrakūṭas, for the Kolhapur and Miraj inscriptions of the Silaharas, the feudatories of the Rāṣṭrakūṭas, refer to the banner of the guilds of the Vira-Balanjas (brave or true merchants) bearing the device of a hill. Umbrellas, *chowries* and banners were also symbols of power delegated to the guilds by the kings, and remind us of feudal charters granted to them in medieval Europe. Like feudal vassals, guilds were under the obligation of supplying soldiers to their sovereign. The Kolhapur record describes the guild of merchants as 'exalted in abundant boldness, embraced by the lady Fame, having their breasts a home for the goddess of victory (won by their arms), lofty in prowess (extending) over the world.'[100] Another record speaks of a similar guild under the Cālukyas a comprising persons, 'whose breasts were embraced by the goddess of perfect impetuosity and bravery.'[101] All this shows that guilds maintained soldiers who probably helped their overlord.

Decentralization, typical of feudal polity, is indicated by the nine military camps of the Palas, who had no fixed capital. But the Rāṣṭrakūṭas had a definite capital situated at Manyakheta or Malkhed. We know of other several military and ordinary camps,[102] from where they issued land charters. Al Masudi informs us that the seat of the Rāṣṭrakūṭa king's government is mostly among mountains, which altekar does not believe.[103] But it might indicate shifting military camps at places of natural defence for the suppression of refractory vassals.

In the end we may draw attention to the feudal elements in the Rāṣṭrakūṭa polity by pointing out that the number of religious intermediaries, enjoying fiscal and administrative rights, was

[97] *IA*, x, 188.

[98] *EI*, xix, no. 4, 1. 12.

[99] Ibid., B. 11. 2-3. This banner of the guild is also mentioned in a Cālukya inscription. (*IA*, v, 344).

[100] *EI*, xix, 34.

[101] *IA*, x, 189.

[102] Ibid., xi, 159, 1. 37; El, vii, no. 19, 1. 32.

[103] Altekar, op. cit., p. 248.

considerable; the right of sub-infeudation was widely recognized; the obligations and privileges of the vassals, who sometimes deposed and installed their overlord, were fairly defined; and even guilds were treated as vassals. Officials were few, and getting feudalized. Local administration was mainly manned by the feudalized officials, vassals, and their families, who probably maintained some link with the village elders. The Rāṣṭrakūṭa capital was, however, fixed, and units of villages generally followed the traditional decimal system than the Rajput pattern based on units of 12 or 16 villages.

Chapter 7

Problems of Peasant Protest in Early Medieval India

The early medieval socio-economic formation was marked by a grossly unequal distribution of land rights and also of the agricultural produce. A large number of landlords were not directly engaged in cultivation but lived on rent, mainly in kind, collected from the cultivators. They also exploited the labour of the peasants for various purposes, including construction and transport. Since trade and handicrafts were languishing and metal money was not much in use in day-to-day transactions, it was difficult for the peasants to go to the market to seek relief.

How did the socio-economic formation characterized by an unequal distribution of land arise? We can identify three processes. The practice of assignment of land revenues or of plots of land for religious purpose was the most important of these. Although epigraphic records indicating such grants for administrative or other services are not so common, land assignments were undoubtedly made for service other than religious. The second process is related to the transformation of the village headman and other functionaries into landed magnates. Thirdly, in certain cases, specified imposts levied from the peasants were earmarked for the maintenance of fiscal and administrative officers. In course of time, these officers seem to have acquired permanent control not only over these imposts but also over the land which was the source of such income.

What led to the wide prevalence of the practice of assignment of land and revenues? In all probability it was the outcome of bitter social conflicts, though we can make only very general statements. The earliest passages which refer to the Kali age[1] in the Purāṇas date to the last quarter of the third and the first quarter of the fourth centuries. A good part of their descriptions of Kali age becomes conventional in later times. But the passages, when they occur first, cannot be dismissed as figments of imagination. They show that peasants were oppressed with taxation, and the Vaiśyas and the Śūdrās refused to perform the functions ascribed to them. Such things happened earlier also. Examples of popular revolts against oppressive rulers appear in the Buddhist birth stories called the Jataka, which belong to 500–200 BC. According to B.C. Sen, 'Whenever a story is told of a popular victory over royal absolutism or acts disapproved by the people, it is shown to be the result of an amalgamation of the Brāhmaṇas, the Kṣatriyas and the Vaiśyas. The voice exercised by these communities was made effective by the joint use of physical force.'[2] But the king was supposed to represent the Kṣatriyas, and it seems that in several cases the Brāhmaṇas led the revolt. In one instance, both town and country folk joined in the revolt, and the king was beaten to death along with his priest.[3]

We can better appreciate the significance of the Kali phenomenon if we bear in mind the nature of the socio-economic formation which seems to have been upset by it. In spite of the presence of some rich landowners in the Buddhist birth stories, in ancient times we do not find unequal distribution of the chief means of production, that is land, on any large scale. We however find unequal distribution of agricultural products as well as the forcible use of the labour power of Śūdrās for the cultivation of land and other proposes. A good portion of the produce of the land went as taxes to the rulers, who were called Kṣatriyas. Another portion went to the Brāhmaṇas and other religious elements in the form of gifts.

[1] For details see R.S. Sharma, 'The Kali age: A Period of Social Crisis', in *India: History and Thought* (Essay in Honour of A.L. Bashan), ed. S.N. Mukhaerjee, Calcutta, 1982.

[2] B.C. Sen, *Studied in the Buddhist Jatakas,* Calcutta, 1974, pp. 77–97.

[3] Ibid.

For supplying labour to the three higher varnas including the Vaiśya peasants and merchants, the Śūdrās were considered to be the common source. Śūdrā labour seems to have been utilized more by land-owning village communities or individuals comprising the Ksatriyas and Brāhmaṇas, who were exempted from taxes. This kind of social formation, in which the Vaiśyas were the principal taxpayers and the Śūdrās supplied the main source of labour, was certainly driven with contradictions. Many instances of deviation from this norm could be cited, but by and large until Gupta times this kind of production relations existed in its essentials.

The social conflicts indicated by the passages describing the Kali age leave no doubt that the rulers found it difficult to collect taxes; apparently the Brāhmaṇas together with various types of renounces could not receive gifts. Thus the Kali social disorders affected those who exercised authority but did not produce directly for themselves. In order to put down the disorders effective use of force or violence was recommended. *Danda* was glorified in a manner in which it was never done before. From the fourth century onwards payment for service through grants of land revenues became a significant factor in a good part of the country. Although the texts do not clearly connect the widespread practice of land grants with the preceding social crisis, the former seems to have followed from the latter. From the fourth and fifth centuries onwards land grants on a large scale served to solve the problem of tax collection and its disbursement to non-producing classes engaged in military, administrative and religious services. Much remains to be done about the area, period and the dynastic kingdoms or personalities involved in the resurrection of the machinery of surplus collection in a new garb. However, as early as the fourth and fifth centuries, some of the kings who claim to have restored dharma also issued land grants for religious purposes. The social formation that emerged out of the widespread practice of land grants was dominated by the landlords. The royal charter which gave lands tended to deprive a large number of peasants of communal rights which they enjoyed in respect of pasture grounds, pathways, fisheries, forests, orchards, etc. The new assignees had the right to enjoy these communal resources at the cost of the village or the tribal community. The assignees were given the right to collect not only fixed taxes which hitherto went to the king but were also empowered to levy fresh taxes. The list of land taxes in early medieval charters gets longer and longer. On the one hand it presupposes agrarian expansion and increase in productivity.

On the other, it shows that the burden of taxes was becoming heavier and heavier in the areas directly governed by the State but more so in the benefits granted by it. The charters worsened the production relations. There could be conflict between one beneficiary and the other, between the king and his vassals, and above all between the landlords and the peasants.

These conflicts could assume various forms. One important form was litigation to which obviously only the beneficiaries and advanced sections of the peasantry could resort. The landed beneficiaries and some other landed elements who may have acquired land by force or custom may have been involved in lawsuits. Apparently, it was the needs of settling land disputes in favour of the grantees that a new provision was inserted and emphasized in the *Dharmāśāstras* or the law books. According to it, the claim based on royal charter would override the claims based on custom, agreement and religion. In other words, a *rajsasana* would prevail over *dharma*, *vyavahara* and *carita*. This particular provision first appears in verse form in the *Arthasastra* of Kauṭilya, which is mostly written in prose; the provision therefore may have been inserted in it at a later stage. It occurs from the fifth to the tenth century in the law books of Narada, Brhaspati and Katyayana, and also in the *Agni Purana*. It is obvious that the claim to land made by the peasant or any other party on the basis of custom, contract or even religion was not sustainable in the face of the charter-based claim of the beneficiary.[4]

In addition to litigation, peasants protested in various other ways. They took advantage of royal visits to complain to the king. When Harsa's army was passing through the countryside, a large number of rural folk came out to welcome him, but at the same time they complained to him against the oppressions of the *bhogpatis* who had been given the right to enjoyment of revenues from the villages. Self-immolation, particularly in south India, was another form of protest. People registered protests by killing themselves in public. A dancing girl threw herself from the temple tower to fight for the right of her relations to till the land assigned to her for her maintenance. More importantly a Brāhmaṇa immolated himself to establish the right of the temple guards and

[4] The Problem had been discussed in detail in R.S. Sharma, *'Rajasaana'*, *Proceedings of the Indian History Congress,* Calicut Session, 1976.

servants who also died for the same thing.[5] Many Jain believed that they would attain salvation by subjecting themselves to physical hardships leading to the end of their lives. Perhaps these religious methods of ending life for the sake of salvation adopted by the Jains were repeat performances of the actual methods adopted by the peasants to articulate their protests against the exploitation of feudal landlords in south India. It seems that self-immolation prevalent in south India till recent times such as one on the occasion of the death of M.G. Ramachandran is a survival of the practice of protest against unbearable conditions of life.

Several instances of violent conflict between the landlords, who were Brāhmaṇas, and the peasants in the eleventh to thirteenth centuries in Karnataka and Andhra Pradesh have been cited. The peasants launched armed attacks on Brāhmaṇa landlords, and the landlords burnt a whole village and the standing crops, and carried on war against peasant villages.[6]

Many commemorative stones were raised in south India in order to record the acts of bravery performed by those who laid down their lives in defense of the of the Brāhmaṇa's land or those who died in violence unleashed by the landed religious elements or others. Such stones are called *viragala* or *virakala* (hero stones) and are found not only in Karnataka but also in many other parts of southern India. An inscribed hero stone from Hasan district in Karnataka shows that in 1212 the Chief of Hanche fell fighting against the people of Kerehalli for a pond, for which a stone was raised in his memory.[7] In the eleventh to fourteenth centuries many inscriptions in Karnataka mention not only the endowment, construction and maintenance of tanks but also speak of battle for their possession. All this was natural since the tank formed the chief means of irrigation. The case referred to above suggests that the peasantry in the whole village was pitted against the chief who wanted a larger share of water for himself. It would be worthwhile to map such 'hero stone' inscriptions area wise and period wise and to work out their implications from the point of view of rural conflicts.

[5] N. Vananalai, 'Consolidation of Fundalism and Anti-Geudal Struggles during Chola Imperiated Rule', *Proceedings of the Second International Conference Seminar of General Studies,* III (Madras, 1968). 242-43 quoted in D.N. Jha (ed.), *Feudal Social Formations in Early India,* Delhi: 1987, pp. 21–2.

[6] R.N. Nandi, 'Growth of Rural Economy in Early Feudal India', Presidential Address, Ancient India section, Indian History Congress forty-fifth Session, 1984, Annamalai University, Annamalainagar pp. 64–7.

[7] *Epigraphic Carnatic,* V, Hasan Taluq, Inser. No. 42 (Eng. Tr.).

Numerous instances of peasant protest occur in the Chola and other inscriptions found in Tamil Nadu and the neighbouring areas. I have consulted the summaries of these inscriptions published in the *Annual Reports of South Indian Epigraphy* (*ARE*). Even these summaries give a fair indication of the strong reaction of the peasants to the oppression of the landlords and occasionally of the royal agents during the first half of the thirteenth century under the Chola King Rajaraja III. We find that his vassals benefited from the discomfiture of the Chola monarch at the hands of the Pandyas. The Pandya invasions were followed by troubles and agitation (*ksobham*) marked by insecurity and damage to property. Temples were deserted, images removed and, what is more significant, land records and title deeds destroyed. All this happened in the heart of the Chola kingdom in Tanjore district.[8] Records and title deeds may have been destroyed by vassals and rival beneficiaries, but the temple tenants and other peasants who suffered from oppressive taxes would be nonetheless interested in doing so. In such cases sometimes the temple managers took the side of those who were engaged in the service of the temple. An inscription from Shirangam in the ninth year of Maravarman Sundara Pandya who came to the throne in 1216 shows that the temple managers colluded with the *Ottar* to the detriment of the income of the temple. Venkataramayya takes the word *Ottar* as *Offiya* (people of Orissa) and postulates a Kalinga invasion as far as Shrirangam around *c.* AD 1224.

But according to Venkatasubba Ayyar the term *Ottar* must be taken to mean 'those who have undertaken to do a thing or given an agreement to the temple'. The people of Orissa are referred to as *Oddiyar* in Tamil inscriptions and not as *Ottar*.[9] Ayyar's interpretation of *Ottar* apparently refers to the servicing sections which included artisanal groups and agricultural labourers who were given land for their maintenance. These also might include *devadanakammi*, that is, serfs attached to temple lands. It seems that the managers of Shrirangam temple took up the cause of the servicing sections and rose against the temple head; their action reduced the income of the temple and upset its normal routine. Eventually the managers were expelled by the Pandya King *Maravarman* Sundara. Lasting for two years, evidently it was a major protest of the temple artisans and land labourer who were led by its managers.

[8] *ARE*, No. 141 of 1926 (yr 16-1); 213 of 1925 (yr 19); 309 of 1927 (n.d.).
[9] V. Venkatasubba Ayyar, *Epigraphia Indica*, XXVII (1947-48), p. 193, ft. 4.

Records full of cases of turmoil, social disorder and anti-State activities are found towards the end of the reign of Rajaraja III. On account of such cases there are many instances of confiscations and public sale of property. A record of the twenty-third year of Rajaraja from Tanjore district gives details which can be considered typical of several others of its kind.[10] According to it, two temple priests who were called *Siva Brāhmaṇas* were punished by the congregation of *Saiva* worshippers called *mahesvaras* who were joined in this act by the village assembly (*ur*) consisting of the non-brāhmaṇas. The temple priests were punished for *raja-droham* and *siva-droham*, that is, treason against the king as well as *Siva*. The accused had handed over to a concubine the jewels of the goddess, misappropriated the temple funds placed in their charge, refused to pay dues on the lands held by them and had misbehaved in other ways. They ignored royal commands and ducked the king's messengers. They had committed indescribable sins through the Kannadigas and are said to have collected 50,000 *kasus*. For all this they were expelled from the temple and ostracized, and the property, movable and immovable including servants, was confiscated by the State.[11] This record shows non-brāhmaṇa *Saivas* to be enthusiastic supporters of the temple grant system which was being violated by some Brāhmaṇa priests serving in the temple of *Siva*.

In the nineteenth year of the reign of Rajaraja III, a document registered the renewal of the title deeds through the village assemblies to all the residents who enjoyed lands in the several hamlets of the village up to the eighteenth year of the king. This renewal was effected by two functionaries with the surname of Pillai, whose names suggest that they held high positions in the State. This action had to be undertaken because old registers and documents had been lost in the disturbed state of the country in the fifth, eleventh and sixteenth year of the reign of the king. All this relates to the temple of Sankhanarayanesvara which was located in Tanjore district.[12]

What has been told above shows that the reign of Rajaraja III was punctuated with rural revolts, especially in the first quarter of his rule even in the heart of the Chola kingdom. In every case the records relating to land were lost, suggesting that the peasants were not prepared to accept the religious beneficiaries. In the case of Sankhanarayanesvara,

[10] *ARE,* No. 279 of 1927; *ARE,* 1927, part II, para 13.

[11] *ARE,* 1927, part II, part 30.

[12] *ARE,* No. 213 of 1925, p. 86.

eventually the village assembly comprising the assignees had to renew the titles of those who enjoyed lands in various hamlets of the villages.

A similar case of protest is found in the twenty-third year of Rajaraja's reign. The record states that at the time of a famine a person called Andaranda in combination with others opened the coffers of the temple, mutilated the image of the deity and mismanaged the temple lands. For all this, according to the decision of the judges and other residents of the village, his lands, as well as those of his associates were confiscated. All this happened in the district of Tanjore.[13] This cryptic account leaves many things untold. It is not clear in what ways the leader and his supporters mismanaged temple lands; obviously they settled lands with agriculturists or remitted rent on account of the ravages of the famine. Apparently, because of this 'mismanagement' the income or advantages from the temple, lands were directed to the tillers in times of famine. Eventually the leader and his supporters were punished with the deprivation of their lands.

We have also a case of *raja-drohins*, that is traitors, being punished, but it is not clear whether they acted against the local landlords like the Siva-Brāhmaṇas and their followers; certainly they had acted against the king. This anti-king conspiracy was put down through the ethnic device of divide and rule. According to record,[14] Kulottunga-Chola III, when encamped in the Pandya country, called one of the chiefs and ordered him to accept the chiefship of a village in the Tondaiamandalam. The Pandya chief accepted the offer and coming to the village he punished the traitors to the king *raja-drohin*. One of the reasons for asking a native of the Pandya country to rule over a village of Tondai was evidently the disturbance caused by the traitors whom the new chief must have eventually expelled from the village.[15]

I am sure that many more instances of rural tension and violence can be collected. Though none of these cases clearly indicates the revolt of organized peasant groups against the State or the landlords, yet the destruction of land records and titles, which were usually based on charters granted to the temples and the Brāhmaṇas, is of special significance. The peasants would certainly take advantage of the rivalry between the various types of beneficiaries, religious and non-religious, and also of the rivalry between beneficiaries and the State. Since the

[13] *ARE*, No. 225 of 1927.

[14] *ARE*, for 1913, para 39.

[15] Ibid.

peasants themselves were not enlightened enough, they were invariably led by such priests as were either enlightened or disgruntled.

We have a few instances, particularly of tribal peasants, rising in open revolt against the landed powers. Around the sixth century in south India, we have the famous case of the revolt of *Kalabhras*, who seemed to have been tribal people. Nilakanta Sastri, who refers to this revolt in several of his writings,[16] has never a single good word for the *Kalabhras*. They are considered the scourge of humanity and the enemy of civilization. The Kalabhra chiefs are called evil kings, and they are charged with the resumption of brahmadeya lands enjoyed by the beneficiaries. The Pandya inscriptions of the eighth and ninth centuries speak of the loss of such lands in the wake of the *Kalabhras* aggression and also of the encroachment of the Śūdrās on a donated village.[17] The period for which the *Kalabhras* dominated the scene in Tamil Nadu, especially at the cost of the Cholas, is called a dark age. Although their rule lasted only for 75 years or so, they upset the existing social and political relationships. The Pandyas brought to an end the so-called dark period inaugurated by the *Kalabhras*.

In eastern India we may refer to the revolt of the *Kaivartas*. They were both fishermen and cultivators. As a tribe the *Kaivartas* were absorbed in brahmanical society as a low mixed caste. According to Manu (X.34), the *Kaivarta* was a boatman. But in east Bengal most of them seem to have been peasants, and as such were identical with the *Mahisyas*, who were considered to be the offspring of a Ksatriya father and Vaiśya mother.[18] Some Kaivarta chiefs were given land as service tenures by the Pala rulers. These lands were resumed by Mahipala I around the end of the tenth century,[19] and the Kaivartas were oppressed with taxes. Eventually they revolted against Mahipala II and wiped out the Pala authority for a considerable period of time.[20] Hitherto the Kaivarta revolt has been seen either as a popular upsurge against

[16] K.A. Nilakanta Sastri, *History of India Part 1 - Anuent India,* Madras: 1950, pp. 147–8; *A History of South India,* OUP 1958, pp. 138–9.

[17] Rajen Gurukkal, 'Non-Brāhmaṇa Resistance to the Expansion of Brahmadayas: the Early Pandya Experience, *Proceedings of the India History Congress,* Forty-fifth Session, Annamalai University, Annamalainagar, 1984, pp. 161–3.

[18] R.C. Majumdar, *History of Ancient Bengal,* Calcutta, 1971, pp. 437–8.

[19] *Epigraphia Indica,* XXIX, 5.

[20] Chapter II of the *Ramacaritam of Sandhyakaranandin,* ed. H.P. Sastri and serviced by R.C. Rasak. Calcutta, 1969 (hereafter RC), deals with this revolt.

tyranny[21] or as a civil disturbance against an established and legitimate authority upsetting law and order;[22] the first view is intended to justify democratic rule and the second to support the status quo and discourage revolts under all circumstances. In the process the peasant dimension of the *Kaivarta* problem has been overlooked.[23]

There is need for analyzing the character of the few revolts that are known to us. It appears that so far we have no examples of revolt in settled and clearly caste-divided areas. Both the *Kaiabhras* and the *Kaivartas* were tribal peasants least infected with caste ideology or brahmanization. The *Kaivartas* were a fierce tribe. In their revolt against the Palas they did not possess any chariots.[24] On the other hand they rode buffaloes and fought with bows and arrows.[25] It is significant that the buffalo appears as the *vahana* or conveyance of Lord Yama who is the God of Death. The fact that the buffalo was also associated with the Kaivartas shows them to be as fierce as Yama. At any rate it is clear that the Kaivartas retained their tribal identify under the leadership of Bhima. We find repeated references to the slaughter of the kinsmen of Bhima in the Ramacarita of Sandhyakara Nandi.[26] Although Ramapala is depicted as one who never caused any injury to his kinsmen, he put down the *Kaivartas* not with the support of his kinsmen but a large number of vassals called *samantas*, of whom fourteen are specifically mentioned in the text.[27] Many of these vassals were tribal chiefs ruling over forest tracts.[28] It therefore appears that the protracted struggle between Ramapala on the one hand and the Kaivartas on the other caused a dent in the supra-tribal solidarity, with the result that the Kaivartas were left alone to fend for themselves. Hence the problem of the extent of the kin-based solidarity in these revolts has to be examined.

[21] This seems to be a new one by Jadunath Sarkat, R.P. Chanda and U.N. Ghoshal. Majumdar, op. cit., p. 187, fn. 197.

[22] This is a new by R.C. Majumdar, op. cit., p. 197.

[23] R.S. Sharma, *Indian Feudalism, c.* AD 300–1200, (2nd edn.), Delhi: 1980, pp. 127, 220.

[24] RC, II 40. At one place, however, the commentary speaks of the elephants, houses and buffaloes of Brina (II. 33).

[25] RC, II, 42.

[26] Ibid., II. 48–9.

[27] The names mentioned in the text amplified and associated with various regions in the country which seem to have belonged to the twelfth century. See commentary to Ramacarila, II. 5-6,

[28] Ibid. The term *Samart-atavika-sananta-cakra* is significant.

In analyzing the nature of these revolts one has also to locate the role of religion in mobilizing peasants against their oppressors. Clearly the *Kalabhras* were anti-brahmanical, and they are called Buddhists. Reference to the Kalabhra *Kula* is found in the writings of a Buddhist monk[29] of about the seventh century or so. Similarly the Kaivartas were Saivites, and they were pitted against the Palas who were very much pro-Buddhists. Although Narayanapala granted land to the *Pasupatas* and erected temples for them[30] in the tenth century, in later centuries Buddhism and Saivism were locked in opposition in eastern India. The iconography of eastern India shows aggressive Buddhist gods. Trailokya Vijaya from Orissa (tenth century) is a Buddhist deity trampling Saivite divinities underfoot. Similarly a tenth-century pantheon from Nalanda shows the dominance of the Buddhist deity Aparajita over Saivite and other deities.[31] This religious conflict cannot be isolated from the social situation in which the Buddhist monasteries enjoyed huge landed properties at the cost of both the Brāhmaṇa beneficiaries and the ordinary peasants following Hindu religion. Bhima, the Kaivarta chief, was a devotee of Siva and Bhavani,[32] and his community may have been Saivite. It is significant that when Ramapala gained victory over the Kaivartas, he constructed a large number of Siva temples in the newly founded capital Ramavati in order to pacify the people,[33] who were obviously Kaivartas.

The situation was different in south India where the Saivites and the Vaisnavites persecuted the Jains and the Buddhists. The competing claims for grant of lands may have been an important cause; the Jains were granted lands for the *vasadis* and the Buddhists for *viharas*. In the long run such antagonisms ended in reconciliation. Since references to these revolts are not found in non-religious or secular idiom, it is all the more necessary that their social dimensions be examined.

Sometimes those discontented Brāhmaṇas who were not fortunate enough to receive grants also led revolts against Brāhmaṇas, who were granted lands, by mobilizing the peasants. It is significant that in the Jataka stories revolts are led by Brāhmaṇas with the backing of the common masses. They result in the replacement of the tyrannical king by another ruler who promises to govern according to the norms set by religion and society.

[29] K.A. Nilakanta Sastri, *History of India, Part I, Ancient India,* p. 118.

[30] RC, Introd., p. 23.

[31] These pantheons are housed in Patna Museum.

[32] RC, II, 26.

[33] Ibid., III, 41.

It is not easy to identify the aims and objects of the peasant revolts and the issues involved in them. Mostly the issues were of immediate concern to those who revolted. The Kaivartas apparently wanted the lands that had been resumed from them by Mahipala I and transferred to the Buddhists. They also sought relief from oppressive taxes imposed on them by the Palas. The brief period for which they supplanted the Pala rule did not bring about any transformation in social and political relationships; only the place of the Pala ruler was taken by the Kaivarta chiefs Dibyoka and his son Bhima.

The revolt seems to have raised the ritual status of the Kaivarta community. Formerly a Brāhmaṇa could not accept the food of a Kaivarta, who was called an *antyaja* (literally last-born but really untouchable). But later the myth of his origin from the union of a Ksatriya father and Vaiśya mother was popularized,[34] and he was considered a *sat sūdra* who could perform certain ceremonies and whose food could be accepted. It is stated in a text of the sixteenth century attributed to Vallalasena (twelfth century) that he raised the social status of the Kaivartas and prescribed menial or domestic service as their livelihood. Mahesa, the headman of the Kaivartas, was honoured with the rank and title of *mahamandalika*.[35] Sridharasvami (*c*. AD 1400) in his comment on a verse from the Bhagavata Purana also shows that the Kaivartas gained in status.[36]

The *Kalabhras* who supplanted the power of the three Tamil kingdoms for a short spell in the deep south do not seem to have left much trace of the nature of their rule. They seized the lands granted to the Brāhmaṇas and were probably more egalitarian. The Kaivartas also may have been inspired by the egalitarian spirit. But neither of them can be credited with any vision for recasting social relationships or production relations through revolts.

Whether peasant protests and revolts undermined the existing socio-economic formation needs investigation. The possibility of their linkage with the revival of trade and handicrafts from the eleventh century onwards in many parts of the country has been suggested but not explored.[37] We also cannot state whether these revolts were spontaneous

34 R.C. Majumdar, op. cit., pp. 437–8.

35 Extracts from the *Vallalacarita* (compiled in the sixteenth century) quoted in Majumdar, op. cit., p. 252.

36 *Bhagavata Purāṇa*, ed. J.L. Sastri, Delhi: 1983, XII.325; also see Introd., p. 7.

37 On this point see Nandi, op. cit.

or organized. These questions cannot be answered for lack of sufficient sources and adequate research.

One thing is, however, clear that by the twelfth century or so the enormity and ferocity of the various types of evils and oppressions associated with land grants had been sufficiently publicized and realized. This seems to be particularly true of south India where we find some preemptive protests. In one instance, during the twelfth century a whole village refused to be converted into a religious/educational grant called *agrahara.*[38] This open opposition to being placed at the mercy of landed beneficiaries may have encouraged other villagers to act similarly.

In spite of instances of peasant protests assuming varied forms in early medieval times, by and large the peasants lived in a state of reconciliation and resignation with the situation imposed on them as a result of the rise of landlords and the erosion of their communal rights. This state of affairs can be explained in different ways.

In certain parts of the country; particularly in backward areas, serfs were tied to the land granted to the beneficiaries, but serfdom was not a general feature of Indian feudalism. Wherever the serfs worked on the land, they existed in small numbers. The lack of numbers weakened their position and division into castes hampered organization. The difficulty was further compounded by wide spatial distribution. But in one case in Karnataka the bonded labourers attacked a Brāhmaṇa benefice, and the warrior who fought in its defence claims to have killed many of these labourers (*besa-vagal*) in the fight.[39]

Perhaps the corporate unity of the village community mostly kept the peasants at bay. If the landlord and the peasants belonged to the same village the common belongingness would be used to keep them under the same umbrella. If they belonged to the same kin and caste, the illusion of corporate unity would be stronger. At least for four centuries or so, from the sixth century onwards, this belongingness was strengthened by the blending of agriculture and handicrafts based on the *jajmāñī* system, a phenomenon which has been debated repeatedly under the title of the Asiatic mode. The initial stage of agrarian expansion meant the multiplication of numerous self-sufficient villages and provided a congenial climate for 'corporate' life.

[38] *Epigraphika Carnataka,* VIII, Sorat, Nos. 252 and 253 quoted in ibid. p. 26.

[39] S.J. Janabiah 'From Varna to Caste through Mixed Unions', in *The Character of Kinship,* ed. Goody, p. 207.

Equally important seem to have been the ideological and ritualistic factor. Land seizures do not seem to have been infrequent. The donors constantly feared that the land granted by them could be either seized by their successors or resumed by the existing peasants who had been in possession of it for a long time. In order to forestall such possibilities all kinds of curses were heaped on those who would dare violate the provisions of the land charters granted to the beneficiaries. It was repeatedly stated at the end of the land charters that those who violate them live in hell for 60,000 years and those who observe them live in heaven for the same period. It will be interesting to find out how hell and heaven were deliberately visualized to indoctrinate the mass of the peasants and other people in the norms of feudal patriarchal society. One of the main reasons why the illusion of hell and heaven was developed very much in early medieval times seems to have been to protect the landed property of the Brāhmaṇas and others against encroachment by their equally entrenched rivals and also by the mass of the peasantry.

Connected with the concept of hell and heaven was the Vadanta theory of Karma. The Karma theory emphasized the point that if people performed the duties assigned to their stations by their birth, they could look forward to social promotion in the existing social framework in the next birth. The theory of *punarjanma* or rebirth therefore was preached to the peasant masses and others through numerous religious stories which were recited as kathas. Hence the belief that there was no escape from the consequences of birth and heredity was ingrained in the minds of the people in ancient times but more strongly in early medieval times when social classes became more and more unequal.

Further, the varna theory handed over from ancient times was refurbished in a new manner. One of its greatest proponents was Kṛṣṇa who taught in the *Bhagavad Gītā* that people should carry out the functions assigned to them by their respective varnas. As time went on, the teachings of the Gita received more publicity and increasingly came to be regarded sacred. However, complications were created by the rise of many landed groups or powerful families who would not fit in the fourfold traditional system. In order to absorb them and contain social discontent, new provisions were made in the *Dharmasastras*. If some powerful indigenous tribal families or foreign tribes managed to capture power, they came to be recognized and legitimized as Kṣatriyas. This theory was put forward clearly around AD 400 by Sabarasvami who wrote a commentary on Jaimini's *Mimamsa Sutra*. Now the theory prevailed that any raja could be recognized as a Ksatriya, that is *Kṣatriyo raja ucyate*.

Similarly when land grants helped annex numerous tribals to the Brāhmaṇical system, the new peasants came to be considered Śūdrās. In a way the Śūdrās who served mainly as domestic servants, slaves, artisans, and agricultural labourers in ancient times were now called peasants in some texts, and more so in foreign accounts. The number of *samskaras*, that is domestic ceremonies, was increased and those which were not associated with Vedic mantras could be performed by the Śūdrās. Obviously many Brāhmaṇa priests officiated in these ceremonies although their status may have been low in society. But those Śūdrā peasants who could afford to perform these *samskaras* would certainly have a feeling of social promotion and of closeness to the highest varna.

It would therefore appear that attempts were made to give ritualistic recognition to the social changes that were taking place in production relations. The rituals served to satisfy the vanity and psychological aspirations of the Śūdrā peasants and to make them resign to the new situation, in which they had been deprived of their egalitarian tribal rights.

What distinguished the early medieval period was the proliferation of the cast system; particularly the Śūdrā peasant castes proved to be numerous. Based on regions, clans and tribes, they were arranged in some ritualistic gradation. The theory of the origin of these Śūdrā castes was known as the theory of mixed castes, which attributed the origins of numerous peasant castes to the union of the existing castes in the reverse order, that is in the *pratiloma* order. This theory was conceived in such a manner that almost every mixed caste was either inferior or superior to the other caste.[40] Thus, although the peasants were exploited more or less in the same manner, they were the victims of endless division caused by the castes based on ritualistic distinctions of inferiority or superiority. The element of ritualism tended to distort the reality of exploitation to which the peasants were subjected. Therefore the solidarity of the peasants against the landlords could not be achieved easily.

[40] R.S. Sharma, 'Material Milieu of Jantrism', in *Indian Society*, eds. R.S. Sharma and V. Jha, Historical Probings in Memory of D.D. Kosambi, Delhi, 1974.

The two important religious movements that influenced the thinking of the peasant masses in early medieval times were Tantrism and Bhakti. Tantrism emphasized the worship of the mother goddess, many of whose names sound non-Sanskritic. Its rituals and ordination were open to both men and women without any distinction. Though tantrism affected Saivism, Vaisnavism, Jainism and Buddhism, it really originated as a result of land grants to Brāhmaṇas and others in the outlying areas inhabited by tribal and non-brahmanical people. The super-imposition of a class of beneficiaries substantially took away the rights of the tribals to land and communal resources, but their egalitarian ritualistic rights were recognized in a tantric garb. Even the brahmanized peasant castes who did not enjoy such rights under the varna system could perform tantric ceremonies.[41]

Tantrism enjoyed a large following, particularly in the backward tribal areas. With the accommodation of the mother goddess in the Hindu set-up and her elevation to a very high status in it, the exponents of the tantra system obviously succeeded in reconciling the tribals to the hardships resulting from the land grants. The initial appeal of the tantra to the tribals may have petered out in the long run when the tantric hierarchy was modeled on the feudal hierarchy, and when war and sex, with which the landlords were obsessed, were given prominence in the tantra system.

But a more powerful factor that helped to contain and channelize the discontent of the peasant masses was the medium of bhakti. Originating in a new incarnation in south India around the seventh century it affected Vaisnavism as well as Saivism. The Bhakti movement in the early medieval period was inspired by the feudal social set-up. But when it crystallized it seems to have acquired an autonomous character. The peasant devotees offered the same allegiance to their landlord as they offered to their god. They seem to have sincerely believed in the 'invisible realities' resulting from the blessings of the all-powerful and ever, compassionate god. The idea of complete surrender to the god was developed further in late medieval times. The god was conceived as father, mother, kinsman, companion, wealth and learning. His constant imaginary company was considered a great solace for those who experienced exploitation and hardships arising out of the increasing burden of taxation in medieval times.

[41] This point has been discussed in my book *Indian Feudalism*.

Various other methods were used to keep the peasants and the landlords together. Special mention may be made of *vratas* or religious vows including festivities which were prescribed for all sections of society, high and low. More importantly, *tirthas* and temples, which diluted distinctions between landlords and peasants, became a common feature. There is no way to compute the number of rituals that were actually performed by various princes, chiefs, landed magnates and temples in the early medieval period. But rituals were considered necessary for legitimizing quick changes in authority and social status. This partly accounts for the provision of a large number of *vratas* in medieval texts. A ritual was an occasion not only for making gifts to the priests but also for holding sumptous feasts and distribution of *prasada* by the temple and other authorities. This meant sharing of common food both by the landlords and the peasants and artisans attached to them. In a way rituals offered opportunities for 'redistribution' in medieval times. Thus the process of integration and reconciliation was promoted through different devices in which arousing hopes for the next world and rituals of legitimacy and 'redistribution' played an important part.

The measures mentioned above were communicated to the people through the written or the spoken word. The written word may have been confined to a few literates, but the spoken word through the citation of the Purana stories reached even women and Śūdrās. The ideological and ritualistic propaganda was backed by the medium of art. Social and religious ideals were articulated in representations of gods and goddesses in numerous pieces of sculpture in stone and bronze. Their number in early medieval times is so large that one encounters them in almost all the settled parts of the country.

CHAPTER 8

Usury in Early Medieval Times

1. ATTITUDES TOWARDS USURY

Literally the term usury means the practice of lending money at an exorbitant rate of interest, especially at a higher rate than is allowed by law. This, however, seems to be a later meaning. In many ancient societies the very idea of taking interest was considered to be reprehensible, and the act of charging interest, high or low, was thought to be immoral, so that the term usury has a tinge of something socially and religiously undesirable about it. In early medieval Indian society it is not always possible to draw a precise line between usury and interest, and hence the subject can be best studied by examining the data on interest and moneylending.

The present study covers a period of about 800 years, and is mainly based on Smṛti texts. In about the fifth and sixth centuries, Bṛhaspati and Katyayana present to us fairly developed laws regarding debt. Fragments of law ascribed to their successors add precious little. The subject is also dealt within the compilations on debt in the legal digests of the twelfth and fifteenth centuries.

The *Dharmasastra* material can be supplemented by some epigraphic evidence, but even all this stuff does not enable us to treat the whole question in successive stages. Hence we propose to study its important aspects separately but in sequence of time wherever possible.

Ancient and medieval Indian Sanskrit texts convey the idea of interest or usury by *kusīda, vārdhuṣa, vṛddhi* and *vyāja,* of which the last seems to be of later origin. Since these terms were used indiscriminately by lawgivers, it is difficult to establish whether they used one for usury and the other for interest. Baudhayana, a lawgiver of about the fifth century BC, prescribes taking interest as a source of livelihood for the Vaiśya[1] and condemns a Brāhmaṇa who practices *vārdhuṣa* as a Śūdrā.[2] On the other hand Gautama permits *Kusīda* to a Brāhmaṇa who does not do it himself.[3] Manu does not demarcate between *vṛddhi* and *kusīda,* and lays down that the *vārdhuṣika* (one who lends at interest) should take *vṛdhi.*[4] In the opinion of Vasistha a *vārdhuṣika* is one who taking cheap lends it on condition of receiving a greater quantity.[5] Whether this applies to grain is not clear from the text. But Narada defines *vārdhuṣa* (usury) as interest on grain.[6] According to him, interests on grain can rise three times the principal, but it can be regarded as usury only when it is demanded at the rate of 5 per cent on grain given through friendship.[7]

Bṛhaspati's concept of usury was different. According to him, the use of a pledge after twice the principal has been collected from it, compound interest, and the addition of the interest to the principal constitute usury and are to be condemned.[8] Brhaspati seems to identify *kusīda* with usury and defines it as that which is taken fourfold or even eightfold without any qualm of conscience from a poor person who is serving or distressed.[9] He gives a fanciful grammatical interpretation of

[1] *Baudhāyana Dharmasūtra* (Kasi Sanskrit Series, no. 104, Banaras, 1934), 1.10.22.
[2] I. 10.25.
[3] X. 5–6.
[4] VIII. 140.
[5] II. 41–42.
[6] IV. 110. *vṛddhistu yoktā dhānyasya vārdhuṣam tadudāhṛtaṃ,* quoted in *HDS.* III, 417.
[7] I. 109–10.
[8] XI. 12.
[9] XI. 2.

the terms *ku* and *sīda,*[10] which indicates the attitude of derision in which the lawgivers holds usurious rates of interest. The idea is reproduced in the ninth century by Medhatithi, according to whom the term *kusīda* means that which is followed by evil persons, and also the persons themselves.[11] Almost all the legal texts disapprove of what is not considered *dharmyā vṛddhi,* legal interest, but they do not seem to use any special term of opprobrium for it. Nevertheless, they exhibit a tone of venom against exorbitant interest, which continues into late medieval times. The *Vivādacandra,* written by Misaru Mishra of Mithila in first half of the fifteenth century, condemns the food of the usurer (*vārdhuṣikasyānna*) who waits a for long for the increase of his interest a nigh-soil.[12]

The legal texts from ancient to medieval times show a changing attitude towards charging interest by members of various social classes (varnas). Lawgivers of the fifth-third centuries BC permits lending at interest only to the Vaiśya. Vasistha lays down that a Brāhmaṇa or *srotriya* shall not act as usurer.[13] In particular a Brāhmaṇa usurer (*vārdhuṣika*) is condemned as a Śūdrā[14] and is not to be treated even as a Vaiśya. Vaishtha states that if Brāhmaṇa murder and usury are weighed in balance, the murderer of a Brāhmaṇa rises to the top while the usurer trembles.[15] Similarly, Baudhayana declares that if interest (*vṛddhi*) and abortion are weighted, the destroyer of womb rises while the usurer sinks.[16] Usury is therefore considered even worse than the murder of a Brāhmaṇa or abortion. Coming as all this does from Brāhmaṇa lawgivers, it shows an intense hatred for usurers, who probably did not spare the Brāhmaṇa. However, Baudhayana[17] permits the first two varnas to charge interest from one who neglects his sacred duties, from a miser, from an atheist, or from a very wicked man, but these cases are exceptional and do not ordinarily allow a Brāhmaṇa to practice usury. Gautam[18] permits

[10] *SBI,* XXXIII. 320.
[11] On *Manu*, VIII. 152.
[12] Quoted in *HDS,* III. 423, fn, 691.
[13] *Vas.*, II. 40.
[14] *Baudh.*, 1.10.25.
[15] *Vas.*, II.46.
[16] 1.10.24.
[17] 1.10.26.
[18] X. 5–6.

a Brāhmaṇa to lend at interest provided he does not do it himself. But it is doubtful whether this injunction formed part of his original law book.[19]

Manu, the most important lawgiver of post-Maurya times, states in unequivocal terms that the Brāhmaṇa or the Ksatriya should not take interest even in times of distress, but should pay some interest to people of mean avocations (*pāpīyase*) out of legal necessity (*dharmartham*).[20] On the other hand Manu enjoins the king to compel the Vaiśya to practice lending at interest and other occupations.[21] Narada seems to concede this practice in favour of the Ksatriya but lays down that a Brāhmaṇa must never resort to usury, not even in a state of extreme distress.[22] Similarly Katyayana states that a Brāhmaṇa (*dvija*) who is a cowherd, trade, artisan, bards, servant, and an interest-taker should be administered the same ordeal by the king as a Śūdrā.[23] Thus the law books of the post-Maurya and Gupta periods roundly prohibit a Brāhmaṇa to live on interest. It is curious that they do not allow even as much latitude to the Brāhmaṇas in this respect as Baudhayana does.

About three centuries later the situation seems to have changed. In the ninth century, commenting on Manu, VII. 140, Medhatithi states that the good Vasistha, who possessed knowledge of all the three ages and was free from various weaknesses including greed, accepted interest at the rate of 1/80 of the principal. He therefore declares that this rate increases wealth, and is not associated with the weakness of greed (*lobha*). From this it follow that if Vasistha charged interest, the Brāhmaṇas were justified in doing so. The position came to be clearly recognized by the twelfth century, when the *Garuda Purana* was compiled. The text permits the Brāhmaṇas and Ksatriyas to practice

[19] Gautama is considered to be one of the earliest lawgivers, if not the earliest. It has been shown by me elsewhere (*Śūdrās in Ancient India,* Delhi, 1958, pp. 83-4) that he should be dated much later on the basis of his provisions on social matters. His regulations regarding debt confirm my earlier view, and it seems that these were interpolated into Gautama's law book some time in Gupta or post-Gupta times. His enumeration of six kinds of intersest are not found in any law book earlier than that of Brhaspati, whose section on debt is the most developed. Again, his provision that a Brāhmaṇa can lend (money) at interest is not found in this form in any early law book; on the other hand it is found in post-Gupta texts which allow this to a Brāhmaṇa only in distress.

[20] VIII. 410.

[21] I.111.

[22] *Kātyāyana Smṛti* (ed. and tr. P.V. Kane, Poona), verse 423. Here the term *dvija* is taken by kave as a member of the three higher cases, but the word Brāhmaṇa would suit the context better.

[23] Quoted in *Vācaspatyam,* III. 2159.

Kusīda in times of distress.[24] It considers *kusīda* to be the most effective of all the mode of livelihood prescribed by sages in abnormal times. Agriculture is hampered by want of rains, royal terror, and the depredations of the mice, etc., but not *kusīda* which keeps on growing at all times and under all circumstances.[25]

Whether Brāhmaṇas actually practiced money lending in northern India is difficult to say. Speaking of the eleventh century, Alberuni states: 'Usury or taking percentages is forbidden. Only to the Śūdrā is it allowed to take percentages, as long as his profit is not more than (a) fiftieth of the captial'.[26] It is not clear whether 'usury' is the correct word used by Sachau in his translation. But since all the legal texts authorize the Vaiśyas to charge interest, there is no reason to believe that this was confined to the Śūdrās in Alberuni's times. Probably Alberuni's picture is rather idealistic, and projects Islamic ideas which do not permit such percentages.

But in south India temple management dominated by priests and the Brāhmaṇas did invest gold with the village assemblies and others, and received interest thereon for the maintenance of worship, perpetual burning of lamps and similar other purposes. All this was done on religious grounds, and we have yet to find examples of moneylending carried on by the Brāhmaṇa for secular purposes.

2. RATES OF INTEREST

From the fifth century BC onwards metal money came into use, and loans were given in both cash and kind. Some early lawgivers, such as Baudhayana[27] and Gautama,[28] clearly mention the percentage in terms of coins, which shows that money lending was practiced. Some later lawgivers do not clarify it, but the rates they laid down apparently refer to loans in cash, for in regard to loans in kind they do not indicate the rate but merely prescribe the maximum to which the interest can rise.

The rates of interest laid down by the legal texts show a tendency towards gradual increase. Baudhayana prescribes 10 per cent per year,[29]

[24] Ibid.
[25] Ibid.
[26] *Alberni's India,* ed. and trans. Edward C. Sachau, London: 1910, II. 150.
[27] 1.10.22.
[28] XII. 29.
[29] 1.10.22.

but Gautama, whose law book was compiled later, raises it to 15 per cent, [30] which is supported by Vasistha.[31] This rate is endorsed by not only the *Arthasastra* of Kautilya[32] but also by the law books of the first six centuries of the Christian era.[33] Medieval lawgivers and commentators held that it applied only to loans for which securities were furnished. Vyasa, whose code was compiled some time between AD 600 and 900, laid down that the monthly rate of interest was 1/80 of the principal (15 per cent) when a pledge or mortgage was given against the loan, 1/60 (20 per cent) when a surety was offered, and 2 per month (24 per cent) when money was lent on personal security.[34] Harita, whose law book belonged to this period, also prescribes 24 per cent in case of absence of security.[35] Vrddha Harita adds that double the normal interest (30 per cent) may be taken when there is nothing pledged to secure the debt.[36] Thus by about the ninth century there seems to have taken place an appreciable increase in the rate of normal interest, which in general rose from 10 per cent in the fifth century BC to 24 per cent in the ninth century AD. The strikingly lesser use of coin during the four centuries following the Gupta period leads us to think that the supply of cash was limited and consequently the rate of interest higher. Decline in foreign trade may have been an important reason for want of cash.

The rules quoted seem to apply for ordinary transactions in normal times. Money lent for purposes of trade is charged higher interest. Kautilya characterizes 15 per cent as legal but lays down 60 per cent for those who are engaged in ordinary trade, 120 per cent for those traders who traverse forests, and 240 per cent for those who carry on maritime trade.[37] Exactly the same rates for the three grades of traders are laid down by Yajnavalkya,[38] whose eleventh-century scholiast, Vijananesvara, explains the reasons for it. According to him these exorbitant rates are justified by the danger of the loss of even the principal as the debtors may perish on account of shipwreck or the attacks of

[30] XII. 29.

[31] II. 51.

[32] III. 11.

[33] *Manu,* VIII. 1400; *Yaj.,* 11.37; *Nar* 1.99; *Br,* XI.3.

[34] *HDS,* III. 421.

[35] Quoted in Caṇḍśvara Ṭhakkura's *Gṛhastharatnākara* (*Bibliotheca Indica,* Calcutta, 19.8), 447.

[36] *HDS*, III. 420–1.

[37] AS, III. 11.

[38] II. 38.

robbers and wild beasts.[39] Since these rates seem to be too excessive for the Maurya period, it seems that they were introduced into the *Arthasastra* at a later stage. The other possibility that Yajnavalkya might have borrowed from Kautilya seems to be remote.

Besides loans for trade, in certain other cases the interest prescribed is high. Katyayana, a lawgiver of about the sixth century, ordains that what is lent through friendship, a deposit, balance of interest, and unpaid purchase money, if not returned on demand, begin to carry interest at 5 per cent per month,[40] which works out at the rate of 60 per cent annually. The same rate can be inferred from a provision of Narada.[41]

The early lawgivers Gautama, Baudhayana, Apastamba, and Kautilya do not introduce any consideration of varna in the payment of interest, which is done for the first time by Vasistha,[42] and followed by the lawgivers of the early centuries of the Christian era.[43] Brāhmaṇas are required to pay 24 per cent per year, Ksatriyas 36 per cent, Vaiśyas 48 per cent, and Śūdrās 60 per cent.[44] According to the medieval commentators (the comment of Nanda Pandita to Visnu VI.2) it applies to loans without pledges, but this does not account for varna discrimination in fixing interest. It might, however, explain a higher rate, that is 24 per cent even for the Brāhmaṇa which considerably exceeds the normal legal rate of 15 per cent. On the other hand differences in rates according to the varnas might be explained on the ground of the helplessness of the members of the lower orders, whose economic position was generally worse than those of the higher varnas.[45] The practice is followed even now in villages where Śūdrās are charged higher rates of interest. According to the *Sarasvativīlāsa,* a work of the sixteenth century, these discriminatory laws do not apply if the debtor and the creditor belong to the same caste; in that case the interest shall be at the flat rate of 24 per cent per year. Thus if a Ksatriya gives loan to a Ksatriya he will charge 24 per cent, if to a Vaiśya, 36 per cent; and if to a Śūdrā, 48 per cent.[46] Similarly if a Vaiśya gives loan to a Vaiśya, he will charge 24 per cent; and if to a Śūdrā 36 per cent.[47] The provisions

[39] *Mitākṣarā on Yāj.,* II. 38.
[40] Verses 505–6.
[41] 1.109.
[42] 11.48.
[43] *Manu,* VIII. 142; *Viṣṇu,* VI. 2; *Yaj* II. 37; *Nar., 1. 100.*
[44] Ibid.
[45] R.S. Sharma, *Some Economic Aspects of the Caste System in Ancient India* (Patna, 1952), pp. 16–21.
[46] *Sarasvativīlāsa,* quoted in *DK,* I, part 2, 620.
[47] Ibid.

indicate a softening of the varna distinctions in matters of interest in late medieval times though it would be wrong to think that they were followed to the letter in early medieval time. At least the available epigraphic material does not indicate any social distinctions in the levy of interest.

During post-Maurya times in northern and western India endowments in money were invested with guilds, which undertook to pay a certain amount of interest for carrying on worship and meeting the needs of the monks and other religious people. In a Nasik inscription of the second century AD the rate of interest prescribed for payment is lower than that recommended by Manu.[48] The inscription indicates 12 per cent per year, but Manu recommends 15 per cent. The clearest hint of interest rates is thrown by the south Indian inscriptions of the early medieval period. Several tenth-century endowment from the Tamil country under the Cholas suggest 15 per cent as the usual rate of interest. Two inscriptions of the reign of Parantaka I, one of AD 936[49] and the other of AD 937,[50] can be interpreted in this light. In one case $4^1/_2$ *kalañju* of gold per year was charged as interest on 30 *kalanju* which was endowed for burning a perpetual lamp[51] in honour of mahadeva. In another case gold was invested with the residents of a settlement who agreed to pay interest once in six months at the rate of the three *mañjāḍi* per *kalañju* annually.[52] Since one *kalañju* is equal to 20 *mañjāḍi,* it works out at the rate of 15 per cent per year. Again, an inscription of AD 986 records that in the reign of Uttama Chola 200 *kalañju* of gold was deposited with the inhabitants of four settlements on a perpetual interest of 30 *kalanju* per year, which again amounts to 15 per cent.[53] These three instances would show that on gold invested by temples and similar religious institution, which they received as endowment, the village Assemblies paid interest of 15 per cent annually, which was the legal rate (*dharmya*) prescribed by the law books of ancient and medieval times.

But we also come across certain variations, which generally exceed 15 per cent and rarely fall below it. Thus an epigraph of AD 979, belonging to the reign of Uttama Chola, records that the assembly of a settlement received 24 *Kalañju* and agreed to pay an annual interest of one *kalañju*

[48] D.C. Sircar, *Sel. Inscr.,* book, II, no. 58, line 1-3; cf. *Manu,* VIII. 139–42.

[49] *SII,* III, part 3, 237.

[50] Ibid., 237.

[51] Ibid., 236.

[52] Ibid., 237.

[53] Ibid., 274.

and four *mañjāḍi* of gold, which amounts to 5 per cent per year.[54] However, as early as the eighth century AD gold given for the perpetual burning of lamp in a temple in the Bana kingdom carried an annual interest of 20 per cent, 4 *Kalañju* of gold being fixed as interest on 20 *kalañju.*[55] A century later an epigraph of AD 940, belonging to the reign of Parantaka I, shows that a yearly interest of 40 per cent was charged on a deposit for religious purposes.[56] These examples show the temples as moneylenders and roughly indicate that the rate of interest in south India generally corresponded to the early Dharmasastra rate of 15 per cent and not the later rate of 24 per cent.

The epigraphic evidence for the rate of interest in northern India during the same period is slender. An inscription shows that the Mahajanas of Sivapura paid 25 per cent interest on the deposit of 6 *gadyānas*,[57] nearly the same as recommended by Vyasa[58] and Harita,[59] who prescribe 24 per cent per year. The same rate is mentioned by Alberuni in the eleventh century. He states that only the Śūdrā is allowed to take percentages as long as his profit is not more than a fiftieth of the capital.[60] Hence in early medieval times 24 per cent seems to have been the normal rate of interest on loans in cash in northern India. This was obviously much less than later rates which allowed the principal to double itself in three years. Later lawgivers do not prescribe any such time-limit, and hence the principal can double in six years and eight months at the rate of 15 per cent annually. But in the ninth or the tenth century, when the normal interest came to be recognized as 24 per cent, it was laid down by Harita that the principal is doubled after four years and two months at the rate of 8 *paṇas* per month for 25 *purāṇas,*[61] one *purāṇa* being equal to 16 *paṇas* according to it.

Nonetheless, the limit of interest being equal to the principal is generally accepted by all lawgivers. Narada, however, adds that in some countries a loan grows to twice the principal, in other 3, 4, or 8 times.[62] It is not clear whether the things referred to here are in terms of cash or

[54] Ibid., 273.

[55] EI, XI, 228–9.

[56] 1/4 *puttakkam* was the interest charged on 1 *ilakkāsu* for one month, and 1 *ilakkasu* was equal to 7½ *puttakkām.* SII, III, part 3, 239.

[57] EI, XII. 273.

[58] *Gṛhastharatnākara,* 447.

[59] Ibid.

[60] Ed. and tr. E. Sachau, II, 150.

[61] *DK,* I, part 2, 608.

[62] *Nar.,* I, 106–7.

kind. Bṛhaspati simply states that the loan and its recovery should be regulated by local custom,[63] which may mean the same thing as Narada's provision. In the later medieval period a passage ascribed to Gautama states that the principal is doubled in sixteen months, which raises the rate of interest to 150 per cent. Thus the tendency to reduce the period in which the interest can reach the maximum seems to be fairly strong in medieval times.

As pointed out earlier, the maximum amount of interest that could be claimed by the creditors was equal to the principal—what is known as *dvaiguṇyam* in legal texts. But if double the principal (including principal and interest) was not paid in time, further interest could be charged. Thus Manu seems to suggest that if the interest becomes equal to the principal and is not paid, it should be compounded with the principal.[64] Katyayana lays down that if the creditor does not get twice the amount lent by him, to which he is always entitled, this should be compounded with the capital on which further interest shall accrue.[65] Commenting on Manu, VIII. 155, Medhatithi states that the rate of interest on the new principal should be reduced and continued till such time as does not render it oppressive, the idea being that it should be lower than the former rate. The maximum limit of the interest, more than double the principal, is also contemplated by Vijananesvara. Commenting on Yaj., II. 39, he stipulates that if the interest is recovered daily, monthly or yearly and is not claimed in a lump sum at one time, then the total interest received by a creditor may be even more than double the principal lent. This provision is not confined to certain areas or certain articles, as done by Narada and Brhaspati, but made a general rule, which shows that by the eleventh century whatever little prejudice there existed against the maximum accumulation of interest had disappeared, and it could cross the normal limit (double the principal). The law can be better appreciated if we bear in mind the needs of trade which revived in Gujarat and Rajasthan. Since the eleventh century we also find considerable trade in Karnataka and Tamil Nadu.

The idea of compound interest occurs in Gautama,[66] but since none of his contemporaries mentions it, it may not have occurred in the original law book. The provision, however, recurs in Manu,[67] Narada[68] and

[63] XIII. 24.
[64] *Manu,* VIII. 155.
[65] Verse 509.
[66] XII. 34–5.
[67] VII. 156.
[68] *DK, I,* part 2, 625.

Brahaspati.[69] Curiously enough it is not referred to by Katyayana, whose laws on interest are very elaborate. Asahaya, who flourished some time in the eighth century, defines and illustrates the practice of compound interest at great length. According to him, one *dramma* lent as principal can be multiplied by 500 times, and the process of compound interest can continue for 33 years and 4 months.[70]

Considering the nature of the economy in ancient and early medieval times it would be reasonable to expect more loans in kind than in cash. The practice of lending grain was as old as the time of Gautama and Vasistha. The ancient lawgivers down to the time of Manu seek to regulate the return of a few articles given on loan, but these provisions become more detained in the law books from Gupta times onwards. Vasistha lays down that the return on grain, roots, fruits, and fluids shall be three times, and that on things that can be weighed shall be eight times.[71] It appears that the articles which can be weighed were meant to be loaned to small traders by big traders or producers. Gautama prescribes a higher rate, although, he does not differentiate between various kinds of articles. According to him, on loans of grain, fruits, wool, and beasts of burden, and products such as ghee and milk from cattle, the total recoverable cannot exceed in any case five times the capital.[72] The provision is literally repeated by Manu.[73] Here, again it appears suspicious whether the provision formed a part of the original law book of Gautama, because his near contemporary vasistha mentions a rate of only 3 times on grain. Visnu[74] and Narada[75] lay down the following schedule more or less on similar lines:

gold	2 times
grain	3 times
cloth	4 times
liquids	8 times
women and cattle	one issue

Brhaspati's provision regarding gold is exactly the same as that of the two lawgivers but is somewhat different regarding other articles, as would appear from the following.[76]

69 XI. 4–9.
70 *DK*, I. part 2, 625.
71 II. 44–47.
72 XII. 36.
73 VIII. 151.
74 VI. 11–15.
75 106–7.
76 XI. 13–15.

gold	2 times
cloth and base metals	3 times
grain, edible plants, cattle, and wool	4 times
pot-herbs	5 times
seeds and sugar cane	6 times
salt, oil, and spirit	8 times

Katyayana's provision on the point is detailed. According to him, precious stones, pearls, corals, gold, silver, fruits, silk and wool increase by two times; base metals by five times; and oils, liquors, ghee, raw sugar, salt, and land by eight times.[77] That the loan of land increases by eight times is also confirmed by Pitamaha, who is assigned to AD 600–900.[78] Here the striking thing is the provision for the loan of land, on which eightfold return would mean eight times the produce from one harvest.

Viṣṇu and Bṛhaspati mention certain articles on which increase in interest is unlimited. Viṣṇu states that on wool, cotton, thread, leather, shield, weapon, bricks, coal, etc., there is no limit to interest[79] (*akṣaya*). Brahaspati declares that on these articles no interest is ordained.[80] The tem *akṣaya,* used by Viṣṇu, is interpreted in another context as 100 times by the *Smṛticandrikā,*[81] which refers to flowers, fruits, roots, etc., in this connection.

It is difficult to account for the difference concerning the maximum accumulation of various articles given on loan. As regards grain, difference in rate ranged from three times prescribed by Vasistha, Visnu and Narada to five times prescribed by Gautama and Manu. In between comes Bṛhaspati, who makes it four times. Katyayana does not mention it. The difference does not seem to be temporal but regional, for Narada points out that in certain countries interest grows three, four or five times.

It is obvious that for day-to-day use the common folk would be more in need of grain, seeds, cattle, etc., than in need of cash. This would be particularly true of the early medieval period up to the tenth century for it was marked by less of trade, urbanism and coinage. High rates charged

77 Verses 510–12.
78 *DK,* I, part 2, 634.
79 VI. 16.
80 XI. 16.
81 *DK, I. part 2, 609.*

for cereals and other articles remind us of similar rates prescribed for Vaiśyas, and particularly Śūdrās, in giving them loans in cash. Apparently, in extending loans to the common folk the lawgivers had in mind their inability to pay in time. Another factor that led to the demand for a higher return in the case of some articles was their perishable nature. Since gold and silver were more lasting and valuable, they could increase by two times. On the other hand there was no limit to interest on cheap articles of common use such as ferment (*kiṇva*), cotton, thread, leather, shields, weapons, bricks, charcoal, all enumerated by Narada and Brhaspati, and roots, fruits, flowers, etc., added by the *Smṛticandrikā*. It is remarkable that fruits, on which according to earlier lawgivers the return ranged from two to five times, came to be considered in the medieval age as a source of exploiting the people who borrowed it. We may add that other articles which were intended to secure a return of 100 times were also to be used by the common people, who, in consequence of their borrowing, could not be free from the internal obligation of serving their creditors in various ways. What might explain the provision for return on certain marketable commodities such as base metals, salt, raw sugar, liquor, ghee, oil, and other materials, is the fact that these were borrowed by retail traders who were supposed to earn more profit on them. The provision for borrowing land and giving eightfold return on it, given by Katyayana and corroborated by Pitamaha, seems to be unique in early medieval India. It looks like the practice of temporary sub-infeudation, for the land so borrowed would have to be returned to the creditor. In effect it would mean adding to the number of temporary tenants. Perhaps such a law refers to a period of economic or political crisis when the distressed and uprooted peasants approached the landowners for some plots of land in search of livelihood.

Very few lawgivers set the time-limit for reaching the maximum in regard to articles given on loan, although it is reasonable to expect such a limit. Commenting on a passage of Harita,[82] Candesvara points out that if payment is made with the gathering of the next harvest within two to three months, grain (taken on loan) becomes double; if it is not given back at that time, it becomes treble but not more than that,[83] an explanation also given in a work of the fifteenth century.[84] According to

[82] *tule tu dviguṇam dhānyaṃ triguṇameva vardhate. DK,* I. 608.

[83] *Vivādaratnākara,* quoted ibid. 608–9.

[84] *Vivādacandra* of Misaru Mishra, quoted ibid. It seems that the principal is to be collected in addition to this.

Harita, this also applies to wool and cotton given on loan.[85] Ghee, salt, and raw sugar increase eightfold in a year according to Harita and the commentary of Caṇḍesvara in his *Vivādaratnākara* on him.[86] It appears that in medieval times this time-limit of one year was prescribed for all articles made over as loan except grain, wool and cotton for the return of which two or three months were allowed.

3. KINDS OF INTEREST

It is curious that the forms of interest seem to be fairly well-developed in the law book of Gautama, ascribable to the fifth-third centuries BC. It mentions six kinds of interest: compound periodical, stipulated, corporal (*kāyikā*), daily and pledge-using.[87] But Manu, who is placed later than Gautama, mentions only four kinds,[88] which raises doubts about the antiquity of this provisions inserted in Gautama. Whatever be the precise dating of these provisions, it is definite that the various forms of interest were defined in detail some time between the fifth and seventh centuries AD. Thus Narada not only[89] enumerates four kinds of interest but also defines each one of them in some detail.[90] According to him the *kāyikā* (corporal interest) means the milk of a pledged cow or animals used by the creditor, which thus excludes the exploitation of the physical labour of the debtor by the creditor. Periodical interest (*kālikā*) means monthly payment. Stipulated interest (*kāritā*) implies the interest promised by the borrower over and above the normal interest in times of distress. Compound interest (*cakravṛddhi*) is interest received everyday; it does not cease growing except on the loss of the head of the state. Interest-bearing pledge (*bhogalābha*) is interest by enjoyment, such as the use of a mortgaged house, the produce of field, etc.[91] Brhaspati adds that hair-interest, corporal interest, and interest by enjoyment shall be taken by the creditor as long as the principal remains unpaid.[92] We do not know why this rule does not apply to periodical (*kālikā*) and

[85] Ibid.

[86] Ibid.

[87] *cakrakālavṛddhiḥkārtiakāyikaśikhādhibhogaśca.*XII.31–2, quoted in *DK*, I, part 2, 607.

[88] VIII. 154.

[89] II. 87-9, quoted in *DK*, I, part 2, 624–5.

[90] XI. 4–9.

[91] Ibid.

[92] XI.II.

stipulated (*kāritā*) forms of interest. Perhaps the first four forms of interest are deducted from the capital, but neither of the last two reduces the capital in any way. A later lawgiver, Katyayana, does not mention all the six forms of interest, for periodical and compound varieties are left out by him. He, however, devotes seven verses (502–8) to *akṛta vṛddhi*, unagreed interest, not found in other texts. There he contemplates imposition of interest under various conditions. Thus when a person takes a temporary loan and goes to another country before repayment, it begins to acquire interest after a year.[93] If a person after taking a loan goes to another country without repayment even when pressed by the lender, that loan begins to acquire interest within three months.[94] When the borrower of a thing does not return it on demand, the king should make him pay interest since the day of demand, though it was not agreed upon when he was in the country, and though he be unwilling to pay interest.[95] It is apparent that all the cases carry an interest of 5 per cent.

In about the eighth century, Asahaya, commenting on the four forms of interest prescribed by Narada, deals at some length with each one of these. *Kālikā* or periodical interest is that where payment is made every month.[96] *Kāritā* is that which is agreed to by the debtor in times of distress according to the interest laid down by the law books; here the debtor agrees to pay a higher interest, say 10 per cent more.[97] *Kāyikā* is explained by Asahaya at some length. Herein the capital (*dravyapiṇḍa*) is considered to be *kāya,* and the daily interest that accrues on it in the form of *paṇa* or a *pāda* does not reduce it in any way, and the capital remains as it was. According to Asahaya, this interest is paid by the debtor in the form of daily wages (*divasabhāṭaka-vṛddhyācāreṇa*), which incidentally does not amount to more than a *paṇa* or *pāda*.[98] *Cakravṛddhi,* as shown earlier, is explained in detail by Asahaya. Here the capital can increase 500 times and the king is instructed to make the debtor pay the interest.[99]

Of the forms of interest prevalent from the beginning of the Christian era onwards there is some confusion about the interpretation of the *kāyikā*. Though the lawgivers do not clarify whether the bodily labour

93 Verse 502.
94 Verse 503.
95 Verse 504.
96 *DK*. I, part 2, 625.
97 Ibid.
98 Ibid.
99 Ibid.

of the debtor could be exploited by the creditor in lieu of interest, the commentators imply this clearly. Asahaya indicates that the interest had to be paid in the form of daily wages, which obviously would accrue to the debtor as his remuneration for working for the creditor.[100]

An early medieval lawgiver, Vyasa, explains *kāyikā* as that which is accompanied by milching and carrying (*dohyavāhya-karmasaṃyutā*).[101] This is explained by Caṇḍesvara as pledging cows and oxen.[102]

Medhatithi, commenting on Manu, VIII. 153, made it clear that the *kāyikā* interest has to be cleared through bodily labour.[103] This is roundly supported by Govindaraja (eleventh century),[104] and Haradatta (1100–1300).[105] Sarvajnanarayana, who belonged to the same period as Haradatta, commenting on Manu, VIII. 153, states that bodily service should be rendered gradually till the principal is not cleared.[106] A verse quoted in the *Smṛticandrikā* of Devaṅṅabhatta (1150–1225) states that *kāyikā* is based on performance of work.[107] In the ancient period failure to pay debts (which would include both the principal and the interest) was an important source of slavery. The provision to make the debtors work in lieu of interest so long as the capital was not paid implies some kind to bonded labour in early medieval times. Such rules leave clear scope for enjoying the manual labour of the debtor in return for interest and remind us of the continuing practice according to which several generations of the same family are reduced to the position of hereditary ploughmen in consideration of a paltry sum advanced to them. Therefore, in view of the paucity of coins in the four centuries following the fall of the Gupta empire, *kāyikā* should be considered an important and widely prevalent form of interest. However, only the members of a case lower than that of the creditor could be subjected to bodily labour for recovery of loans, and consequently the incidence of this interest fell more heavily on the members of lower orders.

In the economic context of early medieval times the practice of giving pledge for interest deserves as much attention as *kāyikā*. Mentioned in the earlier law books of Gautama and Manu, pledge became obligatory

[100] Ibid.
[101] *DK,* I, part 2, 634.
[102] *Vivādaratnākara,*quoted ibid.
[103] *kāyakarmaṇa saṃśadhya.DK,* I, part 2. 616.
[104] Ibid., 617.
[105] *Gautama Mitākṣarā,* quoted ibid., 607.
[106] Ibid., 611.
[107] *kāyikā kāyakarmaṇā, DK,* I, part 2, 635.

and prevalent from Gupta times onwards. Brhaspati lays down that a creditor should never lend money without having first secured a pledge of adequate value or a deposit, or some trustworthy security, nor without a bond written by the debtor himself.[108] Along with Narada,[109] he[110] provides for the enjoyment of pledge in lieu of interest. According to him, the pledge which was not given in lieu of interest lapses to the creditor a fortnight after the date when the principal is doubled or the stipulated period has expired.[111] On the contrary, according to Narada, the foolish fellow who enjoys the pledge without the authorization of the owner should enjoy only half the interest.[112] Again, the creditor who enjoys the pledge (*bandhaka*) without the term (period) of the debt being complete out of greed is not entitled to any profit, for such a pledge should be protected like deposit (nyāsa); if it is not, interest is destroyed.[113] The same idea is expressed by Narada according to whom a pledge should not be used by force; if the creditor does so he should surrender the interest due to him from his debtor. Moreover, he must compensate the owner for the pledge or else he is considered a thief appropriating the pledge.[114]

Early medieval law books represent fields as an important form of pledge; this form is not mentioned by Gautama and Manu or any other early lawgiver. In his provisions regarding pledge Yajnavalkya gives no indication, whatsoever that field was given as pledge for enjoyment in lieu of interest, nor does Narada[115] specify it. The first to include fields as a source of interest is bṛhaspati. According to him, the use of a mortgaged house or the produce of a field is termed *bhagatābha* (interest by enjoyment).[116] Together with Katyayana he lays down several provisions regarding the enjoyment of fields. Katyayana provides that the boundaries of the house or the land to be pledged and the villages or the countries in which they are situated be defined.[117] The details about the identity of villages made over as religious gifts were given, and the

[108] XI.1.
[109] 1. 129.
[110] XI. 7–8.
[111] *Br,* XI. 27.
[112] I. 28.
[113] *Br, quoted* in *DK,* I, part 2, 350.
[114] IV. 127 (quoted in *DK,* I, part 2. 650).
[115] 1.125.
[116] XI. 7–8.
[117] Verse 522.

procedure may have appeared in secular transactions. Bṛhaspati ordains that one field mortgaged to two creditors at the same time shall belong to that mortgagee who was the first to obtain possession of it.[118] If both have possessed it for an equal length of time, it shall be held in common (or shared equally) by them.[119] Bṛhaspati ordains that when a field or other immovable property has been enjoyed and the principal and interest actually got out of it by the creditor, the debtor receives back his pledge.[120] This shows that land was given towards the payment of both the principal and the interest. Katyayana adds that the debtor can get back his field, etc., given for enjoyment as interest, from the creditor on paying back the amount he had taken.[121] On the contrary, according to Brhaspati, when a house or field is mortgaged for use and the period fixed for such use does not expire, the debtor cannot recover his property nor can be creditor recover this loan.[122] But when the stipulated period has elapsed both parties are at liberty to do so. Nevertheless, even before the stipulated period has expired they may make a special arrangement for recovery by mutual consent.[123]

The practice of mortgaging land for interest, which began towards the end of the Gupta period, continued widely for another three or four centuries. Thus Asahaya (700–7500), commenting on two kinds of pledge mentioned by Narada, cities a house and a field as instances of a pledge for use.[124] Similarly, commenting on *Manu*, VIII. 43, Medhatithi states that a cow is given as *adhi* to the creditors for using its milk, and a piece of land or garden is given as *adhi* for enjoying its produce; hence the creditor is not entitled to any interest (*vrddhi* or *kusida*). Vyasa who probably belonged to the same period as Medhatithi explains *adhi* similarly. When somebody accepts money (*dravya*) having settled interest on it and asks the creditor to enjoy his field in return for interest and to apply the excess towards the payment of principal, it is called *adhi* or *sapratyaya bhogyadhih*; it is released when twice the amount of the loan is paid.[125] Even where land is not pledged it can be sold to clear off the debts. According to Bharadvaja, if the debtor is unable to pay,

[118] XI. 34.
[119] *Bṛ,* XI. 34.
[120] *Bṛ,* XI. 23.
[121] Verse 516.
[122] XI. 32.
[123] *Bṛ,* XI. 33.
[124] *SBE,* XXXII, 73 fn.
[125] DK, I, part 2, 658.

his property is to be sold for payment, including his land, fields, garden and house.[126] This again points to the practice of pledging land for the payment of debts. Curiously enough the *mitaksara* does not favour it. But the practice certainly obtained in early medieval times, and must have added to the landed property of creditors on failure of payment of the principal. It is even stated that pledges of land can be enjoyed for one hundred years, like a form of commendation in the feudal context. In medieval Europe the poor people surrendered their land to some lord in return for protection. But here it was done in return for a loan. Commendation in Europe entitled the lord to a share of the produce of land surrendered in return for protection afforded by him, but pledge of land in India authorized him to enjoy its whole produce.

Actual instances of mortgage of land are wanting in India, but the provisions of the law books belonging to AD 600–900 suggest that the practice was widespread. At least two epigraphic records from northern India indicate the mortgage of a village in consideration of an amount advanced to the mortgagee,[127] which might imply pledge in lieu of interest. In this case the mortgagee was given all the rights of collecting taxes,[128] he also appears to have been empowered to hold the village in pledge as long as he wished, probably meaning thereby till all the dues were cleared.[129] The other, the Jaunpur brick inscription of AD 1217, shows that a person borrowed 2,250 drammas on the security of cultivated lands.[130] There may have been more inscriptions of this type.

As shown earlier, numerous epigraphic records refer to the investment of gold by the temples for burning perpetual lamp and performing regular worship, but they do not specify anywhere the mortgage of land by the village assembly or the debtors of the purpose. However, the terms of investment do imply full or partial use of land by the temples in lieu of interest on the principal, mostly made up of a certain measure of gold usually advanced to the village assembly, which set apart a part of the produce of the land as interest for maintaining the offerings on lamps. Thus in AD 877–8 the Pandya kind Varaguna-Maharaja granted to a temple 290 *kāśu* of gold, in return for which the members of the temples assembly undertook to measure out 580 *kalam* of paddy per year (as

126 Ibid. 731.
127 *EI.* XXV, no. 1, lines 10–21.
128 Ibid.
129 The meaning of 1.19 is not clear *EI,* XXV, p. 3.
130 *El,* IX, 91–4.

interest, at the rate of two *kalam* for each *Kāśu*) for meeting the requirements of the offerings for a long time.[131] Significantly enough all the articles meant for offerings and enumerated in a long list given in the Pandya inscription and priced in terms of paddy, indicates that the use of coin was very limited at this state in south India. Thus the interest on the investment of gold was collected in crops, for which it was necessary to set apart certain fields. This can be also inferred from other inscriptions. An epigraph of the reign of Aditya I informs us that a priest of the temple of Airavateśvara received from a Pallava queen the gold assuring her that, from the interest accruing at the rate of 1/8 of every crop on each *kalañju*, he would maintain the charity; the gift was placed under the protection of the assembly of all Maheśvaras.[132] So here also the deposit in gold bears interest in crop. An inscription of AD 910 informs us that the wife of the son of the Chola King Parantaka I gave 60 *kalañju* of pure gold as capital to the members of the assembly of a temple who undertook to supply in perpetuity 60 *kalam* of paddy per year, at the rate of 30 *kalam* per harvest[133] as interest. From the Madras Museum plates of Uttama-Chola we learn that in AD 992 the assemblies of two places received 250 *kalanju* of gold from the temple and agreed to measure every year as interest there on 500 *kāḍi* of paddy.[134] According to a document of the same year 50 *kalañju* was received by the assembly of Uḷai-ūr, which agreed to render annually an interest thereon of 150 *kāḍi* of paddy.[135]

In the eight year of Parthivendravarman a village assembly received 15 *kalañju* of gold for a temple, and agreed to pay an annual interest of 50 *kāḍi* of paddy on that amount.[136] These examples from the ninth to the eleventh century have been cited to show that in return for gold lent to them on behalf of the temples the assemblies provided certain quantities of produce, probably by earmarking certain fields owned by the assemblies for the service of the gods. An epigraphic record of the second half of the tenth century shows that land was sold to the temples for gold. In several cases in the Chola dominions in return for gold the land was made tax-free and its produces transferred to the temples, so that the whole produce of the land was given as compensation for the

[131] *SII*,III, part 3, 227.
[132] Ibid., 229.
[133] Ibid., 273.
[134] Ibid.
[135] Ibid., 363.
[136] Ibid., 263.

principal in gold. All these allied practices fit in well with the custom of using the produce of fields in return for money loaned to their owners, which must have greatly added to the landed property of the temples in south India.

We have hardly any instance of temples in north India lending gold directly for interest collected in the form of crops of land attached to them. But the Ahar stone inscription shows how the revenues of the temple of the goddess Kanakadevi, situated in the town of Tattanandapura identified with Ahar near Bulandshar in western UP[137] invested its revenues in the purchase of houses which were let out on rent. The process covers a period of nearly 40 years from AD 864 to 904,[138] and shows that the rent of the houses was estimated in terms of money, to be spent on regular worship in the temple. In all, the inscription contains eight documents, of which four clearly refer to the rent enjoyed by the temple on the *āvārīs,* houses or shops, let out by it.[139] Particularly, Document X speaks of the purchase of six *āvārīs,* the rent accruing from which was to be religiously applied to the provision of saffron, incense, flowers, lamps, and flags, and to whitewashing and the repairs of the broken portions of the temple, a condition which is attached to the rent derived from another house acquired by the temple with its own *drammas.*[140] Of these four, two documents clearly refer to surety of a house in lieu of 10 viṃśopakas to be paid to the temple every month.[141] This was a limited kind of surety, for in each case the rent of the house was to be enjoyed by the descendants of the donor after they had paid every month to the temple.[142] This would imply that the house was owned jointly by the owner and the management of the temple, who enjoyed it as a form of pledge tendered to them. However, in the second case, according to Document VIII it appears that probably the descendants of the donor were given some money by the temple in consideration of which they made over the entire rent of the house by a deed of ninety-nine years to the holy Kanakasridevi (so that there the rent would be in the form of interest accruing on the principal invested on the lease of the house). In four other cases, that is, Documents V, VI,

137 R.D.R. Sahni, *EI,* XIX, no. 7.
138 *EI,* XIX, no. 7.
139 Ibid., Document nos. II, IV, VIII & X.
140 Ibid., Document no. II.
141 Ibid., Document nos. IV & VIII.
142 Ibid.

VII, and IX, it is not mentioned whether houses acquired out of the funds of the temple were let out on rent, but the context of the inscription leaves no doubt about it. All these instances show that the temple of Kanakasri did not derive any interest on its investments, as did the temples in south India, but received rent from the houses which were purchased with its funds. Rent and interest cannot be taken to be the same, but in substance there is hardly any difference between the two. Rent on houses purchased by the temples was obviously the interest accruing on the money with which the houses were purchased.

In the town of Tattanandapura several other temples seem to have lived on rent. This practice could be linked with increasing trade and commerce since the end of the ninth century in western India. What further distinguishes this town is the fact that rent was to be collected in money, which is not found in the case of south Indian temples which lent the principal in gold but charged interest in paddy or crops. Since many persons from whom houses were purchased by the temple were merchants, Tattanandapura was apparently a great centre of trade and commerce which put considerable amount of money in circulation.

4. EXEMPTIONS FROM PAYMENT OF INTEREST AND DEBT COLLECTION

Exemption from interest on religious ground is allowed by Kautilya, according to whom no interest can be charged where the debtor is engaged in a Vedic sacrifice of long duration, or staying at his teacher's house (*gurukula*) for study, or is a minor, or is a man without substance.[143] We do not know whether this provision, mainly in favour of priest, continued in later times.

Normally, both on money and a commodity, the borrower had to pay interest in early medieval times, though under certain conditions exemption was allowed. No interest could be charged on a short-term loan from a friend unless agreed.[144] It could yield interest only if the debtor refused to restore it on demand by the creditor.[145] So here exemption from interest is governed mainly by the nature of personal relations between the debtor and the creditor. According to Narada, no interest can be charged on wages, on a deposit, on a fine, on that which

[143] AŚ, III. 11.

[144] *Nar.*, I. 108; *Katya.*, verse 505.

[145] *Nar.*, 1. 109; *Katya.*, verse 505.

has been idly promised (to bards and the like), and on the stake won in gambling, unless there is an express agreement to pay interest.[146] Katyayana also lays down a similar but detailed injunction that hides (or armour), crops, wine, gambling debts, the price of commodities sold, the bride price of women and debts incurred as surety do not bear interest at any time.[147] Oddly enough, he recommends, at another place, eightfold interest on liquor,[148] we do not know how to explain it. Certain abnormal conditions invalidate interest. Thus Vasistha declares that interest stops the moment the king dies and begins to run only after the coronation of the successor.[149] Perhaps it is apprehended that in the absence of the king or in a state of anarchy exorbitant interest might be exacted, and hence the basic condition for any normal activity is political order and stability. This provision is elaborated by Prajapati, a lawgiver assignable to the period AD 600–900. He states that 'in famines, countrywide disturbance (*rastrasambadhe*), religious work, and distress, only the principal debt is to be given not the interest; this is definite.'[150] This probably refers to natural calamities, peasant unrest and other crises in early medieval times and runs counter to the view expressed in he *Garuḍa Purāṇa* that interest grows in all circumstances.

In collecting interest and the principal from the debtors, creditors were backed by the authority of both the state and religion. The Buddhist Order did not admit a person who had not cleared off his debts. The Buddhists dwelt on the virtues of paying off debts. Narada declares that if the fellow does not pay off his debt, the amount goes on increasing till it reaches one hundred *kotis* (1,000 million), and the person not paying it is born again and again as a horse, an ass, an ox and a slave.[151] Katyayana adds that such a debtor is born as a slave, a servant, a man, or a beast in the house of the creditor.[152] But these curses are not considered enough to make the debtor pay. The authority of the state is therefore invoked to enforce payment. Narada states that if the debtor, in spite of being wealthy, does not pay out of bad disposition, he shall be compelled to pay by the king who will be entitled to one-thirtieth of the amount in

146 *Nar., II. 36.*
147 Verse 508.
148 Verse 511. Here the term used is *madya* and not *āsava* as in verse 508.
149 II. 49.
150 Quoted in *DK,* I, part 2,715.
151 Ibid.., 695.
152 Verse 591.

question.[153] This is less than the fourth payable to the king according to Manu in case of debt collection with royal help[154] Narada does not make it clear whether this one-thirtieth of the amount in question payable to the king is over and above the interest and thc principal hc had to pay. But commenting on *Manu*, VIII. 176, Medhatithi makes it clear that the creditors shall be paid the whole amount; and the fine, one-fourth of the total debt, shall be paid by the debtor to the king in addition to what he pays to the creditor.

Even if the debtor had no means to clear off his dues, he could not be let off. Manu enjoins the creditor to compel the member of an equal caste or a lower caste to do sufficient manual labour to repay the principal plus interest, although members of higher castes are made to pay gradually.[155] Thus exploitation of the physical labour of the debtor was considered to be an effective legal way of collecting debts. What is important to note is that this had the backing of the king.[156]

In the case of the death of the debtor his son is placed under the obligation of paying the debt with interest up to the expiry of the term,[157] otherwise the property of the deceased person can be put up for sale. Brhaspati ordains that if gold (*hirańya*) lent is doubled and the debtor is dead or destroyed, his wealth (*dravya*) shall be seized and sold in the presence of witnesses. The price so received shall be kept in safety for ten days in the presence of the people, and the amount on account of the debt (*rṇānurūpam*) shall be accepted and the rest returned.[158]

The provisions regarding the recovery of debt enumerated above give the creditor the upper hand. But certain other provisions seem to protect the interest of the debtor. According to Kautilya, those who exceed prescribed rates shall be punished with an ordinary fine, and each of the witnesses to such usurious transactions shall be punished with half as much.[159] Such a punishment is hardly provided by any Smṛti in early medieval times, when rates of interest higher than those prescribed as legal are condemned as usurious and immoral, but except for pious denunciations we do not have anything effective against the offenders.

153 Quoted in *DK*, I, part 2, 724.
154 VII. 176.
155 *Manu*, VIII. 177.
156 Ibid., VIII. 178.
157 *Br*, quoted in *DK*, I, part 2, 707.
158 *Br*, quoted in *Vivādaratnākara*,quoted ibid., 726.
159 III. 11.

On the other hand, according to Gautama and Yajnavalkya, if the debtor offers to repay the loan and the creditor refuses to accept it interest stops when the debtor deposits the money in the hands of a third person.[160] Narada gives a little more protection to the debtor. According to him it the creditor, though pressed by the debtor, does not give an acquaintance for the sum paid to him by the debtor, the sum shall yield interest to the debtor henceforth as it had done to the creditor previously.[161] This law given seems to be favourably disposed towards the debtor.

5. CONCLUSION

It is possible to differentiate between the ancient and medieval systems of lending. In ancient times the Vaiśyas were permitted to live on interest, but in early medieval times even Brāhmaṇas and Ksatriyas were allowed to practice lending on interest, which was generally forbidden to them in ancient times. In south India the temples became important moneylenders.

The laws regarding interest generally seem to favour the creditors in early medieval times. Kautilya prescribes some punishment for charging usurious interest, but in this he is not followed by later authorities. In spite of strong disapproval of usury, particularly of lending grain and charging interest on it, by some lawgivers and commentators of the early medieval period, no attempt is made to protect the interest of the debtors in concrete terms.

The ancient normal rate of interest, 15 per cent annually, was prescribed by the medieval legal texts too, but several lawgivers about the seventh-ninth centuries raised this to 24 per cent, which was more than 50 per cent than the earlier rate. Since the list of returns on account of interest on various commodities, including grain, is given separately, it is reasonable to suppose that the increased rate of interest applied to money lending. In our opinion, this increase does not seem to be so much the indication of a stronger tendency of exploitation or of the growing importance of the entire class as of the comparative absence of metal money and decline of trade in the three centuries following the fall of the Gupta empire.

160 *Gautama,* XII, 33; Yaj., II. 44.

161 *Nar.,* 1. 115.

Varna distinctions in the rate of interest are rare in the more ancient texts, but some post-Maurya texts introduce the principle of the lower the varna the higher the interest. We do not know how far it was observed, but it certainly reflects the lesser capacity of members of the lower order to pay in time.

The detailed laws regarding interest on such commodities as grain, cotton, milk products, salt, sugar, fruits, etc., laid down by the lawgivers of Gupta times and their successors show that these were lent to traders as well as ordinary peasant consumers. They create the impression that loans in kind were more frequent than those in case in early medieval time—a feature in keeping with the largely self-sufficient and predominantly agrarian economy of the period.

An important form of interest that attracts attention in early medieval times is *kāyikā* or bodily interest. First mentioned in Gautama and Manu, it is explained by Narada and Bṛhaspati, and by the medieval commentators. They generally agree that in this case interest must be paid through services rendered either by the debtor himself or by his cows, oxen or slaves. The latter alternative could apply only in the case of men of means; debtors of ordinary rank would be reduced to the position of semi-slaves. Thus paying interest through bodily labour could prevail only in an economy where the use of money was limited on account of decline of trade and urbanism.

What distinguished the medieval mode of interest was the introduction of land in its mechanism. On the one hand, land was mortgaged or its produce earmarked by the debtors in lieu of interest on the principal which they received in money or gold; on the other hand, land was given on loan to the debtors who were required to return eight times the harvest at the maximum. Both cases involve peasant debtors; while the former practice reminds us of commendation, the latter resembles grant of benefices or the practice of sub-infeudation. The second practice presupposes the presence of such families as possessed large acreage and it seems that one of the methods to get it cultivated was to lease plots of land to needy peasants at exorbitant rates of payment in kind. At any rate the two practices fit in with feudal economy in which there was less scope for payment in money.

CHAPTER 9

Urbanism in Early Historic India

I propose to say something on the problem of urbanism in early historic India. It roughly denotes the period from 500 BC to AD 500 to 600, but I would also refer to the next three or four centuries. Whenever we talk of urbanism, we are faced with the difficult question of its definition. There is a view nowadays that size and population are crucial to the concept of urbanization in the Bronze Age cultures in which crafts and commerce did not play a significant part. But it is also argued that commerce played a vital role in Harappan urban life. When we consider the question of identifying a town, it is not only the size and the population which matter, but also the nature of the population. Basically, a town has to be a concentration of non-agriculturists, and unless people living in the hinterland have attained a food-producing economy of considerable scale, unless they are able to supply the towns with food provisions from their produce, it is not possible to have a large population. As far as early historic towns in India are concerned, crafts and commerce have played a considerable role and, therefore, the presence of crafts and commerce has to be looked for not only in the archaeological record but also in literary texts. Further, there is the question of the quality of material life. We have to differentiate between the type of life in the towns and that in the rural areas. Of course, there would be class differentiation in both towns and rural areas. Even so certain articles which are considered interior are used mostly in rural areas and are basically different from those used by the affluent sections in towns. These articles would perhaps also be used in rural areas but not on the same scale. This is my rough understanding of what a town was, and how a town could be identified in the early historical context.

Having said that, we need to differentiate between the types of urbanism in the Bronze Age culture of Harappa and that in the middle Ganga plains lying between Allahabad and Rajmahal where the towns started their career from around the middle of the first millennium BC, throve till AD 300 and lingered up to AD 600 or even beyond. There is an important difference in the geographical or ecological aspect. The Harappan area is an arid, semi-arid zone without much rainfall. The Harappan zone may have floods, inundation and so on but not the type of alluvial soil covered with thick vegetation that characterizes the middle Ganga plains. Since rainfall in that area is slight, the problem of forest clearance does not exist. The Gangetic area on the other hand had a heavy rainfall, creating an entirely different environment. Whereas bronze and even stone tools could be effective in the Harappan area, facilitating large-scale settlements, these tools could not be effective in clearing the thick forests in the alluvial soil to the middle Ganga plain. Thus, we have urbanism in the Harappan area in the Bronze Age, and in the middle Ganga plains in the Iron Age when iron tools appeared for the first time on a considerable scale and boosted agricultural production. They helped in the clearing of forests, and in the production of the surplus much over and above what was needed for the subsistence of an ordinary peasant. This enabled him to save something that could be used for supporting rulers, priests, craftsmen, specialist artisans, army men and others living in the town. This surplus could be in the form of taxes and tributes or even in the form of unequal trade. In other words, what we have in the alluvial plains of the middle Ganga is a new kind of phenomenon as compared to what we have in the arid, semi-arid plains of Sind and Punjab associated with Harappan urbanism.

The other difference is the use of metal money. In the Bronze Age we do come across references to the pieces of silver being used in Mesopotamia though there were various other ways and means of carrying on transactions. But in that culture nothing like coined metal money, standardized, authorized and recognized by the state was used.

That feature appears in the Old World only towards the end of the seventh century BC, and in India, so far as the actual coins are concerned, they are not earlier than 500 BC if we go by archaeological evidence. Coins by themselves do not mean much, but they are an indication of the type of economic activity that began: they show petty commodity production though on a small scale. With commodity production, there was a new type of distribution in which middlemen played a vital part. All this led to trade which was enormously facilitated by the use of coins. Once coins came into being, they led to many changes. The coins became a far more convenient mode for exchange than numerous other objects including cattle. Metalled money was not easily perishable. One could easily add and subtract: book-keeping became easy. It also became possible to transport coins easily from one place to another; it was not easy to transport a large number of cattle. The coins became associated with the towns of the middle Ganga plains on a considerable scale.

There is yet another difference between Harappan urbanism and that of the middle Ganga plains. This relates to duration. The Harappan urbanism lasted shorter than urbanism in the middle Ganga plains, somewhere from 2350 BC to about 1750 BC a period of about 600 BC years. Intriguingly, once Harappan urbanism disappeared there was no urbanism in that part of the country for more than a thousand years. Even more intriguing, once town planning disappeared, the use of bricks also disappeared; we do not find burnt bricks in that part of the country or in other parts, on any scale till the times of the Mauryas, that is, around 300 BC.

On the other hand, the urbanism which started in the middle Ganga plains around 500 BC was never completely extinguished. It lasted much longer. Certainly, it existed from about 500 BC, though some have pushed it back to 600 BC, the difference of a century does not cause much concern particularly to a student of ancient history. So we start with 500 BC and we can go up to AD 600 and even later. Towns did not disappear completely, and go up to AD 1200 and so on. Once towns came into existence in the early historic period they suffered decay and decline but they did not completely disappear unlike the Harappan towns. Archaeological evidence regarding the sudden decline of towns in the ancient period in various parts of the country is piling day by day; and its detailed study deserves attention.

We must therefore study Harappan urbanism in the perspective of Bronze Age culture extending right from Harappa through Iran and Iraq and Asia Minor to Greece and then Egypt, it is one compact geographical area of the Bronze Age culture with many similarities. There was urbanism in this whole area, yet several traits typical of Harappan urbanism are not found in any Bronze Age urbanism outside Harappa. To study Harappan urbanism in isolation from other urban cultures also does not help us much. How else to account for its total eclipse? Why are its specific, concrete traces not found later? That is a problem which needs attention.

In any case, the type of urbanism which developed in the subcontinent in the Bronze Age had a short life while that which developed in early historic times had a much longer life. Furthermore, the urbanism which started around 500 BC reached its peak between 200 BC and AD 300. Archaeological excavations of this period have exposed a large number of towns spread all over the country which of course does not mean that every bit of the country had towns. But still there were a good number of towns in this period. It was also the time when Indo-Roman trade was most thriving, particularly in the first two centuries of the Christian era, and trade with central and south-east Asia was also thriving.

A large number of crafts are mentioned in this period about seventy-five occupations are mentioned in the *Milindapanho* which is attributed to the second century BC, and nearly one hundred occupations each in the cities of Rajagriha and Kapilavastu are mentioned in the *Mahavastu*, a text of around the first century AD. Description of these two capital towns is invariably accompanied by a long list of specialized occupations. In bow-making, there would be a person who just made bowstrings, another was engaged in arrow fletching, and a third made only the bow. Similarly, in dyeing industry were persons engaged in weaving, others in dyeing, and still others in the manufacture of dyes. All these are specifically mentioned in the texts. It was the period when the largest number of crafts are mentioned in literary texts and are attested by the type of excavated artifacts and coins. Thus, on the basis of excavations, we can say there were various types of potters, ivory workers, dyers (because dyeing vats have been discovered), textile workers, glass workers and various types of iron workers (because various furnaces and ovens have been discovered). There were also various types of brick layers and tile makers. All this activity obviously existed in towns.

One great difference between Harappan urbanism and the urbanism in the middle Ganga plains is that the former is characterized by monumental structures and, as Gordon Childe rightly points out, these monuments are symbols of consumption of surplus but where do we look for such symbols in our excavations in the middle Ganga plains? No such monument has been discovered and still we have towns. The structures seem to have been mainly mud structures in the beginning and came to be made of brick from 300 BC onwards. Bricks became more common from 200 BC onwards in north India, but even then mostly mud houses seem to have been used. In the towns there would have been cattle-sheds and doghouses too, which somehow thanks to our archaeologists, have not been discovered in any excavation, as far as I know, in the middle Ganga plains. It does require some archaeological skill or some special method to find signs of such houses also.

At any rate, the main point is that early historic urbanism reached its peak in this country between 200 BC and AD 300. Whether in north India, the Deccan, parts of south India, or in western India, we have the same phenomenon. Rajagriha, Vaishali, Chirand, Majhi, Khairdih, Banaras, Shravasti, Kaushambi and Atranjikhera are some of these towns. Not far from Dharwad is Vadgaon-Madhavapur, a Satavahana site which was excavated by the Karnataka University. There is also Kaveripattinam in Tamil Nadu. In fact, there are any number of sites in this period. I have taken note of 130 excavated sites belonging to the period between 200 BC and AD 300. These sites were prosperous in terms of artefacts, coins, structures and other types of antiquities, including semi-precious stones, ivory, ivory objects, glass articles, bones and so on.

This peak in urbanism could be associated with the growing trade and commerce in this period; and this growing trade and commerce is linked with the use of money, because money is a good and convenient medium of exchange. The numismatic evidence suggests that as many as thirty-five places issued their coins in this period. The name of the place is mentioned on the coin whether it is *Kausambi* or Banaras or any other place. Each place was a mint town. In addition, many dynasties such as the Kushanas and the Satavahanas had their coins. There were fourteen tribes which are called oligarchical states and each tribe had its own coins. In a talk, in Calcutta, I calculated through a formula, which nobody will accept, that there were more than four million coins in circulation during this period. The number of coins actually available to us is very small. Ways and means have to be found to have an idea of the total number of coins current in a period. This has to be further related to the number of people in urban and rural settlements. I added up the coin numbers of ten museums and they came to about 1,25,000.

There are as many as 50,000 Satavahana coins alone in the State Museum of Hyderabad which reflect of the overall picture of trade, commerce and crafts during this period. This is significant, for it is argued that large prosperous towns or prosperous trade can exist only if large states exist. There is some sense in that, because a state collects taxes and tributes, brings them to the towns and disburses salaries to its officials, army men, etc. Thus, there is a lot of exchange activity and distribution at several levels.

On the basis of trade, coins, artefacts and structures, we can confidently say that urbanism reached its peak in ancient India in the post-Maurya period. After AD 300 it declined. There were two phases of decline, one around AD 300 and the other around AD 600. But before we briefly take up the question of decline, a few things about the wider relevance of this urbanism may be noted. What does this urbanism mean to society as a whole? What does it mean to the socio-economic set-up? There are all types of views. Some will argue that these towns were just parasitical entities as their inhabitants did not do any useful work; they were not engaged in production. Besides this old view, there is also the view of some eminent Bronze Age archaeologists that arts and crafts were not so important rather they were peripheral to the existence of towns, and towns did not pave the way for arts and crafts.

It would however appear that while there would have been a good many rulers, soldiers, priests and numerous state officials, who may be regarded as having been parasitical in some sense, a large number of others were engaged in production as a result of which towns could become centres of exchange, manufactures and technology. Thus, the towns had their generative dimension. Moreover, they contributed to polity by facilitating large-scale payment in cash to the state employees who were paid from 48,000 panas to even ten panas. Unless taxes were collected and brought to the towns which were centres of tax collection, how would people receive that money in cash?

The *Arthasastra* of Kauṭilya, which incidentally was discovered in the state of Karnataka, mentions sources of income to the state, and divides them under two headings; one is from the countryside (*rāshtra*) and the other from the fortified capital (*durga*). As many as twenty sources of income from the *durgā* to the state are enumerated by Kauṭilya. The term *durga* may have included towns in general. Some of those who have worked on Roman history argue that so far as the income of the state from trade was concerned the state got only 5 per cent.

We do not as yet have the means to calculate such income in ancient India. How much income was derived from the countryside? How much from the town? How much income did the state derive from trade and how much from agriculture?

Meanwhile, we cannot ignore the role of urbanism in ancient Indian economy. Important segments of people were involved in urban activity, even when a large section of population was left out of it. Urbanism did mean something in terms of economy and something of polity and society inasmuch as soldiers, Brāhmaṇas, artisans and merchants who lived in towns were supported by means of what was gathered by way of taxes and exchange. The towns were equally relevant to the countryside. It appears that food grains were supplied to the towns by the peasants living in the hinterland, while the artisans supplied the tools to the peasants. For example, we hear in a *Jataka* story how somebody deposited 500 ploughshares in a city. The obvious purpose would be to sell them to the peasants.

As to the pattern of settlements in earlier times, it appears that the town was surrounded by a cluster of villages. Because of the obvious difficulty of transportation in ancient times, towns could not receive their day-to-day requirements from distant places. There were intervening forests between one and the other clusters of villages. The Pali texts speak of forests in the vicinity of several towns. But all these are matters which have to be examined further by archaeologists. Settlement archaeology has not made sufficient progress. The spread of settlements and their relative populations need to be studied. The archaeologists have not done any work whatsoever, as far as I know, on the linkage between the hinterland and the towns. Towns did, however, play an important role they were relevant to ancient economy and also to ancient polity. Since these towns declined after AD 300 and again after AD 600 we shall have to explain this phenomenon and also think of the people who lived in towns.

Why did the towns decline? One obvious factor was that the Indo-Roman trade stopped from the third century AD onwards. The Satavahana empire, which brought a lot of gold from outside, also ended; the central Asian trade also tapered off. I may venture a speculation here. There was a kind of social crisis, but not like the *jagirdari* crisis. It is reflected in the passages of the *Vishnu Purāṇa*, *Bhagvada Purana* and some other *Puranas* which are attributed by a great Puranu scholar, Rajendra Chandra of Hazara from Calcutta, to the end of the third century AD and the beginning of the fourth. These Puranas vividly describe what is known as the Kali Age (*Kaliyuga*), which unfortunately seems to be unending in this country.

In ancient India, as elsewhere, social progress was accompanied by social inequality. Certain functions were assigned to certain people. Some people were meant for praying, some for writing books, some for teaching, some for doing theological work, for fighting, for administering, for collecting taxes and for maintaining law and order. Others were the principal taxpayers. P.V. Kane, the great Indologist, is of the view—which is also my view—that the Vaiśya were the principal taxpayers. They were primarily agriculturists; it was only in later times that they became primarily traders. Agriculture remained their principal occupation in ancient times when the Śūdrās supplied the labour power. A careful reading of the Kali passages gives the impression that the whole social order was upset—the Brāhmaṇas behaved like Śūdrās and the Śūdrās like Brāhmaṇas. There was an intermixing of functions. Whenever the Puranas use the term *varna-sankara* (on which Vivekanand Jha has done a detailed piece), it means not merely transcending caste restrictions in marriage, it also means giving up one's prescribed functions. Manu asserts that if members of various varnas do not perform their assigned functions the whole world will fall into chaos. That would be calamitous and to forestall it the king must exercise *danda* or coercive authority.

Also symptomatic of the social crisis were the land grants which began to be made at this time. These had been known earlier too, but now they were being made on a substantial scale. The Puranas, of course, do not state that *Kaliyug*a or social disorder should be put down by making land grants, but the point is that if it became difficult to collect taxes, to bring these to towns and then to disburse salaries to officials and soldiers and to give gifts to the Brāhmaṇas in terms of money or cattle, the state felt obliged to have recourse to land grants which became common from the third to fourth century AD onwards. In the new situation the understanding seems to have been that the state gave a village to a select person; that person fended for himself, collected taxes, maintained law and order in the village and took care of it. The state would not use its regular officers for these functions. In every state there would be a core domain (with occasional land grants) where the state officials could function and a large peripheral area in which land grants were made extensively. With the practice of land grants becoming common, there also began the practice of granting shops; even whole towns were granted, as recorded in inscriptions and also by Hiuen Tsang. The grant of shops, towns and villages meant restrictions of trade and commerce, on the free operation of traders, thus restraining the autonomy earlier enjoyed by them. It was a process of feudalization of towns.

Between the fifth and seventh centuries AD and may be even later, there were nearly fifty states in India. Rather than being political fragmentation, it was a positive development, because the state system arose in those areas which did not witness the formation of the state in earlier times. Every state had its own army, administrative machinery, judicial officers and exercised its sovereign authority through a regular state apparatus. How could this apparatus in the core domain be maintained unless there were more villages and more productivity to provide the necessary surplus for its wherewithal?

So it appears that if towns declined, their technology was diffused. Artisans migrated from the urban to rural areas. There is no archaeological evidence to substantiate this, perhaps because the archaeology of rural sites in early medieval times has not been initiated so far. When the towns declined, the Brāhmaṇas too migrated to the countryside and thus contributed towards the spread of technology. Ramendra Nath Nandi prepared a list of the original homes of the Brāhmaṇas who were granted land in the first phase of early medieval times; most of these original homes were towns. Sneh Lata Anand also prepared a list of such Brāhmaṇas in Gujarat who migrated from towns during the same period to enjoy land grants. This kind of examination, which takes note of the original home of the Brāhmaṇas in the giants between the fifth and eighth centuries AD, has to be pursued further. It may be argued that the original homes given in grants were just old genealogical memory. But even if this memory is a century old or still older, it would mean that their ancestors lived in towns. Diffusion of agricultural knowledge through the Brāhmaṇas who were knowledgeable about the calendar helped agrarian expansion. At the same time, it seems that technology was now thinly spread just as coins also were thinly spread. I counted dynastic coins of the period AD 500–1000 on the basis of ten collections in various museums, and the number was less than 25,000. On the other hand, as already mentioned, the Satavahana coins alone number more than 1,00,000. It is not only difficult in this period to find coins issued by towns but also to come by coin moulds in excavation. Similarly, evidence on guilds in this period is scarce. Seals and sealing of artisan and mercantile guilds, so common in ancient times, almost disappear in the early medieval period. The seals and sealing available are mainly of Buddhist monasteries, and that too primarily in eastern India.

Thus, a different type of socio-economic pattern existed in early medieval India in which a class of landlords collected rent from the peasants as a result of grants and other reasons. Probably most administrative officers also were being remunerated through land assignments. While the towns existed, goods and services were evaluated and obtained in terms of money; but when the towns disappeared, goods and services may have been evaluated in terms of money but they were obtained through land grants. It is most likely that the elements of the *jajmani* system, which may have existed in earlier times as indicated in Panini, were greatly strengthened when the towns declined in early medieval times. The *jajmani* system means that if I am a peasant or if I am a landlord and if I require the services of priests or various types of artisans, including a barber or a potter, I do not pay him in money but I pay him twice in a year at the time of the harvest and he is attached to me. This arrangement is now called patron–client relationship. Besides the strengthening of the *jajmani* system one could also find a few elements of what is called Asiatic mode of production in this period. The early medieval period did not exactly have a self-sufficient economy, but most local needs were locally met. This could be due to what we call an ideal blending of agricultural and artisanal activities. This situation may have lasted roughly up to about AD 1000 when there was a mild revival of urbanism which became prominent by the fourteenth century. But this problem needs to be discussed separately.

CHAPTER 10

Urban Growth and Decline

Towns which were primarily settlements of non-agriculturists distinguished by crafts and commerce, reached the peak of prosperity in the centuries from *c.*200 BC to *c.* AD 300. There is no doubt that for centuries food was available for the large urban population. The presence of food sellers and confectioners in towns clearly suggests the existence of grain merchants who were termed *vaṇik*. Granaries have been identified at many sites, although much smaller in size than their Harappan predecessors. Some of these may have been meant for storing taxes in kind received by the state officials, but others were evidently run by merchants who sold cereals to the town dwellers in return for payment in cash. The excavation of coins in the granaries at Dhulikatta is significant. Although the number of coins discovered in excavations may not be large, they have been unearthed at most urban sites. No other period of ancient Indian history is known for so many varieties of coins and so many coin moulds as the period 200 BC to AD 300. Indian coins were reinforced by Roman coins. Metal money without doubt was a distinctive feature of the post-Maurya urban life, and it played a vital role in Indo–Roman and probably also in Central Asian trade.

The spurt in handicrafts is equally remarkable in post-Maurya urbanism. Apart from the conventional sixty-four arts and crafts mentioned in Vatsyayana's *Kamasutra*, which is the product of urban conditions, seventy-five occupations appear in the *Milindapanho*, and nearly four dozen occupations, organized into guilds, are described in the *Mahavastu* in the context of Rajagrha and Kapilavastu. The *Mahavastu* mentions altogether more than one hundred occupations, mostly of artisans and merchants, in each of the two capital cities of Rajagrha and Kapilvastu. The post-Maurya period was noted for great technological progress. This seems to be the period when the Indians learnt feeding silkworms on mulberry leaves. Although this cannot be attested archaeologically, the production of textiles and the dyeing can be inferred from several dyeing vats found in south India, and from many inscriptions referring to weavers. Similarly, Roman reaction against heavy price paid for Indian cutlery can be linked to production of iron goods is shown by various types of furnaces and huge quantities of slag unearthed at many urban sites. But many more iron goods, particularly tools and weapons, were evidently supplied to soldiers, artisans and agriculturists. The Deccan urban sites are particularly rich in iron objects.

Advanced ironwork substantially contributed to various crafts including bead making and ivory manufacture. Several urban sites show factories for preparing beads and bangles of shell. Beads of semi-precious stones were manufactured particularly in central, western and peninsular towns of the country. These costly beads were exported to South-East Asia. The use of iron tools enabled craftsmen to produce sophisticated ivory objects, which appear in numbers in Begram although only one item, the famous Pompeii statue, has been reported from Italy. There is no doubt that many towns were centres of glass manufacture, which evidently reached its peak in post-Muarya centuries on account of the acquisition of the knowledge of glass blowing by Indians. Although glass factories have been found at many places including that of Kopia, only beads and bangles were manufactured in Indian towns. Bottles and utensils were manufactured at Taxila, but this was evidently due to Hellenistic influence.

It, therefore, seems that craft production together with local and long-distance trade in costly goods and the availability of agricultural products from the hinterland boosted urbanization in post-Maurya centuries. Numerous seals and inscriptions attest the growing importance of artisans and merchants who were great benefactors of Buddhism. Increasingly, the influence of an urban milieu is reflected even in the art of the period which produced numerous pieces of terracotta and sculpture in stone.

Urban centres in Punjab, Haryana and western Uttar Pradesh generally suffered sharp decline after the third century. This is true of Sanghol, Hastinapura, Atranjikhera, Mathura and several other places. Even explorations show a clear gap between the cultural deposits of the Kuṣāṇa epoch and that of the Sultanate period at numerous sites in the Indo-Gangetic Divide and the upper Gangetic plains. In the middle Gangetic plains during Gupta times the trend towards sharp decline or desertion is noticed at many sites including *Sravasti*, *Kausambi*, Ganwaria, Khairadih, Manjhi, Chirand, Katragath, Rajgir, etc. Tamluk and Chandrake tugarh in West Bengal and Sisupalgarh in Orissa fall in similar category.

In Madhya Pradesh, Rajasthan and Gujarat as well, after the third century decay starts at many places including Noh, Ujjain and Nagar. Desertion in or after the third century AD occurred at most urban centres in Maharashtra; Pauni, Kaundinyapura, Nevasa, Ter, Bhokardan, Paithan, Nasik, etc., were such towns. A similar position obtained at Vadgaon-Madhavapur and other sites in Karnataka. All these sites are called Satavahana urban centres, which started a century before the rise of the Satavahana power but faded out soon after its fall in the third century. This is true of the majority of towns in Andhra Pradesh. It also applies to Arikamedu and some other towns in Tamil Nadu.

Thus, it will appear that the Kuṣāṇa and Satavahana urban centres suddenly declined in the second half of the third or during the fourth century. This marked the first stage in urban decay, which overlook the majority of early historic towns. It coincided with the fall of the two great kingdoms and the end of the Indo-Roman trade. It also synchronized with the rise of the Gupta power in northern India, with that of the successors of the Satavahanas in central and peninsular parts, and with the rule of the Kṣatrapas in western India. The theory that political power extracts surplus from the peasants and others and makes it available to town dwellers is supported in a way by the provision for deliberate urbanization laid down in the *Arthasastra* of Kauṭilya, but it may not fully explain the presence of towns under the Kuṣāṇas, Satavahanas and their successors. For in the two centuries preceding and succeeding the birth of Christ we find a welter of autonomous states and authorities. This would naturally mean less tax for every state and add to its overhead expenses. Obviously these small states could not ensure security for traders. Collection of customs at numerous points would hamper trade, and yet the towns thrived before the rise of the Satavahanas and Kuṣāṇas. However, the larger kingdoms set up by these two powers may have collected more taxes and offered security to traders.

The Gupta empire in India was larger than each of the two kingdoms, and yet its cities and towns show the general trend of decline. Proceeding from east to west and north, Pataliputra, Vaishali, Katragarh, Ghirand, Khairadih, Manjhi, Varanasi, Kausambi, Sringaverapur, Ayodhya, Hastinapura, Mathura, Atranjikhera, Sonkh, Purana Qila, Noh, Ropar, Sanghol, etc., show symptoms of decline. Varanasi, Kausambi, Ahicchatra, and Taxila, though excavated horizontally, provide a picture of decline in various trenches. Chirand and Khairadih which were dug on a considerable scale are marked by rapid decline in Gupta strata. Vaishali also shows decline although a large area pertaining to the Gupta period has been exposed. More significantly, finds from ancient urban sites dug horizontally may be larger in number but not qualitatively better than their counterparts recovered from those which have been excavated vertically. Whether digging is vertical or horizontal it does not make any material difference to the habitational deposit of the fourth to sixth centuries. The sections prepared by the excavators show that mostly this deposit is thinner than that of the first two or three centuries. Although only stray references in literature suggest decline, Varahamihira's *Brhat Samhita* (AD 505) predicts bad days or destruction for towns, traders and craftsmen. Apparently, the Guptas and their contemporaries were not capable of giving towns the scale of support which they had enjoyed earlier.

Undoubtedly, the decline of long-distance trade which involved Romans, Chinese, Parthians, Kuṣāṇas and Satavahanas was an important cause of urban decay in the late third century and in the fourth century. The end of the Han, Kuṣāṇa, Parthian and Satavahana empires in the third century affected trade which was further diminished by internal dissensions in the Roman empire. But the nature of the relation of trade and politics in the context of India and other countries needs to be worked out. The internal situation of Rome which led to a strong reaction against goods from the East cannot be ignored.

There is no way to assess the loss of income incurred by urban centres on account of languishing trade. We find that Roman coins and goods showed a sudden drop in the third century. Poverty of structures and antiquities both in the north and the south during the post-third centuries bespeak of commercial decline. Loss of trade would mean loss of income to the state, merchants, artisans and others. This could have been made up by boosting production in the hinterland which would depend on technological innovation, but no significant advance occurred in this field between the fourth and the sixth centuries or immediately thereafter. The Harappan decline is sometimes attributed to the wearing away of the landscape, but we at present can only conjecture on the exhaustion of the hinterlands of early historic towns.

The social crisis as reflected in the descriptions of the Kali in the third to fourth centuries appears to be an important factor leading to the decay of towns. The crisis, which amounted to an upheaval in the countryside, was bound to hit the collection of taxes from the peasants and reduce the purchasing power of the priests, soldiers, officials and others who dwelt in towns. This would mean that merchants lost both local and long-distance markets. The social disorder also undermined artisanal activities which centred in towns. Despite the availability of skill and expertise the poverty of the archaeological record in costly objects such as glass goods, ivory objects, beads of precious and semiprecious stones and refined pottery is evident in Gupta and prominent in post-Gupta times. Above all, the paucity of metal money, particularly of gold coins, in the post-Gupta period is a stark reality.

The second phase of urban decay appears after the sixth century and its beginning coincides with the fall of the Gupta empire. This phase was not so widespread as the first one. It covered several important towns in the middle Gangetic plains. Champa, Pataliputra, Vaishali, Varanasi, Bhita, etc., ceased to be towns after the sixth century. The archaeological decline of Buddhist towns after the sixth century is generally attested by the account of Hiuen Tsang and by the lack of such seals and inscriptions as mention artisans and merchants either collectively or individually. It is also confirmed by decreasing attention given to traders and craftsmen in literature. The Buddhist texts of about the first century contain long lists of tradesmen. But, to my knowledge, such lists are strikingly absent in early medieval texts. Some descriptions of trade and towns in post-Gupta Prakrit texts appear as conventionalized descriptions which recall earlier times.

The second phase of urban decay is also linked with the decline of trade. Until the fifth century the Byzantium carried on trade with urban centres in India and also in Sri Lanka. Nearly thirty thousand copper coins of the Roman emperor Constantine, found in Sri Lanka, clearly show trade in the fourth century. Byzantine coins ranging up to the fifth century have been found in south India, particularly in Karnataka, though certainly not as many as early Roman coins. Hence the view that India's trade with the Byzantium was as flourishing as that with the pre-

Byzantine Roman empire is unfounded. Besides spices, silk was an important commodity in the Indo-Byzantine trade in which the Persians acted as intermediaries between China and India on the one hand and the Byzantium on the other. But once the knowledge of feeding silk worms on mulberry leaves was acquired by the Byzantium in the middle of the sixth century silk trade suffered. The silk weavers of Gujarat faced shrinkage of markets even in the fifth century. Similarly evidence for trade between India and South-East Asia during the fourth to the tenth centuries is wanting.

Urban decline meant loss of income to the state which suffered more on account of upheavals in the countryside. Since the standing army ate up a major part of the revenue, alternative methods had to be devised to support them and maintain the administrative apparatus. Now the state shed away its responsibility of policing many villages by granting them to Brāhmaṇas, temples and monasteries. Moreover, it enormously increased its tributary vassals (*sāmantas*), who were obliged to supply their fixed quotas of fighting contingents at the time of war. All this led to the formation of a feudal polity, closely tied up with the decay of towns and trade. The decline of towns forced the Brāhmaṇas to migrate to the countryside in search of new sources of livelihood. The land charters of the fourth to the seventh centuries, and even of later times, show that numerous donee Brāhmaṇas moved from towns to villages. Along with them, artisans probably migrated to the rural areas, where they were attached to their patrons and paid in kind. Instead of operating independently, artisans sought shelter and patronage from temples, monasteries and establishments of the landed magnates.

Temples, monasteries and walled structures of early medieval times were monumental buildings. Though such buildings symbolize the consumption of considerable surplus, overall they do not articulate artisanal and mercantile activities on any scale till the end of the tenth century. Glass goods, ivory objects, and beads of semiprecious stones found at early medieval sites are in much less quantity than those found in ancient urban centres. Coins and coin moulds are practically absent, and so are the seals depicted with coin devices. Early medieval settlements abound in bronze images and pieces of stone sculpture; both of these were used for religious purposes. Ancient Buddhist monasteries were generally located in the suburbs of the town, and owed their existence to the donations of artisans, merchants and other town dwellers including princes and officials. But early medieval religious establishments were maintained by grants of land and villages, out of which they parted plots of land to artisans and others for servicing and other purposes. Many temples in south India came to form the heart of non-agriculturist settlements, and in the long run they generated some crafts and mercantile activity, but not much is visible before the tenth century.

The decline of ancient towns in early medieval times cannot be considered an indicator of decline in overall economic growth. What emerges now is a new type of economy marked by urban contraction and agrarian expansion. Taking the country as a whole, production seems to have picked up in both crafts and agriculture. But its volume was thinly spread over a large area and territory. Urban decline and stagnation resulted in agrarian expansion, which was promoted by land grants made by chiefs and princes. The emergence of numerous states in the early Middle Ages is a significant pointer to agrarian expansion. Nearly, fifty states existed in the fifth to the seventh centuries, and many of them appeared in such areas as had never experienced any regular state machinery. Their land charters show that these states possessed all the essentials of organized political power. Every state evidently depended on a large agrarian base formed by villages bearing Sanskritic and non-Sanskritic names. Agrarian expansion was boosted by the migration of Brāhmaṇas and craftsmen who disseminated advanced knowledge of agriculture and technology. Whether peasants also moved from populated areas to less cultivated areas is not known. But knowledge of agriculture came to be written down in texts belonging to the early Middle Ages. The availability of iron and its metallurgy became so common that this metal came to be used for non-utilitarian purposes such as for erecting Mehrauli and other victory pillars.

The *jajmāni* system was an important element in the social organization which arose in response to urban decline, lesser use of money and agrarian expansion. The regrouping and reorganization of social relationships affected by urban decline led not only to the rise of a class of landed intermediaries but also to the spatial and occupational immobility of the artisans by making them an integral part of the *jajmāni* system. Artisans and others were now firmly attached to the soil and their patrons. They were paid for their goods and services in kind when crops were gathered. What may have prevailed earlier on a limited scale became a common feature in the Middle Ages.

De-urbanization was therefore a feature of the first or the classical phase of feudalism marked by a subject peasantry and a dominant class of landlords in conditions of languishing trade and predominantly agrarian economy. It inaugurated an era of closed economy in which the needs of landed intermediaries were met locally without the effective intervention of traders whose functions were reduced to the minimum. The new situation established direct contact between the consumers on the one hand and the producers on the other. This was because of the rise of intermediaries in land between the state and the peasants. This snapped the direct connection of the peasants with the state which existed in pre-feudal times. State functionaries and its ideological supporters now tended to turn into landed magnates, who mainly lived on rent-in-kind or rent-in-labour collected from the peasants and artisans, and did not depend on taxes which were formerly collected by state officials and disbursed as gifts and salaries in towns. Therefore, the shrinkage of the urban sector was closely connected with the conversion of the tax area into the rent area. Eventually religious and 'secular' non-agriculturist establishments were bound to turn into markets. As centres of consumption they had the potentiality to become centres of production and commodity exchange. In other words, they could become towns and strengthen the mercantile and artisanal classes, but this was not to be for several centuries yet. Mild urban renewal began in parts of the country in the eleventh century, and by the fourteenth century urbanization became a recognizable process.

Chapter 11

The Economic History of India up to AD 1200: Trends and Prospects

The study of early Indian economic history goes back to the middle of the nineteenth century when Christian Lassen devoted fairly long chapters to industry and commerce in his *Indische Alterthumskunde*, published in four volumes between 1847 and 1861. His monumental history of India down to the fall of Vijayanagara emphasized political

ABBREVIATIONS: *ABORI* = *Annals of the Bhandarkar Oriental Research Institute; AHR* = *American Historical Review; BSOAS* = *Bulletin of the School of Oriental and African Studies; IESHR* = *The Indian Economic and Social History Review; IHQ* = *Indian Historical Quarterly; JAHRS* = *Journal of the Andkra Historical Research Society; JAS* = *Journal of Asian Studies; JAOS* = *Journal of the American Oriental Society; JBRS* = *Journal of the Bihar Research Society; JBBRAS* = *Journal of the Bombay Branch of the Royal Asiatic Society; JESHO* = *Journal of the Economic and Social History of the Orient; JIH* = *Journal of Indian History; JRAS* = *Journal of the Royal Asiatic Society, Great Britain and Ireland.*

history, the economic sections occupying a subsidiary place. He was followed by Richard Fick[1] who dealt primarily with the social or caste relationships prevalent in north-eastern India in the age of the Buddha and described occupations and trade guilds in about eighty pages. Fick's work entirely based on the Buddhist birth stories, which were used by Mrs Rhys Davids for a fuller reconstruction of economic life in the sixth century BC.[2] Lassen, Fick and Mrs Rhys Davids were primarily philologists, and whatever they wrote on early Indian economic life was marginal to their main area of interest. Their writings therefore do not indicate any distinct trend in the historiography of early Indian economy.

We see many historians of the nineteenth and twentieth centuries, who wrote under the auspices of the imperial government and had preconceived ideas about the Indian past, set a distinct trend in Indian historiography. As early as 1817, James Mill asserted that Indian society had remained substantially unchanged since its inception.[3] His view was shared by several British administrator historians, including Elphinstone who, under the spell of romanticism, spoke glowingly of the unchanging village communities of ancient India. The administrator scholars of the nineteenth century firmly believed that the British imperial administration could change the Indian socio-economic set-up by legislation.[4] Their study of the Indian society and economy inspired Marx in his reconstruction of the Asiatic mode of production, characterized by the predominance of self-sufficient village economy, the absence of privately owned land, and the complete subjugation of village communities to the stated.[5]

[1] *Die sociale Gliederung im nordostlichen Indien zu Ruddhas Zcit mil besonderer Berucksichligung der Kastenfrage vornehmlich auf Grund der jahala dargestellt* (Kiel, 1897). English translation by S.K. Mitra, *The Social Organization in North-East India in Buddha's Time*. Calcutta, 1920.

[2] Rhys Davids, 'Notes on Early Economic Condition in North India', *JRAS*, 1901. The article was expanded into a chapter on Economic Conditions according to Early Buddhist Literature contributed by her to the *Cambridge History of India*, i (1921).

[3] *History of British India*, London, 1817.

[4] For a discussion of the growth of the idea of the village community in nineteenth-century British writings on India see Louis Dumont, 'The Village Community from Munro to Maine', *Contributions to India Sociology*, no. 9, December 1966, pp. 67–89; cf. S.N. Mukherjee, 'The idea of the Village Community and the British Administrators', *Enquiry*, New Series, iii, 3, Winter 1971, pp. 57–67.

[5] Daniel Thorner, 'Marx on India and the Asiatic Mode of Production', *Contributions to Indian Sociology*, no. 9, December 1966, pp. 33–66.

The best known exponent of the imperialist view of Indian history was Vincent A. Smith. Trained in more advanced techniques of historical research than were available to his predecessors, Smith devoted himself to the study of the general history of ancient India. But in 1904 he made a significant observation that in ancient times land was owned by the king.[6] This theory suited the British colonial interests and was upheld by several other British historians, who apparently wanted to make out a case for introducing agrarian changes by the British government in the late nineteenth and early twentieth centuries.[7]

On account of their interest in foreign rule, British writers after Smith gave special attention to India's connections with Europe and the Greek rule in India. In numismatics, the study of the Indo-Greek coins received their chief attention and in the study of trade they were attracted by India's commerce with Europe. In 1916, H.G. Rawlinson wrote his *Intercourse between India and the Western World*, which covered India's commercial contracts with the Graeco-Roman world from the earliest times to the fall of Rome. In 1928, E.H. Warmington produced a full-scale study of the subject on the basis of Greek and Latin sources. His *Commerce between India and the Roman Empire* (Cambridge, 1928) underlines the importance of the discovery of the monsoon in AD 48 for the Roman navigators and enumerates articles of export and import between India and the Mediterranean region of the Roman empire. Indo-Roman trade continued to attract the attention of British scholars till the 1950s. In 1951, Charlesworth resurveyed the evidence relevant to this theme.[8] Three years later Mortimer Wheeler published *Rome beyond Imperial Frontiers* (Pelican, 1954), which mentions the Roman objects found in Arikamedu and other places in south India as a result of excavations since 1946. By implication all these writers provide some justification for the commercial enterprise of the European nations in India in modern times and support the British exploitation of the Indian resources. A necessary corrective to this tendency is provided by Motichand's Sārthavāha (Patna, 1953) in Hindi, which recounts ancient trading activities mainly on the basis of indigenous texts and stresses the role of the trading communities, the Vaiśya, seṭṭhis and *gahapatis*,

[6] *Early History of India*, 2nd edn., Oxford, 1908, p. 128.

[7] For a summary of views on landownership see E.W. Hopkins, *India Old and New*, New York, 1901, pp. 206–29.

[8] 'Roman Trade with India: A Resurvey', in ed. P.R. Coleman-Norton, *Studies in Roman Economic and Social History in Honour of Allan Chester Johnson*, Princeton University Press, 1951.

in promoting trade and commerce. This, however, does not mean that the British impact on indigenous writings on early-Indian trade has been altogether eliminated. In a recent work,[9] Adhya states that most Indo-Roman trade was carried on by foreigners who came to this country by land and sea routes, collected commodities and sold them to foreigner consumers. He finds no evidence of the participation of Indian merchants in this trade, and describes them as an unenterprising lot. This impression could have been modified by a detailed analysis of India's commercial contacts with South-East Asia, but its treatment in Adhya's book is quite basic.

The main challenge to the historical models put forth by British historians came from Indian scholars, who, under the influence of the growing nationalist movement, wrote in conscious opposition to the imperialist view of Indian history. The development of nationalism and political consciousness at the turn of the century made the Indian scholars keenly aware of the economic exploitation of India by the British, which formed the theme of the writings of Dadabhai Naoroji and R.C. Dutt. The strong nationalist movement that followed the partition of Bengal in 1905 gave a great impetus to the study of the economic conditions of ancient India.[10] One of the first words which contested the British notions of India's economic past was R.K. Mukherjee's *Indian Shipping and Maritime Activity* (Oxford, 1912). In contrast to Rawlinson and Warmington, he drew his material from both Indian and foreign sources. Deficient in intelligent discussion of the economic and technological aspects of the problem,[11] the book sought to prove that 'the ancient Indians fully utilized the opportunities presented by nature for the development of maritime activity and established their colonies in other Asian countries'. A more forceful

[9] G.L. Adhya, *Early Indian Economics,* Bombay: 1960, Chapter III. Two works on the history of India's trade have appeared in recent years. They are : H.P Chakraborty, *Trade and Commerce of Ancient India* (200 BC–AC 650) (Calcutta, 1966), Balaram Shrivaslava, *Trade and Commerce in Ancient Times* (from the earliest times to AD 300), Varanasi, 1968. But both are compilations of the more or less already known data and assimilated into any analytical framework.

[10] Thus appeared in 1911 two books relating to the subject. They are: N.S. Subba Rao, *Economic and Political Conditions in Ancient India,* Mysore: 1911; C.P. Venkatarama Ayyar, *Town Planning in the Ancient Deccan,* Madras: 1911.

[11] The technological and organizational aspects of shipbuilding in early India has been recently discussed by L. Gopal, 'Art of Shipbuilding and Navigation in Ancient India', *JIH*, xl (1962), 313-27. Cf. A.L. Basham, 'Notes on Seafaring in Ancient India', *Studies in Indian History and Culture*, Calcutta: 1964, pp. 146–66.

attack on the imperialist writers came from K.P. Jayaswal, who was considered a potential contributor to 'the seminaries of sedition' and was made to resign his post in the postgraduate teaching department of Calcutta University by the Bengal government in 1912–13. His articles contributed to the *Modern Review* between 1912 and 1915—which later appeared in the form of his famous book *Hindu Polity* in 1924—were clearly directed against the imperialist historical thinking. He strongly criticized Smith's view on the ancient Indian land ownership. A staunch nationalist, Jayaswal did not like British interference with the landed possessions of the big zamindars and therefore argued that in ancient India there prevailed the individual ownership of land. He did not write any monograph on early Indian economic history himself, but he was followed by a host of Indian scholars who flooded Indian journals with numerous articles on the subject.

The period between 1916 and 1925, coinciding with the post-war nationalist and revolutionary movements sweeping across Europe and Asia, marked the peak of our nationalist movement. It saw the publication of several monographic studies of early Indian economic institution. One of the earliest of these was R.C. Majumdar's *Corporate Life in Ancient India* (Calcutta, 1918). Majumdar sought to establish 'beyond doubt that religion did lot engross the whole or even an undue portion of the public attention . . .' in ancient India. This countered the popular European cliche about India that she had put all her energy into metaphysical speculation[12] Majumdar tried to demonstrate the importance of corporate economic activities in the form of guilds and criticized Mrs Rhys Davids, who did not come across 'any corporate

[12] The notion of India's other-worldliness was best expressed by Max Mueller (*A History of Sanskrit Literature*, London, 1859, p. 3), though it was popular even before him and suited the interests of the British ruling class. It has been rightly suggested that the historiographical stereotype of India's other-worldliness has also conditioned much of the current debate on economic under-development of this country (Romila Thapar, *The Past and Prejudice*, The Sardar Patel Memorial Lectures, 1972, mimeographed; p.18). For example, Vikas Mishra, *Hinduism, and Economic Growth*, Oxford University Press, 1962; William Kapp, *Hindu Culture; Economic Development and Economic Planning in India*, New York: Asia Publishing House, 1963; Thomas W. Shea, Jr, 'The Economic Development in Traditional Societies: Malabar, A Case Study', *Journal of Economic History*, xix (1954), 504–22; Gunnar Myrdal, *Asian Drama: An Inquiry into the Poverty of Nation*, 3 vols., The Penguin Press, 1968; A. Maddison, *Class Structure and Economic Growth: India and Pakistan since the Mugals*, London: George Allen and Unwin, 1971.

organization of the nature of a guild or Hansa league' in the jataka literature. Two years later R.K. Mukherjee published his *Local Government in Ancient India* (Oxford, 1920), which covered the same ground in more detail. In contrast to Majumdar, he utilized the bulk of accessible epigraphic material, especially from south India, though a separate study of guilds in that region was made by K.R.R. Sastry.[13]

Though several specific themes of early economic history attracted the attention of Indian scholars in the 1920s,[14] comprehensive surveys of early Indian economic institutions and practices were attempted by J.N. Samaddar,[15] M.A. Buch,[16] N.C. Bandyopadhyaya[17] and later by S.K. Das[18] and Pran Nath.[19] Based on literary texts, Buch's book discusses property rights, currency and prices, trade and transport, public finance, etc., though it does not give any idea of the development of the different features of early Indian economy. Bandyopadhyaya seeks to make 'a systematic study of economic development' in ancient India with special reference to the land system, agriculture, industry and trade. He claims to have divided the economic history of India into periods 'from a consideration of the economic forces and phenomena characterizing them'.[20] But Das tags on economic history to the political. With the possible exception of Samaddar and Pran Nath[21] all these writers were consciously or unconsciously inspired by a feeling of nationalism, and they tried to present ancient Indian economy in a better light. They argued against the idea that ancient Indians had nothing to do with the problem of material life. They sought to prove the modern practices such as banking, partnership, etc., obtained in early Indian society. They

[13] *South Indian Guilds*, Madras: 1925.

[14] R.S. Vaidyanath Ayyar studied the agrarian and commercial problem: on the basis of Manu (*Manu's Land and Trade Laws*, Madras, 1927). In. 1926 Balkrishna wrote his article: 'Interest and Usury', *Sir Asulosh Memorial Volume*, Patna, 1926.

[15] *Economic Conditions of Ancient India*, Calcutta: 1922.

[16] *Economic Life in Ancient India*, Baroda: 1924.

[17] *Economic Life and Progress in Ancient India*, i, Calcutta: 1925.

[18] *Economic History of Ancient India*, Calcutta: 1929.

[19] *A Study in the Economic Condition of Ancient India*, London: 1929.

[20] Op. cit, preface, p.v.

[21] Samaddar believed that 'a real regeneration, civilization and advancement of India, materially, morally and politically, depends upon the long continuance of the British rule' (op. cit., p. 160). Pran Nath did not, however, suffer from the pro-British bias and compared the economic conditions of India with those obtaining in feudal Europe and devoted separate sections to the landowing classes, the labouring classes, taxes, impositions, etc. (op. cit.).

tried to show almost invariably that economic conditions in ancient India were better than those of their own times.[22]

The Indian nationalist economic historians benefited considerably from a significant new body of evidence made available by the efforts of the British administrators who turned Orientalists. The decipherment of the Brahmi script by James Prinsep in 1837 opened up the epigraphic sources. The appointment by the Government of India of Alexander Cunningham as Archaeological Surveyor or in 1861 promoted official and unfold search for them.[23] By the 1920s a good deal of epigraphic material was made available.[24] But what came as a great boon to nationalist historians was the discovery and the partial publication of the *Arthasastra* of Kautilya in 1905 in the *Indian Antiaquary* by R. Shamasastry. The full text of *Arthasastra* was first published by him in 1909, and its first English translation in 1915. The impact of the discovery of this text was so great that from 1910 to 1930 most Indian historians contributed to the literature on it. There followed a spate of books and articles which glorified early Indian economic life, partly in reaction to imperialist thinking and partly as a step towards the building up of national self-respect.[25]

One of the earliest writing on the economic content of the *Arthasastra* was by H.C. Rays[26] who detected in Kautilya's social and economic policies the elements of modem state-socialism developed in Germany by the social legislation of Bismarck. The Kautilyan legislation, according to Ray; embraced all types of production and sought to protect labour against exploitation. He held that to the ancient Indian king the welfare to the people was more important than that of his own. In 1927, Rao Bahadur Rangasvami Aiyangar postulated that the socio-economic idea of the *Arthasastra* was a combination of state socialism and a

[22] Bandy Opadhyaya, op. cit, pp. 276–7; Buch, op. cit, pp. 192–3.

[23] Many inscriptions appeared in such periodicals as the *Asiatic Researches* and the *Journal of the Asiatic Society* (both published by the Asiatic Society, Calcutta), the *Indian Antiquary* (started by Burgess in 1872) and various others.

[24] For progress of epigraphic studies see D C. Sircar, Indian Epigraphy, Delhi, 1965, pp. 8–10.

[25] R.S. Sharma, *Aspects of Political Ideas and Institutions in Ancient India,* 2nd edn., Delhi: 1968, ch. 1; Romila Thapar, 'Interpretations of Ancient Indian History and Theory', *History and Theory*, vii, no. 3, 1968, p. 326.

[26] 'Was State-Socialism Known in Ancient India? A Study in Kautilya's *Arthashastra*', *Sir Asutosh Mookerjee Silver Jubilee Volumes*, iii, pt. I (Calcutta. 1922), 429–46; 'Idem, Economic Policy and Functions of the Kautilyan State', *Journal of the Department of Letters*, Calcutta University, xiii, 1926, 1–30.

laissez-faire policy.[27] In his view Kautilya's economic theory guarded against the 'fallacies which have cropped up in western economic theory'.[28] Therefore he opined that a knowledge and study of ancient Indian economic thought could 'counteract the modern tendency to import some of the socialistic doctrines of the West into India'.[29]

Of the Indian scholars of the 1920s U.N. Ghosal handled his sources most critically. His *Contribution to the Study of the Hindu Revenue System* (Calcutta, 1929) was the first serious study of the taxation system of India from the Vedic age to *c.* AD 1200, but it gave maximum space to the Maurya period because of the ready availability of the *Arthasastra* material. Ghoshal states that the principles of taxation formulated in early times surpass the achievement of classical antiquity and tend to approach the ideas of European thinkers of the seventeenth and eighteenth centuries.[30] In his opinion, the early Indian view (as found in the law books) that taxes are the king's wages for the services of protection is identical with 'the fashionable doctrine of the seventeenth and eighteenth-century Europe, namely, that taxes are the price paid for the services of the public authories'.[31] Refuting V.A. Smith he states that 'there is little, if any positive evidence' to prove that 'the burden of taxation in ancient and medieval periods was so heavy as to leave the cultivator a bare margin for subsistence'.[32] The idea is repeated by Ghoshal in *The Agrarian System in Ancient India* (Calcutta, 1930), where he states: '. . . the glimpses which the observations of the foreign travellers furnish into the actual condition of the people generally indicate a happy and contended peasantry'.[33] To landownership Ghoshal devotes a full chapter and asserts that the brahmanical law not only had a clear notion of the concept of ownership in general but also of the essential qualities and attributes of private ownership of land.[34] He does not give any credence to the foreign accounts which indicate the prevalence of royal ownership land in ancient India.[35] A more eloquent glorification of early Indian taxation system came from M.H. Gopal in his *Mauryan*

[27] *Aspects of Ancient Indian Thought,* Manindra Chandra Nandy Lectures 1927, Benares Hindu University, Banaras, 1934.

[28] Ibid., p. 149.

[29] Ibid., p. 152.

[30] *Hindu Revenue System*, pp. 273–9.

[32] Ibid., p. 278.

[33] *The Agrarian System in Ancient India*, Calcutta: 1930, p. 80.

[34] Ibid., p. 89.

[35] Ibid., pp. 98–9.

Public Finance (London, 1935). Drawing almost exclusively on the *Arthasastra*, Gopal compared early Indian economic ideas and institutions not only with those of the ancient world (especially Athens) but also with modern principle and practices.[36] The *Arthasastra* has continued to inspire nationalist economic historiography till recently, as can be seen in K.M. Saran's *Labour* in Ancient India (Bombay, 1957).[37]

Obviously the nationalist writings of the 1920s and 1930s regarded the ancient period of Indian history as one of considerable prosperity and general contentment. The patriotic bias often resulted in an exaggeration of the self-sufficiency of the early Indian village out of all proportion, and a greater emphasis on the 'socially productive aspects of the corporate institutions (caste included) of pre-British India' than warranted by available historical evidence.[38] By presenting an encouraging picture at the past, Indian historians sought to fill the people with self-confidence which was essential to sustain the freedom struggle and viewed the British influence in India as a malevolent force that destroyed the moral and social basis of Indian life.[39] But they often tried to cover up the social inequalities characteristic of the early Indian society by vague philosophical platitudes.[40] The nationalist economic

[36] Gopal, op. cit., p.15.

[37] Articles on specific aspects of the *Arthasastra* economy have continued to appear in various journals. See H.N. Pathak, 'Some Economic Concepts in Kauṭilya's *Arthasastra', Proceedings of the Alt-India Oriental Conference*, 17th Session, 19.53, pp. 401–8; G. Harihara Sastri, 'Salaries and Allowances in the *Arthasastra* of Kauṭilya', *Journal of Oriental Research*, Madras, xvii 1958–9, 11–25. The latest study of economic content of the *Arthasastra* is B.C. Sen, *Economics in Kautilya*, Sanskrit College, Calcutta, 1969. For an assessment of the impact of the *Arthasastra* on Indian historical research see Johannes H. Voigt, 'Nationalist Interpretations of *Arthasastra* in Indian Historical Writing' in, *South Asian Affairs Number Two,* ed. S.N. Mukherjee, St.Antbony's Papers No. 18, London: Oxford University Press, 1966, pp. 46–66.

[38] Morris D. Morris and Burton Stein, 'The Economic History of India: A Bibliographic Essay Journal of Economic History, xxi, 1961, p. 182.

[39] Illustrations of this argument may be found in B.D. Basu, *The Rise of Christian Power in India,* Calcutta: 1931 and *Ruin of Indian Trade and Industries* Calcutta: 1935.

[40] R. Shamasastry, 'Economic Philosophy of the Ancient Indians', ABORI, xii, 1930-1, pp. 25–39; N.G. Kalelkar, 'Distribution of Wealth in Ancient India', Proceedings of the All-India Oriental Conference, 7th Session, 1933, pp. 279–90; R.K. Mukherjee, 'The Economic History of India', *The Journal of the U.P. Historical Society*, xiv. pt. 2, 1941, pp. 91–6; Motichand, 'Rationing and Other Famine Relief Measures in Ancient India', ibid., xvii, pts. 1–2, 1945, pp. 18–30.

historiography, however, brought to light certain important facts such as the existence of the guild system,[41] the diversification of mechanical arts and occupations, moneylending,[42] agriculture and irrigation,[43] land system, etc.

The nationalist economic historiography stimulated interest in regional and local histories. In the 1920s and 1930s appeared an impressive number of books and articles dealing for limited periods with the various regions of the Indian subcontinent. We may first mention A.S. Altekar's *History of the Village Communities in Western India* (Bombay, 1927), which deals with the rural economy of the region in the early centuries before and after the Christian era. His *Rāṣhṭrakūṭas and their Times* (Poona, 1934) concentrates on political history, but it gives a chapter to industries and crafts, trade, exchange ratio of various exchange-media, prices of commodities, cost of living, etc. Sketchy in the extreme, the chapter ends with the assertion that 'the people were better off than they are at present'.[44] In the absence of adequate contemporary source-material, Altekar often relies on earlier (*The Periplus of the Erythrean Sea*) and later (the accounts of Al-Idrisi, Marco Polo, Ibn Battuta, etc.) sources. Particularly lacking in critical scholarship, Altekar's formulations are now generally untenable.

The real impetus to the study of economic history of the peninsular region came from the writings of K.A. Nilakanta Sastri, whose works have created a new awareness of the history of the subcontinent by

[41] Most of the books on early Indian economic history written in the 1920s and 1930s give considerable space to the study of ancient Indian guild system.

[42] Two important studies of early Indian banking and usury are: Brijkishore Shargave, *Indigenous Banking in Medieval India,* Bombay: 1943; Principal Balkrishna, 'Interest and Usury', *Sir Asutosh Memorial Volume*, Patna, 1926.

[43] This aspect of early Indian economic life came to occupy an important place in most general works produced by Indian historians during the period of the freedom struggle. But it also formed an independent theme of several economic studies, for example, V. Venkayya, 'Irrigation in Southern India', *Archaeological Survey of India: Report 1903-04*, Calcutta: 1904; R. Ganguli, 'Cattle and Cattle Rearing in Ancient India', ABORI, xii (1931), 216–30; R. Ganguli, *Agriculture and Agriculturists in Ancient India* Serampore: 1932; S.E Raychoudhuri, *A Short Account of Agricultural Methods Practised in Ancient India*, Calcutta: 1941; A.K.Y. Narayan Aiyer, *Agriculture and Allied Arts in Vedic India*, Bangalore, 1949. For a recent and systematic, though brief, treatment of the early Indian agriculture see D.M. Bose, S.N. Sen and B.V. Subbarayappa (eds.), *A Concise History of Science in India*, Indian National Science Academy, New Delhi: 1971, pp. 350–70.

[44] Altekar, *The Rashtrakutas and their Times,* Poona, 1934, p. 398.

bringing the history of the south into perspective.[45] Primarily interested in the general history of south India, he did not neglect its economic aspect. In his *Coḷas*, taxation, agriculture and land tenure, industry, trade coinage, and weights and measures receive separate sections. Drawing largely on the Chola inscriptions, he describes the economic conditions during the time of the Chola rulers, but does not pinpoint those features of the socio-economic institutions which are peculiar to the period. But Nilakanta Sastri brings to light some interesting and new pieces of evidence, and systematizes the mass of details bearing on the land tenure, industry and trade, and the economic importance of south Indian temples. He however ignores the inconvenient facts of the past. In spite of considerable evidence to the contrary he attributes to the *Chola* society a wonderful social harmony based, not on equality of classes or individuals, but on a readiness to give and take, a mutual goodwill that had its roots deep down at the foundations of commercial life.[46]

The tendency to praise the past is less pronounced in C. Minakshi's *Administration and Social Life under the Pallavas* (Madras, 1932), which gives a sketch of taxation, weights and measures, irrigation, famines and rural economic life in south India during" the time of the Pallavas. Similarly K. Gopalachari's *Early History of the Andhra Country* (Madras, 1941) surveys the towns situated on the eastern and western coasts, and the land system, and guilds in the Andhra region in the early centuries AD. The reconstruction of economic life in early south India is far from adequate in the above-mentioned works. Principally concerned with dynastic histories, these works lack perspective in treating economic life and institutions.[47]

More detailed studies of early south Indian economic history were undertaken by K.M. Gupta (*The Land System in South India between* AD

[45] *The Pandyan Kingdom* London: 1929; *The Colas* Madras: 1935; *Historical Method in Relation to Problems of South Indian History,* Madras: 1941; *The Culture and History of the Tamils* Calcutta: 1964; *Cultural Contacts between Aryans and Dramdians,* Bombay: 1967.

[46] *The Colas*, p. 542.

[47] This also applies to the relevant sections in the various works on different regions and ruling dynasties of India. See, for example, M. Arokiaswami, *The Kongu County* Madras: 1956; P. Bhalia, *The Paramāras,* Delhi: 1970; J.D.M. Derrett, *The Hoysalas,* Madras: Oxford University Press 1957; B.N. Puri, *The History of the Gurjara-Prātihāras,* (Bombay, 1951); Idem, *India under the Kuṣāṇas,* Bombay: 1965; D. Sharma, *Early Chauhan Dynasties,* Delhi: 1959; K.J. Virji, *Ancient History of Saurashtra,* Bombay: 1952.

800 and AD 1200, Lahore 1933) and A. Appadorai (*Economic Conditions in Southern India, AD 7000–7500*, 2 vols., Madras, 1936). Gupta gives us the first full-length study of the agrarian system of south India in early medieval times. He treats the subject under four main divisions, the habitat, the cultivated tracts, the general waste lands the forest tracts. His book provides some new information on lands and tenure and the revenue system but does not compare the south Indian land system with that of the north. On the contrary, his uncritical lumping together of literary and epigraphic material from the north and the south has obscured whatever regional variations may have existed. Gupta's excessive reliance on Sanskrit literary sources may be seen in his sections on landownership, which are based almost entirely on the Smrti literature. In this respect, Appadorai's work is better. It studies land tenures, agriculture and the nature of south Indian village communities, commerce, guilds, towns, industries and foreign trade from AD 1000 to 1500. Appadorai deals with the economic role of the state and concludes on the basis of the foreign accounts and epigraphic references that taxation may have been oppressive. His treatment is generally descriptive, and does not try to trace the evolution of south Indian economic institutions. However, he does not load his work with citations from north Indian sources and emphasizes the main features of the economic conditions of the region. He shows a general awareness of some of the basic issues of Indian historiogaraphy.[48] The discussion throughout his book, in contrast to that in K.M. Gupta's, is orderly, and his formulations have not been substantially altered by subsequent research. During the three decades following the publication of Appadorai's *magnum opus*, interest in south Indian economic history seem to have languished. The casual and sporadic forays into the subject in the subsequent period do not add substantially to our knowledge except by providing a few pedestrian details.[49]

[48] This is especially evident in the earlier chapters of the book where, agreeing with Baden-Powell, he accepts the existence of joint tenures of land in south India on a limited scale.

[49] Kumuda Ranjan Chatterjee, 'Temple Offerings and Temple Servants in South India', *Proceedings of the Indian History Congress*, Fourth Session, 1940, pp. 156–08; M. Venkateswarlu, 'Land Grants in Medieval Andhra', *JAHRS*, xx, 1949, pp. 12–16; K.V. Soundara Rajan, 'The Kaleidoscopic Activities of Medieval Temples in Tamilanad', *Quarterly Journal of the Mythic Society*, xlii, no. 3, 1952, pp. 87–101; V. Krishnamurthy, 'Temple Endowments in Medieval Andhra', *JAHRS*, xxvi, 1960–1, pp. 113–69; J.D.M. Derrett, '*Kutta*, a class of land tenure in South India', *BSOAS*, xxi, 1958, pp. 61–81.

In recent years, detailed economic studies of the different regions of peninsular India have been undertaken. K. Sundaram, in his *Studies in Economic and Social Conditions of Medieval Andkra* AD *1000-1600* (Machilipatanam and Madras, 1968), gives an account of metal work, jewellery, carpentry, architecture, spinning and weaving, salt manufacture, tailoring, etc., of the artisan communities (especially the Panchala and Teliki communities), and of trade and commerce. He draws upon inscriptions, local traditions, works of Vallabhacharya, Srinatha and Koravi Goparaju and the accounts of Marco Polo, Abdur Razak and Nicolo Conti, but he hardly discusses their credibility. The book is a compilation of useful and fascinating details which often 'float within a thin fluid of unwarranted preconceptions, insupportable assumptions, vague and sweeping generalizations.'[50] Analysis is practically absent also in D.R. Das' *Economic History of the Deccan* (Delhi, 1969), which covers the period AD 100–600. The book is spread over fifteen chapters on geographical background, land revenue system, agriculture, forests, famine and irrigation, towns and cities, associate life in the town and village, mineral resources, crafts and industrial arts, profession and occupation, organization of industry and trade, trade and commerce, banking and currency; but it does not give any idea of the elements of change and continuity. A useful compendium of economic data, it does not tackle some of the basic questions relevant to the understanding of the historical processes. It provides a list of agricultural products in the Deccan during the first six centuries of the Christian era without telling us why and how sedentary agriculture developed in the area during the post-Maurya period and not earlier. Nor does he say anything about the agricultural techniques. He discusses the general layout of towns and cities on the basis of literary and archaeological material but sees no connection between urbanization on the one hand and the growth of commerce and crafts on the other. Each aspect of the Deccan economy is studied in isolation, often on the basis of sources which may have little or no bearing on the period and area covered by Das.[51] He therefore fails to make the economic history of the Deccan meaningful. What may be said of Das's book is largely true of all the studies of the early

[50] *JAS*, xxviii, 1968, 037.

[51] The chapter on forests rests primarily on the Ramayana; and materials from the *Jataka* stories and the commentaries of Vijnanesvara (eleventh century), Apararka (twelfth century) and Kulluka (thirteenth century) have also been used without discussing their possible applicability to the region and the period studied.

south Indian economy with the possible exception of a few recent articles which are based on rigorous analysis of sources and suggest new lines of enquiry.[52]

[52] Burton Stein 'The Economic Functions of a Medieval South Indian Temple'. *JAS*, xix, 1959, 163–76 analyzes the Chola and later inscriptions from Tirupati and emphasizes the role of south Indian temples in the extension of agriculture. He also shows how the south Indian political, economic and social institutions were related to and integrated with the control of land 'Integration of the Agrarian System of South India' in *Land Control and Social Structure in Indian History*, ed. Fnykenberg Wisconsin University Press, 1966, pp. 175–216; Idem. 'Coromandel Trade in Medieval India' in *Merchants and Scholars*, ed. John Parker Mineapolis, 1965, pp. 47–62; Idem. 'Historical Ecotypes in South India', *Proceedings of the Second International Conference Seminar of Tamil Studies*, ii, Madras, 1971, pp. 284–8. On the basis of an intensive study of the Tanjore records G.W Spencer shows that the Tanjore temple was a centre for the redistribution of two key resources in the Indian peasant economy; viz., money and livestock 'Temple Moneylending and Livestock Redistribution in Early Tanjore', *IESHR*, v, 1968, pp. 277–94 and that royal investigation of temple accounts did not generate a large bureaucratic apparatus 'Royal Initiative under Rajaraja 1: The Auditing of Temple Accounts', *IESHR*, vii, 1970, pp. 431–42; cf. his paper entitled, 'Religious Networks and Royal Influence in Eleventh Century South India', *JESHO*, xii, 1969, pp. 42–56. N. Karashimha makes a comparative analysis of the records of a *brahmadeya* and a *non-brahmadeya* village of early Chola times. This, according to him, is necessary for an elucidation of the historical development of south Indian village communities, land tenures and social stratification 'Allur and Isanamangalam', *IESHR*, iii, 1966, pp. 150–62; cf. L. Mannithamby, 'Village and Temple Administration in the Allur inscriptions', *Proceedings of the Second International Conference Seminar of Tamil Studies*, ii, Madras, 1971, pp. 245–50. Karashimha also argues that the brahmadeya villages played a crucial role in spreading brahmanical ideas among the residents of non-brahmadeya villages and were the local nuclei of the Chola power structure 'The Power Structure of the Chola Rule', *Proceedings of the Second International Conference Seminar of Tamil Studies*, ii, Madras, 1971, pp. 233–44. In her recent work based chiefly on inscriptions, a fairly good proportion of which have remained untapped so far, Sister M. Liceria, A.C., systematically discusses such aspects of the economic history of Kamataka as land grants and tenures, growth of intermediaries in land, agriculture and irrigation, trade and commerce, currency and urban settlements (*Social and Economic History of Karnataka c.* AD *1000–1300*, Ph.D. Thesis. Patna University, 1972). She traces (the growth of landed intermediaries in Karnataka (op. cit, pp. 42–74) and thus indirectly supports R.S. Sharma's formulations relating to feudalism in India (infra). But she does not devote attention to the problem of the emergence of serfdom which is a distinctive feature of feudal economy and society. Similarly, her treatment of agriculture and irrigation (op. cit., pp. 75–122) is mainly descriptive and does not seek to prove or disprove Wittfogel's theory of Oriental despotism on the basis of Karnataka evidence.

A broad trend noticeable in the writings on early Indian economic history is represented by those writers who seem to have been influenced by vague socialist thinking and ideas of the materialist interpretation of history. In point of time the first historian of this group is A.N. Bose who produced a study of rural economy of north India in 600 BC–AD 200.[53] Perhaps owing to political conditions in the 1940s, Bose does not confess his indebtedness to Marxism, but in the concluding chapter of his book he discusses class and class-consciousness, class struggle and compromise. In contrast to the nationalist historians, he tries to show that all was not well with the ancient economic system and that according to the Jataka stories the peasants were exploited by the princes.[54] Marxist influence is more explicit in the writings of B.N. Datta, who was associated with the terrorist movement in Bengal. As a young revolutionary living in exile, he visited Moscow as early as 1921 and came in contact with the world communist movement. Datta does not confine himself to any particular phase of early Indian history as Bose does. He takes a long view of the socio-economic developments throughout the ancient period. In his *Studies in Indian Social Polity* (Calcutta, 1944), which deals mainly with the origin and growth of caste, he devotes small sections to the class struggle in ancient India and to the growth of feudalism; the latter theme is assigned a separate chapter in his *Dialectics of Land-Economics in India* (Calcutta, 1952), which seeks to trace the history of the land and its tiller from the Vedic age to the end of the British rule. In 1949 was published Dange's *India from Primitive Communism to Slavery*, which tried to prove the emergence of slave society in the later Vedic period on the basis of material cleverly extracted from the Vedic texts. These writers lack the thoroughness of later Marxist historians, and many of their conclusion have been contested. But their works may be treated as landmarks in the development of early economic historiography. They made a departure from the stereotype nationalist writings and offered new and useful insights into the subject by trying to explain the early Indian economic developments in terms not peculiar to India but of universal application.

[53] *Social and Rural Economy of Northern India c.600 BC–AD 200*, 2 vols., Calcutta: 1942–5.

[54] It may be pointed out that one of the first Indian scholars to openly plead for the application of Marxism to Indian history was D.P. Mukerji, *On Indian History: A Study in Method*, Bombay: Hind Kitabs, 1945, pp. 8–48.

The best representative of Marxist historiography in India is D.D. Kosambi.[55] For him 'history is the presentation in chronological order of successive changes in the means and relations of production'. Any 'personal' episodic drum-and-trumpet history of India, he points out, 'should be enjoyed as romantic fiction' or 'like some Indian railway time-table.[56] It is in accordance with this attitude that Kosambi treats culture as the essential way of the life of the people, and not purely as a matter of intellectual and spiritual value. To him all history is basically economic history. Not surprisingly therefore, he tries to explain the major historical developments on the basis of changes in the mode of production.[57]

The type of history Kosambi seeks to reconstruct is difficult. For the early Indian literature, which has been the basis of all earlier studies, is overwhelmingly religious and ritualistic and deficient in economic data. To counterbalance a purely philological and linguistic approach he uses the anthropological material and shows that throughout the centuries of Indian history there has been taking place a change from the tribal to the peasant economy. Thus, the technique followed by Kosambi is the collation of written records with archaeology and the interpretation of each of these in conjunction with ethnography[58] But the impact of his methodology on Indian historical research has been rather slow, for interdisciplinary cooperation is easier recommended than achieved.

Generally Indian scholars have so far been highly allergic to Marxists, who are often held guilty of blatantly forcing the historical evidence to fit into a supposedly rigid framework laid down by Marx and Engels. Admittedly, some historians like Dange and Hussaini[59] have adhered to the orthodox Marxist scheme of periodization, in reaction to which there has grown up a belief that Marxism stands for a unilinear development

[55] The two books written by D.D. Kosambi are: *An Introduction to the Study of Indian History,* Bombay, 1956 which surveys the course of Indian history from the earliest times till British conquest, and *Culture and Civilization of Ancient India in Historical Outline,* London: 1965 which deals with topics ranging from pre-history to the long process of emergent feudalism. These books sum up the results of Kosambi's historical inquiries published in various journals in the 1950s and 1960s.

[56] *Culture and Civilization*, p. 23.

[57] The Basis of Indian History', *JAOS*, lxxv, 1955, pp. 35–45, pp. 226–37.

[58] See Kosambi's article entitled 'Combined Methods in Indololgy', *Indo-Iranian Journal*, vi, 1963, pp. 177–202. Also see D.N. Jha, 'A Marxist View of Ancient Indian History', *Das Kapital Centenary Volume*, New Delhi: 1968, pp. 166–80.

[59] *Economic History of India*, i, Calcutta, 1962.

of history. But according to Kosambi Indian history does not fit precisely into this rigid framework,[60] and ancient Indian society, unlike the Greek and the Roman, was not based on slavery. In his opinion, chattel slavery did not matter in the relations of production and as a supply of labour for economic production its place was taken by the members of the Śūdrā or lowest caste whose surplus could be appropriated.[61] Thus Kosambi does not show any procrustean adherence to the slavery-feudalism-capitalism scheme. But the denial of the economic importance of slavery in ancient India has been questioned by some Marxist historians, and Dev Raj Chanana's *Slavery in Ancient India* (English Edition, Delhi, 1960) is a major contribution to our knowledge of the origin, extent and nature of slavery during the first six centuries preceding the Christian era.[62]

Kosambi departs from the orthodox Marxian notion of the 'unchangeableness of Asiatic societies'. He points out that the very formation of the village economy with the plough used on a fixed plot of land implies a tremendous advance in the means of production. Self-sufficiency which, according to the founders of Marxism, is a characteristic feature of Asiatic societies, is not possible in the strict sense of the term. For, he tells us, most of the Indian villages produce neither salt nor metals, the two essentials that had to be obtained by exchange.[63] Like Kosambi, most Asian Marxists have differed from Marx's formulation on the 'stagnatory and vegetative' life of Asiatic society. The myth of millenary stagnation of Indian society has been

[60] *Culture and Civilization*, p. 23.

[61] This may be especially true of the Vedic period when the number of slaves was very small and hence could not have engaged in productive activities like their Homeric counterparts. This is corroborated by the fact that whenever the Vedic passages refer to the gifts of slaves they invariably speak of woman slaves made over to the priests.

[62] Also see his 'Ideological Aspects of Slavery in Ancients India, *Journal of the Oriental Institute*, vii, 1959, 389–98; cf. Walter Ruben (ed), *Die Okonomische and soziale Entwicklung Indiens, Berlin*, 1959. A number of articles on early Indian slavery have appeared in various journals : U.N. Ghoshal, 'Slavery' in Ancient India—A Study in India's Social and Economic History' in *The Beginnings of Indian Historiography and Other Essays*, Calcutta: 1944, pp. 85–103; B.C. Law, 'Slavery as known to Early Buddhists', *Journal of the Ganganalh Jha Research Institute*, vi, 1948, pp. 1–10; R.C. Agrawala. 'Position of Slaves and Serfs as depicted in the Kharosthi Documents from Chinse Turkestan', *IHO*, xxix, 1953, pp. 97–110; L. Gopal, 'Slavery in Ancient India', *JAHRS*, xxvii, 1961, pp. 70–89.

[63] Cf. L. Gopal, 'Economic Self-Sufficiency of Ancient Indian Villages', *Journal of the Ganganath Jha Research Institute*, xxvi, 1970, pp. 763–70.

ably exploded by R.S. Sharma who marks definite stages in the development of its economic basis till the beginning of feudalism from the Gupta period onward.[64] Both Kosambi and Sharma, however, agree that by the end of the Gupta period the Indian village became nearly self-contained owing mainly to the decline of trade and urban life, though neither accepts the scheme implied in the theory of the Asiatic mode of production which had within it certain dissolving elements and therefore underwent a series of transformations.[65] The simple structure of the closed peasant village economy, Kosambi appears to believe, was disturbed during the early centuries of the Christian era when kings began to transfer their fiscal and administrative rights over land to their subordinate chiefs, who thus came into direct relation with the peasantry a process he terms 'feudalism from above'. It reached an advanced stage of development during the period of the Guptas and of Harsha. Kosambi postulates that at a later stage 'a class of landowners developed within the village between the state and the peasantry, gradually to wield armed power over the local population'. This process he calls 'feudalism from below'.[66] But it would be wrong to suppose that a class of landowners above the peasantry did not emerge until the later centuries of the first millennium. Sharma has cited Yajnavalkya (fourth and fifth centuries AD), who lays down that land should be assigned to the cultivator (*karṣka*) by the landowner (*kṣetrasvāmī*) and not by the king (*mahīpati*), who, of course, was entitled to the fruits of improvement made on land in the absence of an owner (*svāni*). In the organization of land economy Yajnavalkya introduces three stages, namely *mahīpati* (king), *kṣetrasvāmī* (landowner) and karṣka (cultivator)[67] which is

[64] 'Stages in Ancient Indian Economy' in *Light on Early Indian Society and Economy*, Bombay: 1966, pp. 52–89.

[65] It is likely that in his later life Marx's views on Asiatic societies changed considerably. See Daniel Thorner, 'Marx on India and the Asiatic Mode of Production', *Contributions to Indian Sociology*, No. 9, December 1966, pp. 33–46; Amalendu Guha, 'A Marxist Approach to Indian History', *Socialist Digest*, No. 5, May 1969, pp. 77–8. E.J. Hobsbawan even goes so far as to suggest that Marx's concept of Asiatic mode even implies the possibility of a direct transition from such a society to feudalism (*Precapitalist Economic Formations*, London: 1966, p. 39).

[66] *An Introduction to the Study of Indian History,* Bombay: 1957, pp. 275–6; for his views on Indian feudalism also see his articles: 'Origins of Feudalism in Kashmir', *JBBRAS*, Sardhasalabhi volume, 1956-7, pp. 108–20; 'On the development of Feudalism in India', *ABORI*, xxvi, 1952, pp. 258–69; 'Indian Feudal Trade Charters' JESHO, ii, 1959, pp. 281–93.

[67] *Yajnavalkya*, ii, 158.

roughly corroborated by Bṛhaspati (sixth and seventh centuries AD). The latter lawgiver makes it clear that the *svāmī* formed an intermediate stage between the raja and the actual tiller of the soil.[68] On this basis it may be suggested that the *svāmīs* or landowners leased out land to temporary cultivators and lived on the rent collected from their tenants. In view of this, Kosambi's two-stage theory of feudalism is open to question.[69]

In recent years several scholars have contributed to the literature on early Indian feudalism.[70] But R.S. Sharma's *Indian Feudalism: 300–1200* (Calcutta, 1965) is the only comprehensive work on the subject.[71] It deals with the origins of Indian feudalism (AD 300–750) and studies the feudal polity and economy under the Palas, Pratiharas and Rastrakutas (AD 750–1000) as well as during the two centuries preceding

[68] *Bṛhaspati*, xix, 50-5.

[69] Although there has not been enough discussion of this interesting theory the appropriateness of the expression 'feudalism from above' and 'below' has been rightly questioned. See Irfan Habib's article in Seminar No. 39: *Past and Present*, New Delhi, 1957 and review of Kosambi's *An Introduction to the Study of Indian History in JAGS*, lxxvii, 1957, pp. 220–7.

[70] R.K. Choudhary, 'Some Historical Aspects of Feudalism in Ancient India', *JIH*, xxxvii, 1959, pp. 305–6; ibid, xxxviii, 1960, p. 303 ff.; Idem. 'Theory of Commendation and Subinfeudation in Ancient India', *Proceedings of the Indian History Congress*, Thirtieth Session, 1962, pp. 115–20; K.K. Gopal, 'Feudal Composition of Army in Early Medieval India' *JAHRS*, xxviii, 1962-3; Idem 'The Assembly of *Samantas* in Early Medieval India', *JIH*, xlii, 3964, pp. 241–50; L. Gopal, 'Ownership of Agricultural Land in Ancient India', *JBRS*, xlvi, 1960, pp. 27–44; Idem. 'On Some Problems of Feudalism in Ancient India', ABORI, xlvi, 1963, pp. 1–32; Idem. '*Samanta*: Its varying significance in Ancient India', *JRAS*, pts. I-II (1963), 21–37; Idem. 'On Fedual Polity in Ancient India'. *JIH*, xli, 1963, pp. 405–13; Idem.' Quasi-Manorial Rights in Ancient India', *JESHO*, vi, pt.3, 1963, pp. 296–308; D. Sharma, 'Some Light on Feudal Elements in Indian Polity (AD 700–1000)', *Proceedings of the Indian History Congress*, Twenty-fourth Session, 1961, pp. 79–82. Some of the important Soviet writings on the subject are as follows: L.B. Alaev, *Yuznaya Indiya sotsial 'noekonomicheskaya istoria xiv-xviii vekov*, Moscow, 1964 ; K.A. Antanova, 'K. Voprosu O. Razvitii Feodalizma v. Indii', *Kratkie Sooleschenia Institute Vosokovedeniya*, iii, (A.K. Nauk USSR, Moskva, 1952), 23–32; K.Z. Ashrafyan, 'Some Problems of Feudalism in India', paper presented at the XVIII International Congress of Orientalists (Canberra, 6–12 January 1971); Y.M. Medvedev, 'K Voprosu O Fonnakh Jemlevladeniya V. Severnoi Indii v vi-vii Vekakh', *Problemi vostokovideniya*, i, 1959, pp. 44–61; Idem. 'Origin and Evolution of the Form of Indian Grants' in W. Ruben, V. Struve and G. Bongard-Levin (eds), *Istoriyi drevnei Indii*, Moscow, 1963.

[71] K.K. Copal's *Feudalism in Northern India,* Ph.D. Thesis, University of London: 1966, which deals with the political and administrative aspects of feudalism, is still unpublished.

the establishment of the Sultanate (AD 1000–1200). According to Sharma, feudalism in India, unlike in Europe, began with the land grants made to learned Brāhmaṇas, temples and monasteries for which the epigraphic evidence begins from the first century AD and multiplies by Gupta times when villages together with their fields and inhabitants, fiscal, administrative and judicial rights (with the right to enjoy fines received), and exemption from the interference of royal officials were given to religious beneficiaries. What was abandoned step by step to the priestly class was later given to the warrior class. Religious as well as secular (or service) grants became increasingly popular with the emergence of local and self-sufficient economies marked by lack of commercial intercourse, decline of towns,[72] and paucity of coins. The economic essence of Indian feudalism, like that of European, lay in the rise of landed intermediaries leading to the enserfment of the peasantry through mounting tax burdens, increasing obligations to perform forced labour and the evils of sub-infeudation.

Sharma postulates the existence of serfdom in Gujarat, Madhya Pradesh, Kangra, Andhra, Orissa and Bengal during the sixth and seventh centuries on the basis of epigraphic references to the transfer of individual peasants and labourers of AD 732 to show that the practice of donating villages together with villages to temples and monasteries was fairly common throughout the country. The crucial passage, in his opinion, indicates the general emergence of serfdom.[73] The weakness of Sharma's thesis lies in the inadequacy of the data, to which his critics have drawn attention.[74] For a fuller picture of the feudal developments in India a close examination of the vast mass of south Indian epigraphic material is essential, which Sharma has obviously not done.

[72] 'Decay and Disappearance of Towns in Gupta and Post-Gupta Times', presented to the 33rd session of the Indian History Congress at Muzaffarpur, 1972. A stimulating analysis of urbanization in early India is available in A. Ghosh, *The City in Early Historical India*, Indian Institute of Advanced Study; Simla. 1973; cf. Dilip. K. Chakrabaiti, 'Concept of Urban Revolution and the Indian Context', *Puratattva*, no. vi, 1972, 27–32.

[73] This has been criticized by D.C. Sircar. A Chinese Account of India-732 AD', *JIH*, xliv, 1966, 351–7. But B.N.S. Yadava has brought to light some additional evidence to prove the emergence of serfdom in India. See his paper on the Problems of the Emergence of the Feudal Complex, presented at the Seminar on the Problems of Social and Economic History held at the Department of History, Aligarh Muslim University, 1969. Also see Sister M. Liceria, op. cit., pp. 42–74.

[74] R. Coulbourn, 'Feudalism, Brahmansim and the Intrusion of Islam upon Indian History', *Comparative Studies in Society and History*, x, 1967–8, pp. 356–74.

The appropriateness of the term 'feudalism' to describe Indian situation between AD 700–1200 has been a matter of animated debate.[75] But this cannot minimize the Marxist historians' chief contribution which lies in their challenge to the notion of a stagnant Indian society. They have questioned the validity not only of the imperialist theory of Oriental despotism[76] but also of the Marxist model of the Asiatic mode of production, which, at any rate, should not be taken as crucial to the Marxist historical philosophy. For their interpretation of Indian history the Marxist historians in Indian, as elsewhere, have depended largely on the principles of dialectical materialism. They have, therefore, tried to indicate 'not only the periods of change but also the nature of change' that took place through centuries. In the field of economic history this has led to a fresh study of early Indian agrarian relations,[77] mostly on the basis of early Indian, land grants, which can enable us to answer some fundamental questions relating to the changing agrarian structure and property relations, growth of towns, and arts and crafts.[78]

The wider application of Marxist approach to early Indian economic history may suggest new problems, provide categories for organizing data, supply hypotheses by which the data may be tested and interpreted, and may lay down criteria of proof. Although it has not won general acceptance, it has indirectly influenced recent research leading to a somewhat more objective evaluation of India's past than is available in the pre-Independence indigenous writings. Thus S.K. Maity (*Economic life in Northern India in the Gupta Period,* Calcutta, 1957), through a

[75] D.C. Sircar, *Landlordism and Tenancy in Ancient and Medieval India as Revealed by Epigraphical Records*, Lucknow, 1969; A.K. Warder ii *JESHO*, ii, 1959, p. 217; Buddha Prakash, 'The Genesis and Character of Landed Aristocracy in Ancient India', ibid, ix, 1971, pp. 196–220; Amslendu Guha in *Socialist Digest*, No. 5, 1969, PP. 74–8; J.W. Spellman in AHR, lxxii, 1967, P. 673; Burton Stein in *JAS*, xxvi, 1967, P. 154. For different views see D.C. Sircar, *Land System and Feudalism in Ancient India* (being the proceedings of a seminar held at the Centre of Advanced Study in Ancient Indian History and Culture, Calcutta University), Calcutta, 1966.

[76] D.D. Kosambi, 'The Basis of Despotism', *Economic Weekly*, ix, 2 November 1957, PP. 1417–19; Irfan Habib, 'Anexamination of Wittfogel's Theory of Oriental Despotism', *Enquiry*, no. 6, PP. 54–73.

[77] R.S. Sharma, 'A Survey of Land System in India from *c.*200 BC to AD 650', *JBRS*, xliv, 1958, PP. 225–34;' R.S. Sharma, *Indian Feudalism*, Calcutta, 1965.

[78] R.S. Sharma, 'Land Grants and Early Indian Economic History', in B.N. Ganguli fed.), *Readings in Indian Economic History* (Proceedings of the First All India Seminar on Indian Economic History, Delhi School of Economics. Delhi University, 1961), Bombay: Asia Publishing House, 1964.

greater use of epigraphic and numismatic material than attempted ever before in north Indian economic historiography, concludes that as regards the material life of the common people, the Gupta period was not a golden age—a point supported by another work which suggests that taxes tended to increase in Gupta times.[79] For the subsequent period Puspa Niyogi does not find any evidence to prove that the population as a whole was prosperous.[80] More explicit are the findings of L. Gopal, whose *Economic Life in Northern India* (Delhi, 1965), covering the period AD 700–1200, carefully studies the agrarian system and cites some instances of semi-serfs attached to the soil; he repeatedly suggests that the common people were far from happy and economically well off. A slightly different attitude is adopted by B.P. Mazumdar, who, in his *Socio-Economic History of Northern India* AD 1030–1194 (Calcutta, 1960), tries to explain why northern India succumbed to the Turkish invaders. All these works were produced in the years after Independence when nationalism ceased to remain a source of inspiration and new India's problems attracted attention of their authors. Not surprisingly, they made an attempt to understand the early Indian economic life from a fresh angle. But the impact of the Marxist historiography on their writings has been at best remote; for none of them, except Gopal, shows any acquaintance with the Marxist method of analysis. Nevertheless their works contain very useful economic data, often drawn from hitherto untapped literary and epigraphic sources, and prepare the ground for a detailed analytical study of the limited chronological segments of the early economic history of north India.[81]

In sharp contrast to the West, economic historiography in India has generally remained an obstinate pocket of resistance to the use of economic theory, perhaps mainly because very few economists have

[79] D.N. Jha, *Revenue System in Post-Maurya and Gupta Times*, Calcutta: 1967.

[80] Puspa Niyogi, *Contributions to the Economic History of Northern India from the Tenth to the Twelfth Century AD*, Calcutta: 1962.

[81] It has been pointed out that emphasis on the early economic history of north India has stemmed 'from the historiographical traditions which (along with canons of modern historical scholarship) the Indian historian has inherited from his European predecessor; traditions which emphasized scholarship and research in the venerable Sanskrit law books and commentaries on north Indian Society'. Areas such as south India and parts of central and western India, being marginal to the centre of Sanskritic tradition, have been neglected (Morris and Stein, op. cit., p. 183). But this applies to all types of studies, and perhaps may be explained by the size and general importance of north India.

taken interest in the subject. Whatever little work has been done by such, economists as Pran Nath and M.H. Gopal is out of date both in terms of the questions raised and the methods adopted.[82] Following the publication of their writings, considerable material has come to light, and it awaits fresh examination by historians having knowledge of economic theory which increasingly uses quantitative methods of analysis.[83] In the West the use of mathematics in social sciences is now generally accepted, though this is far from being the case in India. There has been little realization by Indian scholars of the fact that if economic history is anything it is history that asks 'how much', 'what proportions'?, 'how representative'?... etc.[84] Answers to such questions

[82] Pran Nath (op. cit,) deals, among other things, with the rate of interest, prices, population and the cost of living. But he does not go beyond itemizing literary and epigraphic references under various categories. Whatever analysis may be seen in his work (especially in the chapters on territorial divisions and population in ancient India) does not inspire much confidence. Gopal's work (op. cit.) is an example of the abuse of modern theories of taxation and public finance to suit nationalist sentiments. Rangasvami Aiyangar, who was not an economist, has merely compiled literary references under such well-known rubrics of classical economics as production, consumption, exchange and distribution, and public finance (op. cit.).

[83] In England the application of theoretical principles of economics to economic history seems to have become fairly common (*Research in Economic and Social History: A Social Science. Council Review*, London: Heinemann 1971, pp. 25–32), though quantitative history is not as popular in the UK as in the USA. For a discussion of comparative unpopularity of quantitative techniques in England see Donald N. McCloskey (ed.), *Essays on a Mature Economy: Britain After 1840*, London: Methuen & Co. Ltd., 1971, pp. 401–39. David Thomson has described the nature of relationship that should develop between economics and economic history: '. . . Economics and history may enter into a working partnership but never into marriage. They can aid one another, they can suggest techniques, insights, modes of approach to fuller understanding. But they cannot usefully merge. . . . Economic history is not just a hybrid of economics and history . . . it is the main area of overlap in their (economists and historians) activities, an area of common interest a mutual aid' (*The Aims of History*, London: Thames and Hudson, Reprint, 1970, pp. 75–6).

[84] Morris D. Morris, 'The Economist As Economic Historian', paper submitted to the Seminar on Social and Economic History of India, Indian Institute of Advanced Study, Simla, 1966.

cannot be provided without a serious attempt at quantification[85] All this should not mean that there is no dearth of statistical material bearing on early Indian economic history. Hard statistical data begin to appear only towards the last quarter of the nineteenth century. In fact the general lack of evidence has been the *bētī noire* of all historians working on early history. The apparent absence of material amenable to statistical analysis should not be overemphasized, for D.D. Kosambi's study of the punch-marked coins clearly indicates the further possibility of the efficacious use of statistical inference in the analysis of the historical data on early Indian economic life.[86]

Research in early Indian economic history has been seriously inhibited by the fact that the bulk of it has been done source wise, especially the monographs relating to the age of the Buddha. Most of the works do not rise above the level of mere inventories of disparate fads gathered from different sources mutually unrelated in their historical context. Naturally continuities and discontinuities in early Indian economy have been obscured. Of course some recent studies in India and abroad recognize several chronological strata in many early literary

[85] Many years ago the French historian Georges Lefebvre stated his famous dictum: *Pour fain de I 'histoire, il faui savoir compter* (to write, history, one must know how to count, cited in David Thomson, op. cit., p. 84). But in recent years several scholars have sought to make a well-reasoned case for the use of economic theory and statistics in the writing of economic history For example, Alfred H. Conrad and John R. Mayer, *Studies in Econometric History*, London: Chapman and Hall, 1965, pp. 3–40; Richard Stone, *Mathematics in the Social Sciences and Other Essays*, Chapman and Hall, London, 1966, pp. 1–18. For actual examples of the application of statistical method to specific historical themes in the West see D.K. Rowney and J.Q. Graham (eds), *Quantitative History*, The Dorsey Press, Homewood, Illinois, 1969. Cf. J.H. Hexter, 'History the Social Sciences, And Quantification', paper presented at the XIII International Congress of Historical Sciences, Moscow, 1970.

[86] Infra.

texts.[87] But their methodological implications have not been fully appreciated by some researchers who still continue to think in terms of the Epic age, the Buddhist period and so on.[88] The persistent tendency to cling oddly to the outdated ideas on Indian chronology has to be positively discouraged and combated. It will be helpful if we introduce some sense of periodization into the economic history of early India and try to mark the main stages in the economic developments from the beginning to AD 1200 on the basis of 'the substantial changes in economic organization, direction and pace of activity'.[89] This will require a careful

[87] R.C. Hazra, *Studies in Puranic Records on Hindu Rites and Customs*, Calcutta, 1944; B.B. Mishra, *Polity in the Agni Purana*, Calcutta, 1966, D.D. Kosambi, 'The Text of the *Arthasastra*', *JAOS*, xxviii, 1958, pp. 169–73; Thomas R. Trautmann, A Metrical Origin for the Kauṭīlya *Arthasastra*', ibid, lxxxviii, 1968, pp. 347–9. On the basis of a statistical analysis of the vocabulary of the *Arthasastra* text, Trautmann (*Kauṭīlya and the Arthaśāstra*. A Statistical Investigation into the *Authorship and Evolution of the Text*, Leiden, 1971) thinks that its different parts have different dates, though these are probably not widely separated. Also see R.P. Kangle, 'Some Recent Work on the *Kauṭīlya Arthaśāstra*', *JBBRAS*, New Series, xliii-xliv, 1968-69, pp. 227–38. The Poona critical edition of the *Mahabharata* draws attention to the question of stratification which has also been discussed by R.S. Sharma, *Aspects of Political Ideas and Institutions*, 2nd edn., Delhi: 1969, Chapter I.

[88] P.C. Jain, *Labour in Ancient India*, Delhi, 1970. D.R. Chanana, Agriculture in the Gangetic Valley' *Contributions to Indian Economic History*, ii, pp. 101–18) makes a departure from the usual approach and recognizes various stages of economic development in the *Ramayana*.

[89] Morris D. Morris and Burton Stein, op. cit., p. 180. A beginning has been made in this direction by R.S. Sharma ('Stages in Early Indian Economy', *Light on Early Indian Society and Economy*, pp. 52–80), but he does not integrate the south Indian evidence into his scheme. Here it must be emphasized that 'periodization for India as a whole is impossible, except with the broadest margins' D.D. Kosambi, 'On a Marxist Approach to Indian Chronology', *ABORI*, xxxi, 1950, pp. 258–9; cf. Idem. 'Stages of the Indian History', *Journal of the Indo-Soviet Cultural Society*, i, 1954, pp. 40–55. Among Indian scholars during (he last few years (here has been a greater awareness of the problems of periodization as can be inferred from the following writings: D.N. Jha, 'Problems of Periodization in Early Indian Economic History', paper read at the Seminar on Periodization on Indian History, Department of History; Patna University, 1968; R.K. Choudhary, 'Stages in Ancient Indian Political History', *Enquiry*, New Series, iii, no. 1, Spring 1969, pp. 28–49; Barun De, 'Encapsulation as An Alternative to the Difficulties of Periodizing Indian History' in *The Indian Civilization: The First Phase*, ed. S.C. Malik, Simla: Indian Institute of Advanced Study, 1971; B.D. Chattopadhyaya, 'The Chronological and Geographical Scope', ibid., pp. 93–7; B.N. Mukherjee, 'On Periodization', ibid., pp. 98–9; P.B. Desai, 'Chronological Limits for South India', ibid., pp. 104–5; R.V. Oturkar 'Medieval Period of Indian History, in Duration, Nature and Content', in *Studies in Indian History: A.G. Pawar Felicitation Volume*, ed. VD. Rao, Kolhapur: 1971, pp. 41–6.

use of sources such as the *Mahābhārata* whose different chapters belong to different periods. Similarly the temptation to draw heavily upon the *Arthasastra* have to be resisted as also the practice of explaining developments in the twelfth century on the basis of the information available in that text.

Although epigraphic material has also been studied as a source of economic history, there has been a general unwillingness on the part of scholars to subject it to a critical scrutiny. The ever growing accessible body of land charters can now be studied in two possible ways. We may ask major questions regarding self-sufficient economy, ownership of land, rate of productivity, relation between agriculture and crafts, fragmentation or consolidation of holdings, extent of the use of money, etc. Alternatively, we may attempt a thorough analysis of the available economic data in the land grants under well known categories. In our opinion, the second process should precede and form the basis of the first. A detailed study would involve identification of villages granted and the fiscal units in which they were situated. It will mean an examination of the multiple-village fiscal unit introduced by the Rajputs. From an examination of land charters it may be possible to know whether there obtained the same type of village in all parts of the country, including Kerala and Assam, or whether the system differed from area to area.[90]Again, the region-wise charts of the donees prepared in chronological order can give us an idea of the relative numerical and economic strength of the Brāhmaṇas (individuals and in groups), *mathas*,[91] temples, vassals, civil and military officials, who were granted land. A fruitful line of inquiry may be the study of the irrigation system on the basis of inscriptions. The theory that the main reason for the prevalence of despotic rule in Asia was the central control over irrigation

[90] Only a few works ran be cited on the early Indian village: H. Baden-Powell, *The Indian Village Community,* London: 1896; Radha Kamal Mukherji. 'Origins of Indian Village System', *Indian Inheritance*, II, Bombay: Bharatiya Vidya Bhavan, 1956; Abhay Kant Chaudhuri, *Village in North-Eastern India* AD *600–1200*, Calcutta: 1971.

[91] Puspa Niyogi, *Brahmanic Settlements in Different Subdivisions of Ancient Bengal*, Calcutta: 1967, is a case in point. Similar studies of different regions of the country may be undertaken.

will have to be examined in relation to India in early times.[92] Lastly, land grants may be immensely useful in investigating the feudal complex of south Indian temples and their role in the economic life of the community.

The economic studies relating to the early period of Indian history suffer from a curious neglect of the mass of available numismatic material. As a result, the place of coins in the economic life of the people at a particular time and place has still to be determined.[93] The study of coins for this purpose has not advanced beyond testing their specific gravity. But all this can be made far more useful if we are given some idea of the volume of the coins in circulation. The problem of the quantity of coins in India has not received any serious attention. A formula has been used to assess the quantity of the English coinage of the eighth to the eleventh centuries[94] and also of the medieval Islamic coinage in the Near East.[95] Although the applicability of the formula to Indian evidence has been questioned,[96] It may be possible to form a rough quantitative estimate of the coinage in circulation in a particular period and region, which will lend some reality to literary and epigraphic references to the use of coins. The frequency with which coins are used is a no less important aspect of the economic study of coins. Kosambi has attempted a statistical analysis of the punch-marked coins in this

[92] A reappraisal of the theory of Oriental despotism in relation to Ceylon has been attempted by E.R. Leach, 'Hydraulic Society in Ceylon', *Past and Present*, no. 1.5, 1959, pp. 2–25, and R.A.H. Gunawardane 'Irrigation and Hydraulic Society in Early Medieval Ceylon', ibid., no. 53, 1971, pp. 3–27. R.S. Sharma has brought about considerable new material to bear upon the irrigation system of the post-Maurya and Gupta periods (*Light on Early Indian Society and Economy*, pp. 90–101), but has not discussed its theoretical implications. A more recent study is that undertaken by B.N. Puri 'Irrigation and Agricultural Economy in Ancient India', ABORI, Golden Jubilee Volume, 1968, pp. 383–90, but it does nothing to improve our general understanding of the problem.

[93] For a discussion of the relevance of coins to the subject see R.S. Sharma, 'Coins and Problems of Early Indian Economic History', *Journal of the Numismatic Society of India*, xxxi, 1969, pp. 1–8.

[94] D.M. Metcalf, 'How Large was the Anglo-Saxon Currency?', *Economic History Review*, Second Series, xviii, no. 3, 1963, pp. 475–82.

[95] 'Early Islamic Mint Output', prepared by a Seminar at University of Michigan, *JBSHO*, ix, 1966, pp. 212–41.

[96] Upendra Thakur, 'Economic Data from the Early Coins of India', *JESHO*, xiv, 1971, pp. 269–85.

light.[97] But his method needs to be refined and pursued in relation to the other types of coins in different periods and different areas. When a coin passes through so many hands in course of time it undergoes wear and tear and its loses some weight. Therefore something can be done to find out the frequency of the use of coins to get an idea of the period of their circulation.

The area of the circulation of coins has an important economic bearing, which has to be examined in the context of the distribution of the mints.[98] Unfortunately the exact find spots of many coin hoards deposited in Indian and foreign museums are not specified, with the result that their area of circulation cannot be established. By taking into account the find-spots, where they are known, and also the time to which a given set of coins may belong, the numismatic evidence may be used fruitfully in reconstructing the economic life of the area concerned. Thus, the earliest hoards of Roman coins have been found in Kerala in south India, and it seems that they have nothing to do with the trade and commerce of the Satavahana empire with which they are associated. Similarly, if India had trade relations with South-East Asia and China, we shall have to look for Chinese coins, and the few that are available will have to be examined. In this connection, the history of gold in ancient India assumes some importance and could be taken up as an independent subject for investigation.[99] The view that whatever gold

[97] D.D. Kosambi, 'The effect of Circulation upon the Weight of Metallic Currency', *Current Science*, xi, 1942, pp. 227–31. His articles on early Indian currency are full of new insights, even if sometimes of questionable validity. See his following writings on numismatics: 'A Statistical Study of the Weights of Old Indian Punch-marked Coins', *Current Science*, ix, 1940, pp. 312–14; 'On the Origin and Development of Silver Coinage in India', ibid., x, 1941, pp. 395–400; 'A note on Two Hoards of Punch-marked Coins found at Taxila', *New Indian Antiquary*, iii, 1940, pp. 156–7; 'On the Study and Metrology of Silver Punch-marked Coins', ibid., iv, 1941, pp. 1–35 and 49–76; 'Silver Punch-marked Conin's with special reference to the East Khandesh Hoard', *Journal of the Numismatic Society of India,* viii, 1946, 63–6; 'Chronological Order of Punch-marked Coins', *JBBRAS*, XXV, 1948–9), pp. 33–47, XXVI, 1951, pp. 214–18, XXVII, 1952, pp. 261–71.

[98] U. Thakur, *Mints and Minting in India,* Banaras: 1972; Sister Liceria, op. cit., ch. VI.

[99] Marc Block, 'The Problem of Gold in the Middle Ages', in his *Land and Work in Mediaeval Europe* London: Routledge and Kegan Paul, 1967, provides useful guidelines for such a study. The only writing on the history of gold in ancient India is F.R. Allchin, 'Upon the Antiquity and Methods of Gold Mining in Ancient India', *JESHO*, v, 1962, pp. 195–211.

coins India had in the beginning mainly came from Rome or from central Asia deserve further consideration; so does the theory that the Roman gold coins were used as bullion and not as regular money in India.[100] This will also lead to a re-examination of the theory that gold coins involving large transactions travel over a long distance and that coppers meant for the use of the common people are minted and circulated locally.

Numismatic studies may very well be related to foreign trade, whose decline in late Gupta and post-Gupta times will have to be explained in the light of the comparative paucity of coins in the post-Harsha period. Although we have several important ruling dynasties in north India between the seventh and the tenth centuries AD, none of them can be definitely credited with the issuing of any series of coins. On the other hand a preliminary study suggests that trade and commerce, and use of coins revived in the eleventh and twelfth centuries, especially in Rajasthan and Gujarat, which also witnessed some kind of urbanization. One of the tasks of the economic historian, therefore, should be to account for this revival and examine the view whether urbanization was introduced into India by the Turks. The study of coins, trade and commerce may be integrated with that of moneylending, usury, etc.[101]

Although it may not be possible to provide answers to all the questions raised above, most of them may be fruitfully studied in relation to the archaeological material, which is the most direct evidence of the material life of the people but has been almost entirely ignored so far by researchers.[102] The volume of archaeological data accumulated during the last twenty-five years or so may be of great help in reconstructing the history of material culture; whose relevance to early Indian economic

[100] The significance of Roman coins in Indian economic life has been discussed by B.D. Chattopadhyaya, *Coinage and Currency Systems in South India*, Ph.D. Thesis, University of Cambridge, 1969.

[101] R.S. Sharma, 'Usury in Early Mediaeval Ancient India (AD 400-1200)', *Comparative Studies in Society and History*, viii, no. I, October 1965, pp. 56– 67, is a renewed attempt in this direction.

[102] G.L. Adhya, *Early Indian Economics, Bombay*, 1966 and C. Margabandhu, 'Trade Contacts between Western India and the Graeco-Roman World in the early centuries of the Christian era', *JESHO*, viii, 1965, pp. 316–22, illustrate how archaeological data may be utilized for the study of early Indian crafts and commerce.

history has yet to be fully appreciated by Indian scholars.[103] Such studies can go a long way in explaining why a particular region leaped into prominence at a particular stage and became the nucleus of an extensive empire in early India. It may also give us an idea of the formation of different ruling groups and oranizations and of their roles in the diffusion of culture traits. The process of the Hinduization of primitive tribes, noted and emphasized by the writers of the nineteenth-century Census Reports and now conceptualized by Sociologists as Sanskritization or brahmanization, can be better understood only if we carefully examine the material outfit of the vanguard of Aryanization.

On the basis of the available archaeological evidence several questions relating to the material culture down to the age of the Buddha and even later may be raised. It is said that the stimulus to urbanization during the Harappan phase came from the West. Can this view be sustained by a careful and comparative study in a chronological perspective of the material culture of the Harappans and that of the Mesopotamia and Egyptian peoples? Further, how is it that the Harappan settlements were completely obliterated? What was the difference between the material equipment of the Ṛgvedic and that of the later Vedic peoples? Moreover, if the Ṛgvedic Aryans owed their success to the use of bronze weapons, where are those artefacts? We have a large number of copper tools and weapons, ascribable to the first half of the second millennium BC and mostly discovered in the Kuru Panchala area, which became the main centre of activity of the later Vedic Aryans from about 1000 BC. The source and technology of these artefacts and the economic implications of their use in western Uttar Pradesh will have to be explained. A more important question relates to the advent of iron in India. When, where and wherefrom did iron first appear in India? Is it correct to hold that the use of iron came to India from Iran? To what extent the diffusion of iron technology in north India may account for the growth of urban settlements from *c.*600 BC, characterized by development of trade, diversification of arts and crafts, the spread of the NBP deluxe ware and the earliest use of coins. Some of these questions

[103] Outside the Archaeological Survey of India, several Indian universities, notably those of Poona and Baroda, have taken up excavation work. But two main problems handicap the historian. First, Indian archaeologists are finding it more difficult to publish the reports of their excavations than to dig a particular site. Secondly, most excavations done in India are vertical, though horizontal digging may yield more evidence relating to the material culture of a given area at a given point of time.

may be answered if integrated and problem-oriented studies of archaeological remains are undertaken[104] The mass of available material may throw light not only on the habitation history of different places but also on the growth of urban centres,[105] technology (especially arts and crafts, and tools and implements), and transport, whose significance in the economic progress of ancient India has not been adequately appreciated. It may also be of some help in forming a rough idea of the population density of the places where excavations have been conducted.[106] Thus the combination of literary, epigraphic. numismatic and archaeological evidence may give new perspectives to the economic historian of ancient India, who must get rid of his usual insularity and make use of the new and often sophisticated tools of analysis.[107]

[104] The origins of Buddhism and Jainism in the sixth century BC may also be explained in terms of the material developments of the period. See R.S. Sharma, 'Material Background to the Origins of Buddhism', *Das Kapital Centenary Volume*, New Delhi, 1968, pp. 59–66. Attention was first drawn to most of the questions relating to the material culture raised above by R.S. Sharma, 'Material Culture Down to the Age of the Buddha', paper presented at the Seminar on Social and Economic History of India. Indian Institute of Advanced Study, Simla, 1966. Also see his paper entitled 'Gaps in Non-political History of Northern India (*c.* AD 500–1200)', *Light on Early Indian Society and Economy*, pp. 145–51.

[105] A. Ghosh, 'The Kushan Levels at Some Excavated Sites in North India', *Journal of the Ganganath Jha Kendriya Sanskrit Vidyapeetha*, xxvii, 1971, pp. 233–42.

[106] Very few attempts have so far been made to study the population of early India. P. Nath, A Study in the *Economic Condition of Ancient India*, London, 1927, pp. 117–23; K.M. Shambavnekar, 'The Population of Ancient India', *ABORI*, xxxiii, 1953, pp. 82–96; J.M. Dalta, 'Population of India about 320 BC,. *Man in India*, xlii, no. 4, 1962, pp. 277–91 are however, works which should not be ignored.

[107] For a brief discussion of the possible application of new techniques of research see D.R. Chanana, 'Some Problems in the Economic History of Ancient India' in *Readings in Indian Economic History*, ed. B.N. Ganguli, Delhi: 1963, pp. 2–7.